OKINAWA
COLD WAR ISLAND

EDITED BY

CHALMERS JOHNSON

JAPAN POLICY RESEARCH INSTITUTE

Please order *Okinawa: Cold War Island*
($20.00 paperback: ISBN 0-9673642-0-5)
directly from the Japan Policy Research Institute's distributor:

> New Mexico U.S.-Japan Center
> P. O. Box 9678
> Albuquerque, NM 87119-9678
> Tel. (505) 842-9020; Fax. (505) 766-5166 or directly over the Internet through a secure server from:
> <http://www.nmjc.org/okinawa_cold_war_island.html>.

CONTENTS

FOREWORD

During August 1996, the court systems of Japan and South Korea turned in remarkably different performances in terms of delivering political justice for their peoples. By sentencing former president Chun Doo Hwan to death and former president Roh Tae Woo to twenty-two-and-a-half years in prison, the South Korean courts went about as far as any court system can to redress the wrongs done to the people of Kwangju in May 1980.

By contrast, the Grand Bench of the Japanese Supreme Court took one minute to say that the property rights of Okinawans were worthless if they conflicted in any way with the American military bases. One might respond that in both Korea and Japan the supreme courts were acting on the orders of political leaders, of President Y.S. Kim in South Korea and of Prime Minister Ryutaro Hashimoto in Japan. This is without doubt true but I also think it is worthwhile to point out the differences in the orders that these political leaders gave—in Korea, to right old wrongs, but in Japan to shore up the Cold War status quo.

Fifty years ago, without any Okinawan being asked or even being a part of either the Japanese or the American political systems, the American military seized Okinawan property for its numerous military bases, espionage centers, and housing estates for American families. It is important to understand that the Americans did not requisition or pay for this land; they simply seized it at bayonet point and then bulldozed the houses on it.

Any Okinawan who protested this American seizure of land was charged with being a communist, and some "troublemakers" were shipped off to Bolivia and dumped in a jungle area near the headwaters of the Amazon. It was, in Governor Masahide Ota's words, a *kimin-seisaku,* an American military policy of throwing away people who had gotten in the way of its plans. Many in the first group who made it to Bolivia died. The fact that some of the survivors of Colonia Okinawa near Santa Cruz, Bolivia, are today prospering as farmers does not excuse the fact that they got no help whatsoever from the Americans who transported them there.

After Okinawa was finally returned to Japan in 1972 the Japanese Government supported the Americans against its own citizens. The refusal of the Japanese Supreme Court even to acknowledge this history amounts to anything but equal protection of the laws. This amnesia by the mandarins of Kasumigaseki and the Pentagon is also why protestations by the American Air Force and Marines that they want to be "good neighbors" in Okinawa ring so hollow.

There is absolutely nothing the Americans and the Japanese can say today to mitigate their records in Okinawa over the past fifty years. Their only ethical course is to acknowledge that they forced the unlucky Okinawans to pay all of Japan's costs for whatever benefits flowed from the Cold War in East Asia. They must now start trying to make amends, at the very least by finally acknowledging that both World War II and the Cold War are over and by giving up the positions they have occupied since the Battle of Okinawa in the spring of 1945.

The Battle of Okinawa, in which former Governor Ota fought on the Japanese side as a high school boy impressed into service, and was wounded, was the first of four great betrayals the Okinawans have experienced at the hands of the Japanese and the Americans during the 20th century. Even though Emperor Hirohito knew in February 1945 that the war was lost, he ordered one last great battle not fought on the Japanese mainland so as to buy time to negotiate better surrender terms for the Imperial institution. The strategy worked, but the Okinawans paid the price with over 200,000 of them killed, including many civilians who were killed by Japanese soldiers. It is not surprising that the Showa Emperor never visited Okinawa. He would not have been welcome. The Battle of Okinawa was the bloodiest encounter of World War II, and the war memorial built by the Okinawans at Itoman at the southern tip of the main island, reminiscent of the Vietnam memorial in Washington but much larger, is the only such memorial on earth that lists the names of all the people killed, civilian and military, on both sides of the battle.

The second great betrayal occurred in 1952, when Japan won an early peace from the United States but with a price attached: the United States military wanted to occupy Okinawa indefinitely. The Okinawans therefore remained a stateless people, neither Japanese nor American citizens.

6

And Okinawa itself remained under direct American military government, with only minimal Japanese or American civilian oversight. From 1952 to 1972 Okinawa was transformed into a huge military base and safehouse for clandestine operations; no one in the U.S. or Japan knew what went on there because it was all classified and off-limits.

By the late 1960s Okinawa was being used as the Americans' main launching pad for the Vietnam War. The island bristled with nuclear rockets and the B-52 bombers used to pound Hanoi and the Ho Chi Minh trail. This led to violent Okinawan protests and the third betrayal of the Okinawans by Japan and the U.S. In 1972, to defuse the protests, a deal was struck whereby Okinawa was returned to Japanese rule; but the American bases were unaffected, still beyond either Japanese or Okinawan administration. Instead of being an American military colony directly ruled by the Pentagon, after 1972 Okinawa became an American military colony superficially legitimized by the Japanese-American Security Treaty. But nothing changed.

Because of all this, life for Okinawans involves a high level of fear and anxiety that they might be robbed, raped, or killed by American soldiers, or that disasters might descend out of the blue or crop up from nowhere at any time. It also makes a mockery of the declaration, in the preamble to the Japanese Constitution, that "all peoples of the world have the right to live in peace, free from fear and want." Okinawans want the bases withdrawn and the land returned to its rightful owners so that they might use it for the peaceful economic development of Okinawa, not for military adventures plotted in Washington DC.

This situation came to a head in February 1995 when the Americans issued the so-called Nye Report. Written by a Harvard professor working for the Pentagon, this report said that the Americans intended to maintain the status quo in East Asia for yet another 20 years, including the Okinawan bases. Precisely what another 20 years of American occupation would entail was dramatically brought home to all Okinawans and Japanese on September 4, 1995, when three American servicemen abducted and raped a 12-year-old Okinawan schoolgirl on her way home from shopping. Outrageous as this incident was, Governor Ota has noted that the true *hikigane* or trigger of the protests of the late 1990s was not the rape but the Nye Report itself and the prospect of the continued American occupation.

This brings us to the fourth and hardest to justify betray-al—the Clinton-Hashimoto summit of April 1996—in which the U.S. and Japan pretended to offer Okinawa relief. Both Clinton and Hashimoto took credit for their "skillful handling" of the Okinawan situation. In reality, however, they merely tried to divide and distract the Okinawan people. They were surprised by the depth of the Okinawan outrage against 50 years of American military negligence and by their resis-tance to the Pentagon's proposal in the Nye Report that for-eign troops remain on their islands indefinitely. Clinton and Hashimoto may have understood that the rape of Septem-ber 1995 fueled popular anger but they never understood that new policies, not just apologies, were called for.

With this volume, the Japan Policy Research Institute attempts to bring a greater depth of understanding to each of these four betrayals and to relate them to the costs of the United States's perpetuating the Cold War in East Asia long after it ended in Europe. Our primary purpose is to mobilize inattentive citizens to the problem of Okinawa. We want to supply the information needed to correct the wrongs the U.S. and Japanese governments are still today inflicting on the people of Okinawa. Our authors do not necessarily agree with everything said in each of the articles below, but we are all joined in the need to break the hold of official pro-paganda on Okinawa.

As editor of the volume, I would particularly like to express the appreciation of the Japan Policy Research Insti-tute to the following individuals for helping to bring this pro-ject to fruition. During his two terms in office, Governor Ota invited many of our authors to Okinawa to experience for themselves the situation the U.S. government has created there. He is represented in the collection by an important essay he wrote at the time of the fortieth anniversary of the Battle of Okinawa. Kozy Amemiya translated this article from Japanese for JPRI, in addition to contributing two important articles of her own, including her pathbreaking research on the fate of the Okinawans the United States transported to Bolivia. Gavan McCormack drew our attention to the articles by Ota and Sasaki and helped in the translation of Professor Sasaki's important analysis. McCormack's pioneering work on the environmental degradation of Okinawa is also includ-ed. Koji Taira, one of the editors of *The Ryukyuanist*, helped all of us to understand his native land and contributed two invaluable articles to this volume. He also spoke at the JPRI conferences held at the University of San Francisco and at the University Club, Chicago, on security problems in the Pacific and legacies of the Cold War, as did many of the other contributors.

Each of the following individuals contributed in his or her own way to this book, and JPRI is indebted to them: Sumi Adachi, Moriteru Arasaki, Doug Bandow, Barbara Bundy, Bruce Cumings, Robert Hamilton, Jacob Heilbrunn, Carol Jahnkow, Barry Keehn, Masao Kunihiro, Seitatsu Kyan, Wallace Lopez, Ken Miki, Kazuo Miura, Etsujiro Miyagi, Yasuhiro Miyagi, Mike Molasky, Mike Moore, Masao Nakachi, Yoshihiko Nakamoto, Toshi Nakayama, Jean Renshaw, Thomas Royden, Murray Sayle, Spencer Sherman, Tomokazu Takamine, Suzuyo Takazato, Kate Ternes, Robert Wampler, Kenichiro Yamashiro, Chikako Yoshida, and Eiji Yutani.

This volume would not have been possible without the indispensable contributions of JPRI's Executive Director, Steven C. Clemons, and its editor, Sheila K. Johnson. Larry DiRuscio of Self-Publishing Partners was a meticulous guide to the printing and marketing of this book. The Japan Policy Research Institute remains responsible for selecting all the articles, some of which it first published as JPRI reports, and for the organization of the project. Japanese names are given in Japanese order, surname followed by given name, in the articles by Amemiya, Rabson, and Taira on independence, and in Governor Ota's testimony before the Supreme Court. In other articles, Western order is used.

Chalmers Johnson

Cardiff, California
June 1999

I.

JAPAN'S LEGACY:

THE TYPHOON OF STEEL

RE-EXAMINING THE HISTORY OF THE BATTLE OF OKINAWA

Masahide Ota

There has been a persistent demand in postwar Japan from elements in the Liberal Democratic Party, the Self-Defense Agency, and some political and financial leaders that Japan strengthen its own defense system. In this context, I believe it is essential to reexamine the Battle of Okinawa, the only World War II ground battle fought on Japanese soil. Since it is impossible to encompass in this limited space the entire scope of the battle, I will discuss its main characteristics and explore what lessons we can draw from them.

Before I elaborate on the specific characteristics of the Battle of Okinawa, I would like to settle the issue of dating the onset and the conclusion of that battle. It is generally understood that the Battle of Okinawa began on April 1, 1945, when the U.S. troops landed on Okinawa Island, and ended on June 23 of the same year when Lieutenant General Mitsuru Ushijima killed himself and the Japanese defense in Okinawa disintegrated. (American forces hold that the Battle ended on June 22.) Most history textbooks in Japan adopt these dates. In my opinion, however, these dates are inaccurate as well as inadequate to encompass the scope of the Battle of Okinawa. The onset of a war may be marked with a declaration by the involved government and its closing with a signing of the surrender. The dates when the individual battles began, on the other hand, are often disputed: for example, should we regard the onset of air raids or the ground battle as the beginning?

Likewise, the dates of the conclusion can be disputed. Should we regard the conclusion as the date when systematic resistance on the part of the defeated ended or when the terms of the surrender were signed? As for the Battle of Okinawa, I find it most appropriate to consider that it began on March 26, 1945, when the U.S. forces landed on the Kerama Islands, twelve miles west of Okinawa Main Island, to launch the ground offensive, and that it concluded on September 7, 1945, when representatives of the Japanese Defense Task Force of the Southwestern Islands signed the surrender document. To choose these dates is not merely a matter of personal viewpoint; it touches upon significant issues essential to the nature of the Battle of Okinawa.

If one takes April 1 as the date when the Battle of Okinawa began, as most textbooks do, one loses sight of the tragic incident in which nearly seven hundred civilians in the Kerama Islands were driven, directly and indirectly, to acts of mass self-destruction. Another factor that will disappear from the history of the Battle of Okinawa, if we date its beginning on April 1, is that as soon as the United States troops landed on the Kerama Islands, the U. S. Navy issued military directive No.1, suspending the administration and jurisdiction of the Japanese government and declaring the occupied area and residents to be under the military government of the United States. This directive, which was issued on March 26, 1945, prior to the American attack on Okinawa Main Island, should be considered as part of the Battle of Okinawa.

Similarly, it is also inaccurate to mark the conclusion of the battle on June 23. On that date, Lieutenant General Mitsuru Ushijima, who was the officer in command of the defending Japanese 32nd Army in the Southwest Islands, and Lieutenant General Isamu Cho, the chief of staff, realized that an organized defense was no longer possible and killed themselves by allegedly committing hara-kiri. However, while the organized defense effort ceased to exist on June 22, localized combat did not. Moreover, American troops landed on Kume Island on June 26, triggering the terrible "Kume Island Incident," in which the Japanese Defense Task Force slaughtered twenty Kume Islanders and nine other friendly soldiers on the suspicion of their being American spies. By dating the end of the Battle of Okinawa on June 23, this incident, which was quite typical of the nature of the Battle of Okinawa is omitted.

There are other factors as well that make the June 23 date unacceptable. For example, there were nearly four hundred officers, still fully armed, in their headquarters in the caves in the southern part of Okinawa for two months following the suicides of Ushijima and Cho. It was not until August 27 that all of these men surrendered, accompanied by about one hundred civilians. The officers of the Defense Task Force on Kerama surrendered on the night of August 23 and the morning of August 24. About forty men in the

Defense Task Force on Kume Island surrendered on September 7. Moreover, it was August 26 when the General of the Armies in the Far East Theater Douglas MacArthur ordered the Tenth Army under Lieutenant General Joseph Stilwell to receive the unconditional surrender by the Japanese Defense Task Force in the Southwestern Islands. This ceremony of surrender took place September 7 at the headquarters of the Tenth Army in Kadena and was attended by the commander of the 28th Division Lieutenant General Toshio Noomi from Miyako Island and Lieutenant General Toshitada Takada from Amami Island, both representing the Japanese Army, as well as Tadao Kato from Amami Island, representing the Japanese Navy. They signed the six copies of the surrender document. Against this background, the American war historian Benis M. Frank maintains that the last scene of the Battle of Okinawa unfolded on September 7, 1945. I agree with him that September 7 is more appropriate than any other date as the conclusion of the Battle of Okinawa and corresponds with the historical facts.

Setting aside the issue of dates, we still have numerous other issues surrounding the Battle of Okinawa that have not been fully uncovered and need to be clarified. These involve most especially the number of victims and the details concerning the massacres of Okinawan civilians by the Japanese army. I have tried to be as specific and accurate as possible, but there are certain areas that remain incompletely known.

AN ILL-PREPARED, RECKLESS WAR

Over three hundred books have been published in Japanese and English about the Battle of Okinawa. Yet, only a few encompass the entire scope of the battle. Most of the books are simply records of the battle as fought by specific divisions or memoirs of personal experiences. Almost none examines the situations of both the military and civilians on the battlefield, giving equal weight to both, in light of the strategies of Japanese and American troops. However, even the partial or segmented descriptions of the battle make it clear how inadequately prepared the Japanese army was when it plunged into the battle, while the Americans launched their attack with thorough preparations.

The American military historian and correspondent for the *New York Times*, Hanson W. Baldwin, who covered the

Battle of Okinawa, concluded that it manifested the ugliest aspects of the war. He reported that compared to this battle, the Battle of Britain paled in terms of its scope and harshness. A well-known Japanese military historian, Masanori Ito, points to three characteristics of the Battle of Okinawa that distinguish it from others. First, it was the first ground battle fought on Japanese territory. Second, civilians were forced to get directly involved. And third, the all-out air attack by the Japanese was carried out using large-scale suicide (*kamikaze*) missions. Ito emphasizes that while the battle in Iwo Jima was also a ground battle fought on Japanese territory, it involved no civilians, whereas in Okinawa hundreds of thousands of civilians were exposed to the battle and over a hundred and fifty thousand perished.

What then were the characteristics of the Battle of Okinawa? The record at the Self-Defense Forces Academy for Ground Troops cites the key factors of the strategy for Okinawa as follows:

(a) It was a strategy at the last stage of World War II. Both the Japanese and American sides synthesized the lessons they had learned in their previous battles. However, the Japanese troops *had already lost most of their capabilities to carry out the war. In addition, Japan had lost its naval capabilities.* (Emphasis by the author. Subsequent emphases also added by the author unless otherwise specified.)

(b) While it was a battle of powerful strategic frontline troops, it was a strategy for the first battle on our soil since the Mongolian invasion in the thirteenth century. It was also the only ground battle in Japan that involved hundreds of thousands of civilians.

(c) The Japanese launched the largest air force possible (mostly in suicide missions) to defend the air bases on the smaller islands, but they failed to support the troops in ground battle. The ground troops did not fight to stop the landing of the enemy.

(d) It was the battle in which the largest number of troops on both the Japanese and American sides fought against each other in the Pacific War. (Especially, it was the only battle in which the Japanese army mobilized its most powerful battalions against the offensive of the Allied Forces.) However, it was a battle of ground troops (Japanese) with no support from air, sea and reserves, versus ground troops (American) that received direct support from their air force and navy.

Most history books or records of the battle cite these factors as the chief characteristics of the Battle of Okinawa. However, these factors point to the problems of the military and do not indicate what made the Battle of Okinawa unique. I would suggest that several hideous incidents are also characteristic of the Battle of Okinawa. These incidents appear almost inevitable as a result of the lopsided relationship between the central power (the Japanese government and general headquarters) and the remote backwater prefecture (Okinawa), abetted by Okinawa's particular political and cultural conditions. With this lopsided relationship in view, one immediately notices how unprepared and reckless the Japanese military was fighting in the battle in Okinawa. By contrast, the Americans had planned their strategy as early as 1943, with Okinawa as the target, and had set the date of their offensive as the spring of 1945. Based on that plan, the Americans made thorough preparations for the battle considering every eventuality.

To show how well prepared they were, the Americans had collected information that there were 333 sites suitable for landing in the Southwestern Islands. For forty-six of the sites they had collected data regarding the topography, ocean currents and depth of sand on the beach. In addition, they had formed a research team consisting of anthropologists and historians at Columbia University, and involving the army and navy as well, to forge meticulous plans covering all aspects of not only the battle but also the military occupation that would follow. For example, they studied the plans for constructing military bases after landing, actual measures for a military administration to implement, the treatment of civilians under occupation, and so forth.

The American army paid particular attention, albeit out of strategic considerations, to the treatment of civilians. Thanks to their thorough study, the Americans had a good grasp of the Okinawan way of thinking and patterns of behavior, and they took pains to look after the civilians' basic needs for clothing, food and shelter.

Incidentally, the number of American military personnel entrusted exclusively to look after civilian needs reached five thousand at its peak. Not only that, the American military leadership distributed among its rank and file copies of a booklet summarizing Okinawan history, culture, society, and economy before military administration personnel landed.

Had it not been for this American policy toward non-combatants, Okinawan civilians would have paid an immeasurably higher price during the battle. A mere month after the American troops landed on Okinawa Main Island, 128,000 non-combatants—women, children, old people—were placed under the American military occupation. The benefits of the American preparations were easy to see.

Compared to the preparations the Americans made, the Japanese leadership was extremely slow in getting ready for the expected conflict. The 32nd Army in charge of defending the islands south of the 30th parallel was established on March 22, 1944, about a year before the landing of the American troops. However, the main force of this army was ordered by Imperial Headquarters to transfer to Taiwan. A change in strategy also delayed the preparations, leaving the 32nd Army with only three months, from January to March, 1945, to prepare for the anticipated American assault. Furthermore, Imperial Headquarters made all the detailed plans regarding the distribution of troops on the islands, which required close coordination with the air force and navy. The 32nd Army had no freedom whatsoever to alter these plans based on their local knowledge. As early as 1944, the 32nd Army considered the attack on Okinawa by American troops to be inevitable and correctly anticipated that it would take place between April and May 1945. And yet they had no authority to make strategic plans based on their own judgment. This created a conflict of views in the upper echelon of the army, which cast a dark, serious shadow over the entire strategy for Okinawa.

TREATING OKINAWA AS AN OCCUPIED LAND

The unpreparedness of the Japanese army did not manifest itself only in plans for the defense strategy. It was also evident in the battle preparations for civilians. For example, it was urgent for the leadership to establish a system of cooperation between the army, local officials and civilians as well as a system for evacuating non-combatants. It was also necessary for the leaders of both the army and the prefectural office to ensure sufficient food supplies for civilians in anticipation of the battles in the islands. In fact, over ten years before the Battle of Okinawa, in January 1934, the Commander of the Regimental District in Okinawa, Colonel

Torao Ishii, who was in charge of defending Okinawa, sent a classified cable entitled "Measures to Defend Okinawa" addressed to the Administrative Vice Minister of the Army. In this message, Colonel Ishii explained that Okinawa was so dependent on importing most of its daily essentials from the outside that whenever ocean transport was disrupted by a typhoon or the sea routes were shut down by enemy action, many Okinawans were likely to die from starvation. Hence, Colonel Ishii emphasized, it was of ultimate importance to stockpile daily necessities and essential goods in Okinawa. His words of caution were not heeded.

As for a system of cooperation between the army, local officials and civilians, it appears that the army intended at first to keep civilians separated from military personnel. Yet, such a separation was impossible for such a tiny island as Okinawa. Besides, the army had an acute shortage of labor necessary to establish its battle positions. Hence, it had to mobilize an average of fifty thousand civilians a day in order to build an air base. The army was also unable, in terms of time and money, to build new barracks for its soldiers. So it began by taking over schoolhouses to accommodate its officers and soldiers before the air raids intensified. Even that was not enough. Civilian dwellings were also appropriated, and needless to say, such measures worsened the relationship between the military and ordinary Okinawans.

Morisada Hosokawa in his journal *Information Never Reaching the Emperor* recorded in his December 16, 1944, entry the worsening relationship between the army, prefectural officers and civilians.

"I visited Mr. Takamura yesterday, December 15th, at his office in the Home Ministry to hear about what he had observed in Okinawa. According to him the entire island of Okinawa is under air raids from seven in the morning through four in the afternoon. Not even a remote village has escaped assault from either air raids or machine guns. Okinawa, with its population of 600,000 [actually less than 500,000 at the time], now has 150,000 troops. The local residents at first had favorable feelings towards the troops. [However, their feelings have worsened.] They saw only one allied fighter plane take off during the air raids. The rest of the troops occupied the underground shelters of local inhabitants, leaving no room for local residents. The non-combatants in Naha were ordered evicted from the city and evacuated into the mountains forty miles away. These residents had all their homes burned down and had no food. Even now they are left in tatters and provided with no help. On top of such miserable conditions, the troops are totally undisciplined and have confiscated the few houses still standing, *behaving as if Okinawa were their occupied land.* They have no discipline—forcing the residents to live under the same roof with the troops, making use of civilians' possessions as they like, and *raping women.* The officer in command, named Cho, reportedly informed the prefectural office that the troops were there with a mission only to fight the battle according to the strategies they were given, and that as the non-combatants were in their way, they should be evicted to the mountains. However, he proclaimed, *the army is not able to look after them,* and they should be self-supporting."

According to Hosokawa, it was impossible for residents, who had been given an eviction order and whose only possessions were the clothes they had on, to be self-supporting. All the supply boats were sunk, making it impossible for them to receive food and clothing from other prefectures. By that time, the army authorities had lost their self-confidence after the failures of Leyte and other battles. Hosokawa noted that the army was considering taking over the prefectural administration by placing the administrative unit under the military districts and allowing the military commander to take over the governor's office as well. While such a move by the army was carried out in all prefectures in Japan, the army's interference in administration was more evident in Okinawa. Jun Urasaki, who as head of the population section of the Okinawa Prefectural Government was working hard to evacuate the civilians to safety, made this observation:

"There were some officers in the Defending Army who embodied the arrogance of the military as if they were warlords. They not only *made illegal interventions in administration,* but declared they would put Okinawa under military government as if they had mistaken Okinawa for occupied land in China or in Southeast Asia."

In reality, it was not simply a matter of intervention in administration. According to Soosei Gushiken, chief of the Naha Police Department, life in Okinawa at that time was "just the same as under martial law."

Eventually, the antagonism between the Defense Task Force and the prefectural office came into the open. The antagonism was reinforced by the military commanders' strong mistrust of the chief executives of the prefectural government. Also, according to Jun Urasaki, the governor of Okinawa as well as his right-hand man and the head of the home department, were cowards and concerned only with their own safety. After the air raids on Naha City on October 10, 1944, they abandoned their duties at the Prefectural Office and stayed in the cave shelter at Futenma, located in the middle of Okinawa Main Island. Consequently, Okinawa's administration was left unattended and the Prefectural Office existed in name only.

Thus, Okinawa's governor had no contact, official or unofficial, with the military leaders, and was labeled unfit as a governor in a situation anticipating a major battle. This was too much for Mr. Urasaki, the conscientious section chief. When he had an opportunity at the Kagoshima Prefectural Office to meet with a representative of the Diet, he explained the antagonism between the military and the administrative office in Okinawa and asked the central government to take appropriate action. In short, he requested that the governor be discharged and replaced. Considering this situation, the *Okinawa Shimpo* repeatedly argued in its editorials that 1945 would be the year of the decisive battle, and that whether it would be the year of winning the war or not would "depend on whether the military and the civil government and the people are able to unite."

Under these circumstances, the governor of Okinawa made an "official business" trip to Tokyo on December 25, 1944, and never returned to Okinawa. In January 1945, he got himself appointed as governor of Kagawa Prefecture in western Japan, leaving word to his subordinates that, "I would rather meet my death on the mainland." It should be noted that the governor of Okinawa was appointed by the Home Ministry and was always someone from the mainland. Thus, the chief executive officer of Okinawa Prefecture abandoned Okinawa sooner than anyone else.

On January 15, 1945, the head of the Internal Affairs Department of Osaka Prefecture, Akira Shimada, was appointed the new governor of Okinawa. Yoshio Nakano writes in *The Last Governor of Okinawa* that Mrs. Shimada panicked when her husband told her of his acceptance of the appointment, and reportedly blurted out, "What will happen to us? We have done nothing wrong to deserve being sent to

Okinawa! If the Home Ministry treats us like that, you should resign." Governor Shimada, however, resolved to accept his appointment, and reportedly said, "Someone has to go there and since I am asked to go, I must. Look at the young men. They all go into battle, whether they like it or not, with a piece of paper summoning them to active service." The new governor took up his post on January 31, 1945, in full anticipation that Okinawa would soon be invaded by American troops.

Needless to say, the prefectural officials and the people in Okinawa welcomed the new governor's courageous words and action. However, the problem of abandoning Okinawa was not limited to the former governor. The local newspapers argued in their editorials almost daily: "We admonish numerous officials who make so-called business trips outside Okinawa for deserting the frontlines." They also maintained, "Now is a very important time for the military, the administration and the people to be united in defending our land. And yet, there are just too many government officials, teachers and company executives who make one-way trips out of Okinawa in the name of official business. How can you raise people's morale in such a situation?" Mr. Shimada started his duties as governor by admonishing his subordinates: "Adhere to your work by all means necessary and never retreat from Okinawa. Those who violate this basic rule will be strictly punished."

Incidentally, only those over the age of 60 and under the age of 15 were allowed to evacuate from Okinawa. The local newspapers made public the names of others who ignored the restrictions, calling them with full sarcasm, "honorable deserters." Such irresponsible actions by some officials contributed to the disastrous consequences for non-combatants. It also illustrates how unprepared the military, the administration, and the people were in spirit as well as in materials, when they entered into the battle, which I will discuss below.

THE "GROUND PREPARATION" STRATEGY

Why is the Battle of Okinawa called a "reckless battle?" Because by then the Allied Powers were absolutely superior to the Japanese defense forces in terms of number of troops, arms, ammunition, and other materials for military operations. There was no comparison. The Allied Powers arrived off Okinawa's shores with a total of 548,000 soldiers, more than the entire population of Okinawa, in 1,500 ships. In contrast, the Japanese defense forces consisted of no more than 110,000 regular soldiers, including local recruits and students. One American war correspondent reported that the Battle of Okinawa "is a great decisive battle between those who fight in order to live and those who fight in order to die."

The problems of the Japanese defense forces were more profound than merely the matter of numbers. Most serious of all was that general headquarters and the defense forces disagreed over the fundamental definition of the forthcoming battle. Moreover, the army and the navy were sharply divided on how to carry out the strategy. The Japanese forces plunged into the battle without resolving these fundamental problems. It would have taken a miracle for them to win.

Imperial Headquarters had not intended to engage in a final, decisive battle in Okinawa. It regarded the battle in Okinawa, to borrow war historian Saburo Hayashi's words, as the initial battle "in order to facilitate the decisive battles on the mainland."

Sokichi Takagi, author of *The History of Marine Battles in the Pacific*, also argues that Imperial Headquarters considered the battles in Taiwan and Okinawa as "no more than exercises for facilitating the overall strategy for key areas on the mainland." In other words, the Battle of Okinawa was nothing but "ground preparation" in order to buy time for the decisive strategy in the mainland.

Various records suggest that when the Battle of Okinawa began, mainland defense preparations were only sixty percent complete. Hence, it benefited Imperial Headquarters to have the enemy pinned down in Okinawa as long as possible. Originally, however, Imperial Headquarters had planned a strategy to delay the Allied Powers off the coast of Okinawa and to attack and destroy them from the air. Responding to this strategy, the Okinawa Defense Task Force developed a plan to repel and destroy the invading enemy on the beaches by placing its main forces at Yomitan Airfield in the northern part of the main island and at Kadena Airfield in the central part, as well as all over the southern region. They repeatedly carried out rigorous exercises to implement this scheme.

However, prompted by the disastrous failure of the Battle of Leyte Gulf, Imperial Headquarters abruptly changed its strategy toward reinforcing defenses in the Philippines and Taiwan. Thus, Imperial Headquarters withdrew the Ninth Division, which was regarded as the most able, from the Okinawa Defense Task Force without consulting the local leadership and transferred it to Taiwan just before the American troops landed in Okinawa. This naturally resulted in undermining the foundation of the strategy in Okinawa. The Americans had decided, at about the same time, to forego their plan to invade Taiwan and to concentrate on attacking Okinawa. Thus, the Japanese decision turned out to be a grave miscalculation.

Imperial Headquarters had promised to transfer the Eighty-fourth Division from Himeji in western Japan to Okinawa in order to fill the vacuum left by the Ninth Division. But it broke this promise in order to protect the mainland. As a consequence, the Okinawan defense forces had to change their original strategy. They abandoned their defense of the air bases in the northern and the central region of Okinawa, and instead decided on a strategy of holding out in the Shuri district, the old capital of the Ryukyu Kingdom, using the tactics of a "war of attrition" (*jikyusen*). The defense forces also conscripted 25,000 civilians in order to supplement their insufficient troops. In addition, they mobilized, with no legal authority, male and female high school students. This occurred before the Patriotic Military Conscription Law [Giyu Heieki-ho] was promulgated on June 23, 1945, allowing for the conscription of males aged 15 to 60 and females aged 17 to 40 into National Patriotic Combat Units. In Okinawa, 1,779 male students were mobilized into the Tekketsu Kinno Brigade (Blood and Iron Corps) at various schools, and 581 female students were forced to participate in the battle as nurses. Altogether 2,360 Okinawan high school students were mobilized for the battle, over half of whom (1,224) lost their lives.

The Okinawa defense force did consider, after the Ninth Division was transferred to Taiwan, stationing their main force in the mountainous region of the north and sticking to the plan of attrition warfare. However, the leadership calculated that the enemy might simply ignore the force in the mountains and concentrate its attack on the southern region, from which the American troops might then launch their attacks on the mainland, thus bringing down Japan quickly. This calculation led to their decision to remain in Shuri and the southern region of Okinawa.

There was also a psychological factor that contributed to their strategy. Colonel Hiromichi Yahara, the chief architect of the strategy, reflected later that he would have had no hesitation in choosing to take up positions in the mountains if the Japanese military code of conduct had not contained the article on death in battle as honorable and life after defeat as shameful. Without that article, Yahara believed in retrospect, Okinawa might have avoided its tragedy. In other words, the samurai tradition prevented military leaders from making rational decisions.

The price that Okinawan civilians were forced to pay for the sake of "samurai honor" was simply too great. The editor of *The Typhoon of Steel,* the anthology of Okinawan peoples' memoirs of the battle, asserts that the Battle of Okinawa forced more than 400,000 Okinawan civilians to participate in a battle that was a delaying tactic for saving the mainland. Such an assertion is not groundless. The records of the battle kept by the army staff and the analyses by renowned war historians point to the fact that Imperial Headquarters had conceived the expected battle plan in Okinawa as a remote peripheral battle similar to those in Attu and Saipan, and even justified the suicide tactics as those of peoples having no other choice. It is evident that Japanese military leaders did not regard Okinawa as part of the "Imperial land" *(koodo),* but as a sort of "foreign (or outside) territory" (*gaichi*).

Indeed, there are enough indications that the Japanese leaders considered Okinawa as being outside of Japan proper. Shortly after American troops landed in Okinawa, Army Minister Anami issued the so-called "Precept for a Decisive Battle," in which he asserted, "The officers of the Imperial Army should defend the Imperial land to the death. The Imperial land is where the emperor reigns and all our gods and spirits reside. The officers should swear to repel the invasion from the outside and defend the land by any means with all their might and spirit."

In his reference to the "Imperial land," Okinawa was not included. The area south of the 30th parallel was under the charge of the Okinawa defense forces. It was also the target area the Americans chose to attack and separate from Japan. The historian Masanori Ito makes this point clearly. He notes that in January 1945, Imperial Headquarters set up the Tengo Strategy (for the battles in Taiwan and Okinawa) and the Ketsugo Strategy (the final battle in mainland Japan) as the final strategies for the end of the Pacific War. Ito points out that these two strategies were not separate but that "the Tengo Strategy was part of the larger decisive strategy along with the Ketsugo Strategy." And yet, Imperial Headquarters tended to slight Okinawa, rather than putting the mainland and Okinawa together into a larger picture. It considered Okinawa somewhat separate, its view hindered by the distance of hundreds of miles between Okinawa and the mainland.

Ito further argues: "Imperial Headquarters named the strategy for the battle on the mainland as Ketsugo and the one for Okinawa and Taiwan as Tengo in order to indicate the regional differences in preparations for the battles. But it inadvertently displayed the disparity in their own will for the battles in the respective regions."

He also notes that Imperial Headquarters placed three divisions, one brigade, and one artillery brigade in Okinawa, causing criticism within the army: "There were some in the army who said that the value of Okinawa was overestimated. Such a criticism arose from a view that regarded Okinawa as a small island remote from the capital with only loose cultural connections to the mainland. They regarded its position as insignificant. Some on the staff who were sent to Okinawa felt they had gotten the short end of the stick and were quite discontented with their assignment."

Let me now return to the subject of the Imperial Headquarters' decision not to fill the vacuum left by the transfer of the Ninth Division from Okinawa to Taiwan in order to keep enough troops in reserve to defend the mainland. The cancellation of reinforcements shocked Major Yasunobu Haneba, who was the staff officer in charge of the Okinawa theater. He protested that "One division in Okinawa has a value equivalent to two or three in a battle on the mainland. I understand the risk of transporting troops, but even risking a loss of one-third, it will be worth sending the reinforcement." He made the request of the chief of staff, Major General Shuichi Miyazaki, who refused, saying "I cannot rationally allow the risk of losing in transport even one sol-

dier who is a valuable asset in defending the mainland."
Miyazaki also argued that "It is more urgent and effective to
reinforce the forces on the mainland than to increase the
force on a remote island." These statements clearly exhibit
his view of Okinawa. However, the more serious and fundamental problem at Imperial Headquarters was not such a
view, but the fact that their strategy on Okinawa was constructed on the basis of an honorable suicide (*gyokusai*).

THE BATTLE FORSAKEN FROM THE BEGINNING

Both the Okinawa defense forces and Imperial Headquarters expected the Battle of Okinawa to be concluded by
gyokusai (death without surrender). Lieutenant General
Ushijima's predecessor, Lieutenant General Watanabe
reportedly predicted an Okinawan civilian *gyokusai* even
before August 1944. Commander Ushijima had been urged
by the Army Minister and the Army Chief of Staff, before he
left Tokyo for the post in Okinawa, not to rush into ordering
it, but neither did he prohibit it.

The staff officer in charge of planning, Colonel Yahara,
wrote in his private journal over six months before the landing of the American troops that he would be defending Okinawa at around cherry blossom season the following year.
He also recorded several months before the battle actually
began that he had no hope of Japan's winning the Battle of
Okinawa. Moreover, he noted an incident in early 1945, prior
to the Americans' landing, in which a few officers in charge
of intelligence gathering, who were graduates of the Nakano
Army Intelligence Academy, came to the headquarters of the
Okinawa defense forces and publicly declared, "Our duty is
not to participate in battle in Okinawa. We will begin our
activity after the Battle of Okinawa is over and *the 32nd
Army is destroyed.* Our duty is to collect intelligence about
the Americans occupying Okinawa and to report to Tokyo."
Naturally, such a blunt statement that they had no intention
of helping defend Okinawa did not please the staff of the
Defense Task Force. Yahara himself told them sarcastically:
"Then why don't you hide in the smaller islands off Okinawa
and kill time by marrying the local maidens?" What these
intelligence officers did was indeed to hide out in the smaller islands, assuming such jobs as schoolteachers, and some
even married local women. They did intelligence work—not

on American soldiers but on the local residents. Their activities resulted in the murders of some civilians on the suspicion of their being spies. Such suspicions of Okinawan civilians by the military underscores one of the characteristics of the Battle of Okinawa.

The Japanese military's mistrust of Okinawan civilians was manifested above all in the overall defense plan, in which defeat in the Battle of Okinawa was virtually predicted. On April 2, 1945, a strategy meeting between the government and the military took place in Tokyo. It was the second day after the American troops had landed on Okinawa Main Island. In that meeting, Prime Minister Kuniaki Koiso asked the military about prospects for the battle in Okinawa, to which Major General Miyazaki answered, "It is inevitable that the America troops will win the battle, occupy Okinawa, and attack the mainland." On the other hand, the Navy insisted on concluding the war in Okinawa and therefore dispatched the combined squadron to the waters near Okinawa. Imperial Headquarters again refused to send reinforcements in order to save the forces for the defense of the mainland. Major General Toshiyuki Yokoi, chief of staff of the 5th Naval Air Division, noted, "We of the 5th Naval Air Division repeatedly made firm requests for reinforcements. However, Imperial Headquarters not only ignored our requests, but on April 17 even removed Commander Ugaki from his post and ordered him to direct the 10th Naval Division. This meant that Imperial Headquarters had already forsaken Okinawa."

A mainland Japanese citizen, Rei Kiyosawa, recorded in his journal on April 17: "It is evident to everyone that there is no hope of winning the battle in Okinawa. Still, the newspapers make references to 'divine machinery' [the Zero fighter plane], which is of course propaganda by the military. . . . Nowadays newspapers in Japan print what nobody believes." In other words, Imperial Headquarters had secretly abandoned Okinawa on the one hand, while keeping up its propaganda on the other.

On April 20, Kiyosawa noted in his journal: "There are lots of optimistic views going around, thanks to the hearsay that the battle in Okinawa is activating our economy. The stock market has soared. I have heard the rumor that the enemy in Okinawa surrendered unconditionally. Another rumor is that the United States has proposed peace negotiations. Such rumors only show how ignorant people are. They are blindly buying whatever newspapers print." It is hard to believe that there were such rumors going around in Japan while a battle for life itself was being fought on the Okinawan front.

The biggest problem that characterized the Battle of Okinawa was the military's mistrust of local civilians. This mistrust prevented cooperation between the military, the local government, and the people, which was vitally necessary during wartime. Each side made efforts based on their own vantage point, but these bore little fruit. The main reason was the different views of the role of the civilians. While the government and the people believed they were to be protected by the military, the military viewed the civilians as partners in their military destiny. This was evident in the answer of Major General Cho, chief of staff in Okinawa, to a question by a local reporter. Asked how the civilian residents should behave when American troops landed, General Cho replied, "It is too late to say this, but all the civilians should accept military instructions like soldiers. In other words, each civilian ought to have a fighting spirit to kill ten enemy soldiers and destroy our enemy." He also said, "When the enemy lands and our food supply gets cut off, *the military is not in a position to provide civilians with food, even if you plead with us that civilians will starve to death. The military's important mission is to win the war. We are not allowed to lose the war in order to save civilians.*"

While the military thus proposed a common destiny of life or death for the military, the government, and the people, it was, in actuality, only death that was emphasized. In short, the civilians (the government and the people) were regarded as partners of the military, destined to carry out a final "honorable suicide" (*gyokusai*) and were never regarded as subjects of military protection.

THE SPY INCIDENTS

The mistrust the defense forces felt toward Okinawan civilians increased as battle conditions worsened. The military became suspicious of local residents as spies and put them to death. After the war, quite a few Okinawan civilians recalled their horrifying experiences of being suspected as spies. According to a study by the Okinawa School District, more than a thousand civilians were wrongfully suspected of being spies and executed. The most notorious cases took place in the Kerama Islands, Oogimi Village, and Kume Island, but these are only a few that surfaced among many. There are cases of such executions taking place even after Japan's surrender. Even a young child of two or three years of age was executed as a spy. Some cases are simply too gruesome to describe.

Master Sergeant Tadashi Kayama of the Defense Force on Kume Island, who himself carried out the execution of civilians on this island, explains why he did it: "Well, my view is . . . unless we took firm measures, we would have been killed by the local residents before being killed by the Americans. My troops consisted of a mere thirty or so soldiers while there were ten thousand residents. So if the residents had turned on us and sided with the Americans, we would have been finished right away. So . . . we needed to take firm measures. So I conducted executions in order *to keep the civilian residents under our control.*" The most disturbing aspect of such abnormal thinking and actions by individual officers and soldiers was that they were not brought about by desperation borne of defeat but were based on the policy of the Defense Force.

How was this policy expressed? Having set up its headquarters in Shuri, the old capital of the Ryukyu Kingdom, the Defense Force issued the directive on April 9, 1945, that "From now on soldiers and civilians as well are all required to use nothing but standard Japanese. Those who speak Okinawan will be regarded as spies and receive appropriate punishment." The language issue is at the core of suspicions that Okinawans were spies. Okinawans, as is known, spoke their dialect in daily life. It is easy to imagine that elderly Okinawans, in particular, found it comforting to express their own feelings in the language they were most used to under the extreme circumstances of war. Defense Force Headquarters reissued the same directive on May 5, with only the phrase "from now on" deleted. Moreover, it was issued under the name of Major General Cho, the chief of staff. Colonel Yahara notes that there were numerous rumors of spy activities, such as the one that *nisei* (second-generation Japanese-Americans) had landed by submarines or parachute and were engaged in intelligence activities or that women spies were communicating with the enemy by torch signals. However, Colonel Yahara also notes that no one had ever been caught for specific spy activities.

On the other hand, Shinji Mabuchi, a staff officer of the Marines at Imperial Headquarters during the war, reports that there were indeed spy activities. He made a trip to Okinawa after the war as a clerk for the Ministry of Health and Welfare. Afterwards, he was asked by the History Division of the Self Defense Forces Training Academy to do research and write a report on the "facts concerning the behavior of Okinawans during the battle in Okinawa." In this report, he claims that the American military trained a group of Okinawan *nisei* from Hawaii and the Okinawan civilians captured in Saipan and secretly sent them in a submarine to the northern shore of Okinawa for the purpose of intelligence gathering. He also claims that two of these Okinawans were captured in Naha in April 1945. However, he neither identifies the two supposedly captured Okinawans nor clarifies what sort of intelligence activities they were engaged in.

In short, Mabuchi's charges are not substantiated. Moreover, he himself heard about a dozen incidents in which Okinawans had been executed on the suspicion of spying, and he examined those incidents. He concluded that "there were no Okinawan civilians who had lived in Okinawa for a long time who were engaged in spying for the enemy." He further maintains that the executions of civilians as spies were "carried out by those who were at the lowest echelon of the military and were neither wise nor acceptable." The documents on U.S. intelligence activities at the U.S. National Archives that were declassified in the early 1980s made it clear that some officers who were graduates of Tokyo University and taken prisoner by the U.S. provided some detailed information on the Okinawan defense forces. This should prompt us to do more research on alleged spy incidents in order to clarify what really happened.

WHAT THE BATTLE OF OKINAWA TEACHES US NOW

What lessons can we draw from the Battle of Okinawa with all its horrendous characteristics? To put it into one short sentence: military forces cannot protect people. This is particularly true in a small island country such as Japan when it becomes a battlefield.

The *Instructions for Strategy* issued by the Japanese

Army during the war begins, as is well known, with these words: *"The main mission of the military is battle. Therefore, everything should be measured in terms of its relevance to battle.* The purpose of combat in general is to defeat and destroy the enemy and to gain victory as rapidly as possible." Okinawan civilians were forced to shoulder the weight of these words during the Battle of Okinawa. Consequently, they came to share the common understanding that once they were involved in the battle, they could not rely on the military for their protection in any way. Because "The main mission of the military is battle" and "therefore, everything should be measured in terms of its relevance to battles," non-combatants such as the elderly, children and women (whom the defense forces considered incapable of defense) were to be put aside as obstacles to military operations. The military existed only to fight and protect itself.

One prefectural government official in charge of evacuating schoolchildren wrote, as if he understood the true nature of the military, that although the evacuation of children had the same purpose as general evacuation, it carried with it a particular hope for the future of Okinawa. He noted, "The situation is so bad it can no longer be avoided that Okinawan civilians will commit collective suicide (*shudan jiketsu*). . . . Under these circumstances, I believe a top priority is to save the superior progeny of the Okinawans, for the future progress of Okinawa, by transporting schoolchildren to the mainland while such transport is still possible. Even if all those who remain in Okinawa perish, our descendants will grow up on the mainland and rise up in the future to reconstruct our land." Thus he explained the purpose of the evacuations of schoolchildren he organized.

Perhaps his idea contains some aspects that we can hardly agree with today. But what is important is that had the military regarded non-combatants as coming under their protection, evacuations would have been unnecessary and the collective self-killings that took place in the Kerama Islands, Iejima, Yomitan, and Mabuni would never have been carried out. In reality, non-combatants were far from being protected by the military. Instead, they found themselves in a situation where they were attacked by tigers at the front gate (the enemy troops) and wolves at the back gate (their own troops). The table below should illustrate this point. The data is derived from research conducted in 1960 by the Ministry of Health and Welfare concerning the causes of death of 11,483 children under the age of 14 during the Battle of Okinawa.

Death as a result of	Number of deaths
Evacuation of a cave	10,101
Cooking and trying to aid others	343
Self-killing	313
Transporting foodstuffs	194
Cooperating with Japanese troops	150
Being killed together with parents or custodians	100
Transporting ammunition	89
Building up a position	85
Offering food to military men	76
Shot by their own army	14
Running as a messenger	5
Transporting the wounded	3
Others	10

Total number of deaths=11,483

Here, the deaths as a result of "evacuation of a cave" and "offering food" indicate that the children died either because they were driven out of the caves in which they were hiding or because they had their food taken from them by troops of the defense force. "Shot by their own army" literally means the children were shot to death by the Japanese army.

The Ministry of Health and Welfare did this research at a time when adequate data was not available. The actual number of deaths is now estimated to be much higher. Nonetheless, this study is enough to show that the military did not protect non-combatants. And this was not limited to Okinawa. It also applied to the mainland and elsewhere. For example, Morisada Hosokawa, quoted earlier, wrote in his journal on June 11, 1945: "I visited Chief of Police Takamura at the Osaka Prefectural Office this afternoon. He told me about strife in the Diet. He also told me that the Commander of the Army in Osaka was making the outrageous argument that 'Since there is going to be a food shortage all over the country and the mainland will be a battlefield, *it will be necessary to kill all the elderly, the very young, and the feeble. We cannot allow Japan to perish because of those persons.*'"

Such an argument sounds too reprehensible to be believed. Yet, it was not just a monstrous remark by one individual. Rather, it reflected the military's basic position that once the battle began, protecting the people's lives was not its top priority. Some clear examples are found in the document "Absolute Rules to be Observed in the Battle for the Mainland" distributed to officers and soldiers stationed on the mainland. Article 2 states, "The wounded and the sick should not be sent back from the front during the battle. Keep in mind that the greatest thing you can do for your wounded comrades is to annihilate the enemy as quickly as possible. Therefore, you should concentrate on obliterating the enemy. It is not allowed to care for the wounded." Article 5 states, "It is expected that the enemy will use non-combatants, women, children and the elderly as their shields in order to destroy our fighting morale. In such a case, have faith that our compatriots share our hope for our country's victory rather than wanting to have their own lives saved, and do not hesitate to demolish the enemy." Such was the attitude of the military toward civilian safety.

The war historian, Masanori Ito, testified that the army in charge of defending the mainland reached the following conclusion as to what to do with non-combatants in southern Kyushu: "They had a plan around April [1945] to evacuate women, children, the elderly and the sick in Kirishimayama. However, they cancelled the plan after they concluded that it was impossible to secure shelter and food for some hundred-thousand persons and also extremely difficult to transport that many people during the war. As a consequence, they decided not to send the civilians from the battle front to relative safely and to let the *troops engage in the battle with civilians in their charge.*" In other words, their conclusion was synonymous with leaving their destiny to heaven. That would certainly have led to the same result as in the Battle of Okinawa.

Did the mentality of the military change after the war? The answer is definitely No. This is evident in the paper written by Third Major Masami Matsumoto of the Air Self-Defense Force. Entitled "Instructions for Air Defense Force Personnel Facing the Reexamination of the Japan-U.S. Security Treaty," the paper was awarded a prize as the "best paper of 1968" in the Air Self-Defense Force. Third Major Matsumoto asserts in this paper: "It is not the duty [of the

Self Defense Forces] to take antagonistic actions against our comrades and our compatriots. However, recent wars have revealed intraracial strife and psychological chaos among nationals inflamed by ideological conflict. Facing such a trend, the role of the military is becoming more important for maintaining social order and safety."

He also argues, "Each member of the Self Defense Forces must firmly uphold his faith and confidence in order to take strong action against law-breakers among our compatriots. It is imperative for instructors in each class to train members of the Self Defense Forces not to be deterred from taking decisive actions against their compatriots, including relatives and friends." Judging from these passages, we can see very little change in the postwar military's mentality from that of the prewar military. We can assume that not only was the Japanese military unable to protect people in the past, but there is no guarantee it will be able to do so in the future.

There is another lesson to be learned from the Battle of Okinawa, and that is, the scars of war last a long time. The legacy of the atomic bombs is one example; another is the Ishigaki Island Incident. The latter unfolded in the middle of April, 1945. A U.S. fighter plane landed on Ishigaki Island, one of the southernmost islands. The three American pilots were captured, taken prisoner, and killed in a brutal manner by the Naval Defense forces there. After Japan's surrender, the Navy troops feared this incident would be discovered, and therefore they cremated the bodies, put the ashes in a gasoline can, and let it sink in waters three kilometers north of Iriomote Island, about 20 kilometers west of Ishigaki. However, an anonymous letter sent from Kagoshima informed SCAP [Supreme Commander for the Allied Powers] of the incident. Thus, two years after the war, all those who were involved were arrested and tried by a war tribunal in Yokohama. At the end of a lengthy trial, forty-one out of the forty-seven defendants were sentenced to death. Among those who received the death penalty were seven soldiers from Okinawa. Only one of them was a regular soldier, and the remaining six had been farmers and conscripted only two weeks to three months prior to the incident. They were given the harshest sentence for having followed the orders of their superior to stab the American prisoners to death.

The Okinawan Federation in Tokyo immediately started a

campaign for clemency. Its president Zenchu Nakahara presented the Commander of the Eighth Army, Lieutenant General Eichelberger, a long letter of petition for clemency. In this petition, Mr. Nakahara argued that the Okinawans had been a peace-loving people since ancient times and abhorred violence. He made his point by citing his analysis of 142 folk stories and 1,530 poems in the *Omoro soshi* [a Ryukyuan literary classic], in which he found no word referring to killing people and concluded that the Okinawans had no concept for taking a person's life. Thus he argued on behalf of the Okinawan defendants that they had only followed the orders of their superiors, whom they had no choice but to obey. His plea worked, and eventually all the defendants from Okinawa were spared the death penalty. Nonetheless, they had to serve sentences ranging from five years to life. For them, the war continued even in peacetime.

Suffering from bitter wartime experiences, many of the Okinawan people have come to reject the American military bases and everything that is connected with war. Their resolve was expressed, for example, in their slogans during the Reversion Campaign, such as "Return to the Peace Constitution" and "Against War, For Peace." The Okinawans have learned the hard lesson that the military does not protect people. In addition, they are so strongly opposed to ever again being engaged in a war that their resolve is almost like part of their flesh and blood.

Yet, in spite of the Okinawan people's desire, the military bases have continued to occupy a large portion of the land in Okinawa even after the Reversion. Moreover, 75 percent of all U.S. military bases in Japan are concentrated in the tiny island of Okinawa. This is clearly not only a violation of the Japanese Constitution, which guarantees equality under law, but also an act of discrimination by the state. People who live adjacent to the military bases suffer every day from all sorts of ills brought on by the bases. They continue to cherish the Okinawan spirit (*Okinawa no kokoro*) for peace, and they want their basic human rights guaranteed and the autonomy of the prefectural government expanded. They are also working to spread the Okinawan spirit and to create a bright future for everyone around the world in overcoming the crises they face.

I implore those who want to reinforce Japan's armaments to re-examine what transpired in the Battle of Okinawa and to ponder its meanings. I also implore them to consider the Okinawan situation in which the state's will has been imposed upon people's lives. Particularly those who preach the importance of defense of our nation should be willing to accept military bases in their own backyard, or else their argument is worthless.

[Note: A version of this article first appeared in Japanese in *Sekai,* August 1985, pp. 31-47.]

THE BATTLE OF OKINAWA IN JAPANESE HISTORY BOOKS

Koji Taira

In the summer of 1982, there was an international uproar over what appeared to be the Japanese government's attempts to revise, distort, or otherwise falsify the history of Japan's aggression in Asia by means of school textbook screening. Okinawans, too, were outraged by the perceived tendency of the Japanese Ministry of Education (Monbusho) to conceal the wartime atrocities of the Japanese armies in Okinawa. In 1981-82, the Monbusho deleted from a draft high-school history textbook (not Saburo Ienaga's) the following sentence:

About 800 civilians of Okinawa prefecture were murdered by the Japanese troops on grounds that they hindered the fighting.

The official (*tatemae*) reason for the Monbusho's action was that the cited figure was not based on reliable sources. But the real (*honne*) reason was that the Monbusho regarded the book's assertion as unthinkable. A Monbusho official reportedly declared, "It is inconceivable that Japanese could do such a thing to other Japanese."

Okinawans strongly protested. The prefectural assembly unanimously passed a resolution emphasizing the truth of the civilian killings by the Japanese army during the Battle of Okinawa and urged the Monbusho to reinstate the original textbook statement. In 1983, the Monbusho again unfavorably reacted to a statement about Japanese troop atrocities against civilians in Okinawa, this time in a revised edition of Professor Saburo Ienaga's textbook (in English, see Saburo Ienaga, *The Pacific War, 1931-1945,* Frank Baldwin, trans., New York: Pantheon, 1978, a translation of the original edition published by Iwanami Shoten in 1968). Later in the same year, Ienaga brought his third lawsuit against the Monbusho, questioning the constitutionality of textbook screening and alleging illegal excesses in the Monbusho's discretionary authority on a number of points, including the correction demanded on the Okinawa issue.

Ienaga won a partial victory in his third lawsuit in the High Court. He appealed to the Supreme Court, and the Supreme Court ruled on that appeal in August, 1997, in Ienaga's favor on one of the four specific complaints. However, the court sided with the Monbusho on the point relating to Okinawa. For residents of Okinawa it was another disappointment on the heels of many in their unequal relationship with the Japanese state.

THE ISSUE

The Okinawan reactions in support of the original Ienaga footnote and against the Monbusho's correction-order are freighted with perceptions of cultural, historical, and political relations between Okinawa and Japan. Rendering the issue in English is also difficult because of the almost untranslatable semantics of Japanese discourse on the issue, and because these have often been deliberately distorted, shaded, or nuanced for legal or public relations advantages.

Below are reproduced George Hicks's translation, as provided in his *Japan's Wartime Memories: Amnesia or Concealment?* (Brookfield, VT: Ashgate Publishing Co., 1997), p. 116, together with developments which, although not mentioned by Hicks, are nonetheless important. The supplementary material is bracketed in this manner: < . . .>. The italics are also mine.

1. Original Ienaga Manuscript [footnote]: Okinawa became a theater of land combat and approximately 160,000 residents, old and young, male and female, met untimely deaths amid the conflict. *More than a few of these were killed by the Japanese army.*

2. Correction Comment <by the Monbusho>: <Although among the people of Okinawa Prefecture *it was a fact that more than a few were killed by the Japanese army,*> as *mass suicides* were the most numerous among the people of Okinawa Prefecture who fell victim, *the whole aspect of the battle of Okinawa* is not clear without adding an account of *mass suicides.*

3. <Resubmitted Manuscript by Ienaga: Okinawa Prefecture became a theater of land combat and approximately 160,000 residents, old and young, male and female, met untimely deaths *under the offensive of the American army, by mass suicide, by being driven out of the caves by the Japanese army into the crossfire on the battle-ground,*

or murdered **[satsugai]** *as in cases of babies making noise or crying in the caves or persons suspected of being spies.>*

4. <Second correction comment by the Monbusho: The correction submitted is too extensive and greatly exceeds the scope of our correction comment. We merely told you to include mass suicides because these were numerous.>

5. Account as qualified <i.e., approved by the Monbusho>: Okinawa became a theater of land combat and approximately 160,000 residents, old and young, male and female, met untimely deaths by shelling, bombing, or being driven to *mass suicide*. More than a few were *killed by the Japanese army.*

The bone of contention was whether or not "mass suicide" should be mentioned along with the civilian killings by the Japanese army. The primary motive of the Monbusho apparently was to defend Japanese troop conduct in the Battle of Okinawa, which was consistent with the Monbusho's reaction to Ienaga's description of the Nanking massacre. At the 1980 textbook screening, the Monbusho flatly rejected Ienaga's description of the Nanking massacre. But when the same description reappeared in the revised text screening of 1983, the Monbusho acquiesced to the wording while raising new objections. A similar change of mind occurred over Okinawa.

The 1981 screening (not of Ienaga's book) deleted a sentence about Japanese army atrocities in Okinawa and, as we have mentioned earlier, provoked Okinawan protests. Perhaps as a learning effect of this experience, at the 1983 screening the Monbusho accepted Ienaga's statement that "more than a few [Okinawans] were killed by the Japanese army," but it demanded that he add "mass suicide." This again provoked widespread protests in Okinawa. At one time the court even moved to Okinawa for hearings from local witnesses and experts.

Why did Okinawans object so strongly to the concept and use of "mass suicide?" This is not a simple question. Ethics, aesthetics, semantics, deep-seated feelings, and ideologies are all enmeshed in the phrase "mass suicide." In English the meaning of the phrase sounds straightforward, but this is not the case in Japanese. What is rendered as "mass suicide" is the Japanese phrase *shudan jiketsu*, with "mass," or "group," corresponding to *shudan* and "suicide" to *jiketsu*.

ANALYSIS

The usual Japanese word for "suicide" is *jisatsu*. So to call the Okinawan suicides *jiketsu* implies that they were a special kind of suicide. Indeed, *jiketsu* is because of reason, motive, manner, place, timing, and so on, a heroic, awe-inspiring, splendid act of taking one's own life. To call someone's suicide *jiketsu* is to honor and glorify the person who had the extraordinary courage to kill himself or herself in this manner. Calling such cases *jisatsu* would amount to a blasphemy. (Another euphemism for suicide is *jigai*, or hurting oneself, understood to be hurting severely enough to die.)

In the Battle of Okinawa, many Okinawans killed themselves by their own hands or assisted by their relatives or friends. The scenes of such group acts [see George Hicks's book, p. 63, or Norma Field's, *In the Realm of a Dying Emperor* (New York: Pantheon, 1991), pp. 56-67] were anything but glorious. An unpublished memoir by an American who was an eye-witness to a couple of *shudan jiketsu* was recently discovered and published in translation in the *Ryukyu Shimpo* (June 3, 1996). His graphic descriptions of the carnage belie the glorification of *shudan jiketsu* by the Japanese Self Defense Forces.

Shudan jiketsu, then, is a misnomer for the kind of group deaths to which it refers. The group typically included older people, women with children, underage boys and girls, and babies. How would they, many of whom did not even know what it meant to kill or die, kill themselves en masse? Some had been given hand grenades by the army. Several persons huddled around a single hand grenade to enhance its killing efficiency and died by being blown to pieces. Under the circumstances, those who died instantly in this way were the lucky ones.

Hand grenades exhausted, there were no more instruments of killing save what they had with them or found in nature: strings, kitchen knives, razor blades, sticks, rat poison, rocks, stones, etc. Imagine a group of terror-stricken people totally untrained in the art of killing trying to assist one another to die (a euphemism in this case for poisoning, strangling, stabbing, cutting, slashing, or beating one another to death). If one witnessed the scenes in real time and place, even the most battle-hardened soldier would blink and instinctively cry out, "Stop! Stop! Stop!" This indeed was the first reaction of the American soldier whose memoir was recently found.

Descriptions of how Okinawans died in the so-called *shudan jiketsu* evoke no sense of nobility, glory, dignity, honor, or serenity—qualities implied in the idealized notion of the Japanese word *jiketsu*. In hindsight and in view of postwar values, this so-called *shudan jiketsu* amounted to useless, meaningless deaths (*inujini*) of which Okinawans on the whole, including survivors, are deeply ashamed. Those who survived the horror simply clammed up, determined to bury the shame in the deepest recesses of their hearts forever. At some point, however, they began to talk, at first hesitantly and then torrentially.

To some extent, misunderstandings and unacceptable interpretations of the tragedy of the Battle of Okinawa by Japanese governmental agencies, private authors, and movie makers were partly responsible for helping Okinawans overcome their hesitation and begin talking in their own defense. The Japanese said all kinds of things unacceptable to Okinawans, ranging from disingenuous idealization to devastating denigration. For example, the Self Defense Forces took the Japanese word *jiketsu* literally and fantasized that (to quote Hicks, p. 62), "earnestly praying for the fatherland's victory, they in all tranquility collectively dispatched themselves." To Okinawans, this is a blatant lie. *Shudan jiketsu* of civilians in the Battle of Okinawa was not like the story-book suicides of samurai after their last-ditch stand in a lost battle.

A Japanese novelist, Ms. Ayako Sono, romanticized the *shudan jiketsu* and claimed that she had no words, only profound respect for the Okinawans who died such heroic deaths. What should one make of such tender feelings of Japanese toward a people they habitually look down upon? Given the traditional Japanese attitude toward death, perhaps they are sincere. Japan is a country which deifies even its war criminals after death. Besides, *jiketsu* is the kind of word that evokes just such reverential reactions. But no gratitude should be expected from Okinawans.

On the other hand, there are also cynics among the Japanese. In the 1950s, the author Soichi Oya explicitly called the Okinawan self-executions *inujini*, deriving from the word *inu*, meaning "dog," and therefore often translated as a "dog's death." For Japanese a dog's death implies that it was a useless death; Americans, I believe, tend to associate with the phrase that the death was also ignominious and painful. In either case, while Okinawans recognize among themselves that many of them died in vain, they find it intolerable and callous for outsiders so to describe their deaths, particularly when they died in a war that the Japanese state brought to them.

The perception gap between Japanese and Okinawans about the war underlies the Monbusho's insistence on, and Okinawa's resistance to, *shudan jiketsu* being added to any description of the Battle of Okinawa. Safeguarding the honor of the Japanese state is the paramount motivation behind textbook screening. It fits the bureaucratic instinct to say, as an exhortation to all Japanese school-children, that the people of Okinawa died for the glory of the state and the emperor.

It is, of course, an ultimate dishonesty and opportunistic act for the Japanese government to hold up the Okinawans as a model of loyal citizenship. After their own country, the Ryukyu kingdom, was conquered by Japan, Okinawans were subjected to ferocious indoctrination and re-cast into subjects of the Japanese emperor. In the course of becoming Japanese, Okinawans also suffered indignities and discrimination in civil rights, economic opportunities and social standing. In light of this history, for the Japanese government to play with words and suggest that Okinawans are a model for the nation is either a cynical exercise in euphemism or a transparent attempt to cover up past wrongs.

Okinawans dislike the word *jiketsu* not only because it is the wrong word for the kind of deaths they suffered but, more importantly, because it conceals the true nature of the relationship between the Japanese army and the Okinawan population during the Battle of Okinawa. In the eyes of the Japanese army, Okinawans were not like themselves, not the same as people living in the rest of Japan. According to Masaiye Ishihara, professor at Okinawa International University and an authority on Okinawan war memories, the Japanese army was suspicious of Okinawans' loyalty to Japan and considered them potential spies for the enemy. Because of the labor shortage, however, the army drafted Okinawans for work on the fortification of the island. As a result, many Okinawans became familiar with the structure and quality of Japanese defense arrangements.

In order to deny the enemy the possibility of acquiring information on Japanese defense secrets from Okinawans who might surrender or be captured, the army undertook extensive propaganda to prevent such an outcome. The army terrified Okinawans with tales of extreme enemy cruelties and manipulated their minds and feelings in favor of killing themselves in the event they faced the danger of surrender or capture.

Supported by the testimony of Okinawans, Ienaga argued in court that *shudan jiketsu* was caused by the coercion or instigation of the Japanese army and clearly differed from voluntary suicide. Ienaga viewed the Monbusho order to include it in his text as a ploy for minimizing the impact on the reader of the Japanese army atrocities and considered the imposition of such an order on him an illegal abuse of administrative discretion. In essence, he argued that the Okinawans who executed themselves were killed by the Japanese army and were already included in the statement that "more than a few were killed by the Japanese army." The Monbusho did not want that statement to stand alone for fear that it might leave the reader, or student, with the wrong impression about the Japanese army. For the same reason, the Monbusho wanted the description of the Nanking massacre toned down.

THE SUPREME COURT DECISION

In the course of the litigation, the Monbusho apparently retreated from its initial hard line based on the ideal image of *jiketsu* to a view substantially similar to what Ienaga and the Okinawans had argued all along. In the final argument in defense of its position that *shudan jiketsu* should be added to the text, the Monbusho claimed (as reported in the press):

from the statement ". . . killed by the Japanese army" by itself, the reader would ordinarily understand [that all the victims were] *directly* killed by the army. *Jiketsu* [in this case] cannot be considered the same as *direct* killing by the army. Its parallel entry in the text [together with ". . . killed by the Japanese army"] would not cause a misunderstanding that it was a voluntary, noble, spontaneous death (*nin'i de sukona jihatsushi*) (The *Ryukyu Shimpo*, July 19,1997).

Ienaga argued that the Okinawans' so-called *jiketsu* was by "coercion or instigation" of the Japanese army, and therefore implied in the phrase "killed by the Japanese army." The Monbusho obviously invented a stricter standard for being killed—i.e., "directly." Ienaga and the Okinawans argued that coercion or instigation was a sufficiently direct cause for the Okinawans' deaths. For example, the Japanese army, which had previously told Okinawans that they must never surrender and must choose death if they were faced with the prospect of surrender or capture, distributed hand grenades to Okinawan civilians whenever they could afford to do so. Moreover, the army demonstrated in numerous incidents what would become of Okinawans who tried to surrender to the enemy: they were shot or bayoneted to death. Given these examples of "direct" killing by the army, it is not surprising that for most Okinawans the line between being "directly" killed and becoming one's own executioner was very thin.

The Supreme Court, however, sided with the Monbusho. On August 29, 1997, the five justices of the petty bench unanimously decided that in view of the prevailing academic opinion that two special phenomena characterized the Battle of Okinawa—that numerous people were driven to their deaths by the Japanese army, and that numerous people died of *shudan jiketsu*—it was not illegal for the Monbusho to issue a correction comment urging the mention of *shudan jiketsu* in the textbook (The *Ryukyu Shimpo*, August 30, 1997, p. 6).

This correction was one of four that the Monbusho issued in 1983 for Ienaga's text. The four had to do with descriptions of 1) popular resistance to Japan in Korea during the Sino-Japanese War of 1894-95; 2) the Nanking massacre, with special emphasis on the violation of Chinese women by the Japanese army; 3) Unit 731, responsible for medical atrocities in Manchuria during World War II; and 4) the army atrocities in Okinawa. On top of these specific issues there was the overarching question of the constitutionality of textbook screening by the government.

In simplistic "win-or-lose" terms, Ienaga lost on all

counts except the third, relating to Unit 731. The Monbusho's opinion was that the whole reference to Unit 731 should be deleted. The Supreme Court ruled by a three-to-two majority that the correction opinion in this instance was an illegal abuse of the Monbusho's discretionary power in textbook screening.

Because the disadvantages faced by textbook writers vis-à-vis the Monbusho are so overwhelming, Ienaga's modest victory in his third lawsuit was widely hailed as a great victory that stopped the march of the Monbusho juggernaut and reversed the losing streaks of authors and publishers over the last two decades. But in Okinawa, feelings of defeat were pervasive. The Supreme Court refused to expunge the hated expression *shudan jiketsu* and helped to conceal the real nature of it by the vague, potentially misleading statement forced on the textbook by the Monbusho.

FURTHER INTERPRETATIONS

Masaiye Ishihara has tested how readers interpret the revised statement on the Battle of Okinawa in Ienaga's textbook. Underscoring the phrase "driven to mass suicide" in the final, Monbusho version (#5 quoted earlier), Ishihara asked "driven by whom?" and offered respondents two choices: a) the American army, or b) the Japanese army. Fifty-five percent chose a) and only twenty-seven percent chose b). This is of course directly contrary to what Ienaga intended to communicate.

Why is the crucial phrase, "driven to mass suicide," likely to be interpreted as "driven by the American army?" Ishihara argues that since the "shelling" and "bombing" that directly preceded the phrase in question were clearly being done by the American army, it is a natural inference from the logic of the sentence that the same army also drove Okinawans to mass suicide.

The Japanese original is also very vague compared to the translated English version. In fact, it is only one long sentence with words strung together by the ever flexible Japanese conjunctions. A less elegant, but more direct, translation might be:

Okinawa became a theater of land combat and approximately 160,000 residents, old and young, male and female, met untimely deaths by shelling

> and bombing, being driven to *shudan jiketsu, or by
> other causes, not a few among them killed by the
> Japanese army.*

However one reads the statement, "mass suicide" appears to have been a different cause of death from "killed by the Japanese army." That is why Okinawans did not want an explicit mention of mass suicide along with "killed by the Japanese army." By forcing the revision of the text, the Monbusho has succeeded in completely falsifying an important part of the memories of the Battle of Okinawa, and the Japanese army is freed from responsibility for driving people to mass suicide.

Ishihara and others have accumulated enormous quantities of historical material, documentary as well as oral, that leave no question that the Japanese army not only paid no attention to the safety of the civilian residents of Okinawa but encouraged, or in some cases actually ordered, them to die.

The wartime Japanese ideology dictated that suicide was the "duty" of the emperor's subjects when faced with the humiliation of capture by the enemy. This idea had been repeatedly driven into the Okinawans' brains by wartime indoctrination and propaganda. The implicit consensus had been formed among the people that when American troops came into sight it was time to die by charging the enemy or by their own hands. During the war, a massive loss of life after a hopeless battle was euphemistically called *gyokusai* (shattering jewels), aimed at creating a heroic, aesthetic delusion about the glory of massive dramatic annihilations. This is what happened at the Suicide Cliff of Saipan in 1944, and in many other hopeless battles. But these deaths were not called *shudan jiketsu.*

After the war, the wartime rhetoric was discredited and the entire Japanese language, grammar, and usage were reinvented. When Okinawans began to publish their own reports on the Battle of Okinawa in the 1950s, journalists and writers had a problem deciding which expressions to use for many unusual developments during the battle. The mass suicide phenomena would have been called *gyokusai* during the war, but the word had become too distasteful to many by then. Unfortunately, the new expression that replaced it was *shudan jiketsu*, coined by an Okinawan reporter,

Ryohaku Ota of the *Okinawa Times*, in his classic *Tetsu no bofu* (The Typhoon of Steel, 1950).

Norma Field offers a helpful observation on the semantics of *shudan jiketsu* in her book *In the Realm of a Dying Emperor* (p. 61): "[T]he neutral translation . . . might be 'collective suicide.' In this instance, the neutral choice is inadequate. For if the end of life was 'self-determined,'. . . the determination was made under duress, both in the form of the presence of the two armies [American and Japanese] and in the long discipline required for the production of Japanese imperial subjects. For this reason I think of *shudan jiketsu* as 'compulsory group suicide.'" I wholly agree with Field's choice of words.

II.

OKINAWA: THE POLITICAL

AND MILITARY

SETTING

THE BOLIVIAN CONNECTION: U.S. BASES AND OKINAWAN EMIGRATION

Kozy K. Amemiya

In February 1996, Chalmers Johnson, president of the Japan Policy Research Institute, spoke in San Diego about the U.S. military bases in Okinawa. He had just returned from Okinawa, where he had given a lecture at the invitation of Governor Ota. Listening to Dr. Johnson, Thomas Royden remembered what he had heard at the U.S. Embassy in La Paz, Bolivia, about twenty-five years earlier: that a large number of Okinawans had been flown in by the American military and had been dumped in the jungle. Royden had been studying the spontaneous colonization of indigenous people from the Altiplano into the lowlands of Bolivia. "Don't go there," he remembered having been told. "Those Okinawans are very angry and constantly drinking and fighting. It's a dangerous place." Was there a link, he now wondered, between those Okinawans in the Bolivian jungle and the construction of the U.S. bases in Okinawa?

A few weeks later I stumbled onto a book that confirmed the link Royden had asked about. The book was primarily about the immigrant community in Bolivia from mainland Japan called the Colonia San Juan Yapacaní, but it contained a few pages that referred to another settlement of Okinawans in Bolivia. It also noted that the Okinawan emigration to Bolivia was planned in order to deal with the farmers displaced by the construction of the U.S. military bases.[1] Now Royden (my husband) was sorry he had heeded the U.S. Embassy's advice and hadn't gone to the Okinawan settlement, although he knew exactly where it was located. Instead, he had visited the other Japanese settlement, Colonia San Juan Yapacaní. So he suggested that we now visit the Okinawan settlement—he to see it with his own eyes, and I to investigate how the Okinawans ended up there.

I grew up in postwar Japan, enjoying the rapid improvement in living standards, without hearing much about Okinawa. Even when I was a student and began looking at Japan's growing economic strength with critical eyes, I was indifferent to the price Okinawans were forced to pay for Japan's prosperity. Okinawa was simply too exotic for me to consider as a part of domestic Japanese issues and not exotic enough to attract my attention as a part of larger Asian issues. Thus when the Okinawan problem finally entered my consciousness, I felt that as a mainland Japanese (*hondo no Nihonjin*) I had to do something to help right the wrong that Okinawans had endured. The investigation of the link between the Okinawan emigration to Bolivia and the construction of the U.S. military bases in Okinawa provided me with the opportunity to do just that. This is how the JPRI project about Okinawans in the jungle of Bolivia began. In addition to visiting Okinawa and Bolivia to interview scholars and the immigrants themselves, we have also gathered, and continue to gather, as much data as possible in the United States.

Very early in our research I came across several references to the emigration to Bolivia in the context of the construction of the U.S. military bases. For example, Oshiro Tatsuhiro, the winner of the 1967 Akutagawa Prize for *Cocktail Party*, wrote a novella about Okinawan emigrants to Bolivia called *Nanbei-zakura* (South American Cherry Blossoms). The protagonist of this novella remarks about the initial stage of the emigration, "Americans confiscated land in Okinawa and moved all the landowners to Bolivia."[2] One of the most notorious cases of land confiscation by the U.S. military, using bayonets and bulldozers, took place in 1955 at Isahama, which is today in Ginowan city, the location of Futenma Marine Corps Air Station. The book that describes this incident reports that thirty-two families lost their homes and farmlands and were removed to a highland area about ten miles away. Their new land was not suited for agriculture. The book concludes this episode with the statement that most of those farmers, unable to make a living in their new locale, emigrated to Bolivia two years later.[3] In Okinawa, the relationship between the land appropriation by the U.S. military and the emigration to Bolivia appears to be common knowledge. No one in Okinawa I spoke to denied our conjecture about the link between the two, and Governor Ota explicitly confirmed it. The only reservation voiced by some, who echoed our suspicion, was the difficulty of finding solid documentary proof.

In Bolivia I interviewed Okinawans mostly from the first

three groups who came there in 1954 and 1955. I also distributed questionnaires among all the Okinawan residents in Colonia Okinawa and Santa Cruz and made a survey regarding their motives for emigration and their current opinions about the U.S. bases in Okinawa. I also interviewed several people who had emigrated in the fourth group, in 1957, and a few in later groups who emigrated in the early 1960s. In all, I interviewed 36 men (26 in Colonia Okinawa and 10 in Santa Cruz) and 14 women (11 in Colonia and 3 in Santa Cruz). I distributed my questionnaire to all Okinawan households in Colonia and Santa Cruz, but the majority of the 112 responses (66 from men and 46 from women) came from the early settlers.

Among my interviewees, several had indeed had their farmland occupied by the U.S. military. The majority, however, had come from areas that were not taken for the construction of the U.S. bases. It also turned out that the farmers and their families from Isahama had emigrated to Brazil, not Bolivia.

Why, then, have Okinawans come to regard the emigration to Bolivia as so closely related to the land seizures by the U.S. military? Was it a mere coincidence that Bolivian emigration was vigorously promoted with financial support by the U.S. at a time when the U.S. military had constructed the bases and was about to expand them even more? To investigate the issue of Bolivian immigration and American involvement in it, we are concerned with two sets of questions: (a) how did the plan come about, and (b) who were those immigrants and what has happened to them?

HOW THE PLAN CAME ABOUT

The emigration program sent about 3,200 Okinawans to Bolivia between 1954 and 1964. As of 1995, about 800 remaining immigrants and their offspring live in the settlement called Colonia Okinawa and a few hundred in Santa Cruz.[4] The original plan was much more ambitious, intending to send 12,000 immigrants in 10 years. It seems the idea of encouraging more Okinawan emigration to Bolivia may have come from a few prewar settlers there, who had heard of the horrendous devastation of their homeland by the war and wanted to help their compatriots. In 1948 they set up a group to send aid of all kinds to Okinawa and soon started planning to receive more immigrants. By 1950, they were looking for an appropriate site and had found a place in the Department [province] of Santa Cruz, where they began negotiating to purchase 2,500 hectares. Meanwhile, in Okinawa in the same year, the U.S. Civil Administration of the Ryukyu Islands (USCAR) was set up to implement American policies and programs. The Okinawan settlers' efforts in Bolivia caught the attention of some officers, who commissioned James L. Tigner at the Hoover Institution, Stanford University, to explore the possibilities of shipping Okinawan emigrants to Latin America.

Tigner spent ten months in 1951-52 travelling from Mexico to Peru, Brazil, and Bolivia. He took note of the eagerness of the early Okinawan settlers in Bolivia to help their compatriots. The Bolivian government was also receptive to receiving Okinawan immigrants. Its new president, Victor Paz Estenssoro of the National Revolutionary Movement (MNR), was intent on carrying out a social revolution to transform Bolivia, with financial aid from the U.S., and to achieve self-sufficiency in food supply. He was particularly interested in turning the state of Santa Cruz into the granary of Bolivia. The United States was also interested in supporting social reforms in Bolivia in order to keep Communism at bay.

Tigner reported to USCAR in September 1952 with a strong recommendation that the eastern region of Bolivia be chosen as the site for Okinawan settlement. He urged USCAR to set up a budget of US$160,000 for transporting an initial 400 immigrants. Tigner's recommendation was influential with the U.S. military and also helped create a fervor among Okinawans who had been promoting overseas emigration. However, more than a year passed without further serious study of the site, and yet the emigration plan continued to roll on. Meanwhile, in Bolivia, the early Okinawan settlers had secured the 2,500 hectares they had previously located and registered them as the Uruma settlement. They also negotiated with the Bolivian government to release 10,000 hectares of government-owned land adjacent to the Uruma settlement.

In Okinawa there were many who enthusiastically embraced the Bolivia emigration plan. The Ryukyu Government, which was created in 1952 by the United States to perform administrative and legislative functions under the supervision of USCAR, headed by the U.S. High Commissioner, passed legislation in November 1953 providing loans to emigrants. Shortly after that, two delegates—one from the Overseas Association of Okinawa and the other from the Ryukyu Government—were sent to Latin America to "survey the land." Their trip, however, served merely to acknowledge what had already been decided informally—that is, to settle Okinawan emigrants at the Uruma site.

As soon as the survey team had returned to Okinawa, the plan was announced and applicants were solicited through bulletins placed in public offices and newspapers. Each family was promised 50 hectares of free land in an area of rich soil, with no known diseases, and the prospect of railroad access in the near future. Housing was supposedly awaiting the settlers. As a result of this emigration fervor promoted by the Ryukyu Government, four hundred finalists were selected within a month out of some 4,000 applicants, all of them attracted by the prospect of instantly owning 50 hectares of land. Of the 400 accepted, 80 were single men. After a week-long lecture series about emigration in general, the emigrants set out for Bolivia in 1954 with great fanfare.

Both Tigner and the Okinawan emigration enthusiasts repeatedly emphasized the need for emigration as a solution to Okinawa's overpopulation and its shrinking arable land base. Indeed, acute postwar food shortages were experienced by all Okinawans, men and women, young and old. All the immigrants I interviewed said they were eating mostly yams and very little rice. (They told me that yams were the staple and rice a luxury item in Okinawa. The U.S. food aid provided to Okinawans for several years after the war was standard American food, such as canned meat and pork-and-beans, but immigrants claim it did not ease the shortage of their staple food.) Many postwar Okinawans eased their hunger pangs by eating cycads, a primitive Okinawan plant containing both starch and a poison that requires a lot of work to remove. People ate it only when they were desperate for food. Mr. C in Colonia Okinawa recalls that for this reason if you got caught stealing a cycad in order to eat it, you were forgiven.

Okinawa's overpopulation and its shrinking arable land were not entirely a product of nature. Both Tigner and the Okinawan emigration enthusiasts mention only in passing that the appropriation of arable land by the U.S. military exacerbated the problems.[5] Also, whereas in mainland Japan, the Eugenic Protection Law was passed in 1948 for the purpose of virtually legalizing abortion in the midst of the heightened concern about postwar overpopulation (with subsequent revisions in 1949 and 1952, abortion became available on request), the legislature of the Ryukyu Government passed a similar law in 1956 only to have it vetoed by the U.S. High Commissioner.

Two common themes emerge from my interviews with Okinawan male immigrants: (a) nearly all of them were employed at one time or another by the U.S. military bases, doing work called "military labor" (*gun sagyo*), and (b) they developed a strong sense of humiliation and resentment as a result of that experience. The vigorous construction of U.S. military bases began in 1950, turning the whole of Okinawa into one massive fort. The "military labor" demanded by the "construction boom" attracted a large portion of the work force because it paid higher wages than other jobs. For example, a construction worker of the time earned twice as much as a school principal. Yet, Okinawans were paid considerably less than other workers. Mr. C, who taught at a high school before he took a job at a military base, was lured by a wage three times higher but he recalled the pay structure. "Americans were at the top of the pay scale, of course. Next were Filipinos, then the Japanese from the mainland. We Okinawans were placed at the bottom, yet we did the hardest work."

Their resentment seems also to have been triggered by their working conditions. Many of them remember with bitterness that "Americans had us work like slaves." It was less the hard work than the attitude of the American bosses that they resented. Mr. N remembers, "We worked hard, but the Americans always complained about our work." Mr. L puts it more directly: "I just didn't like being bossed around by young GIs." Meanwhile Americans of the time were quite oblivious to such resentments as they watched the Pulitzer prize-winning stage-play (adapted from an earlier novel) and then the immensely popular film (1956) *The Teahouse of the August Moon*, which infantilizes the Okinawans and portrays them as charming, anxious-to-please natives.

Okinawans acknowledge that the Americans as individuals treated them much better than they had expected. "Still, it was unpleasant to live under the U.S. military occupation," summarizes Mr. D about his life in postwar Okinawa. Mr. B is more specific. "The Americans may have been nice as individuals, but politically they would immediately label us as 'reds' if we participated in demonstrations."

The situation worsened as the construction boom faded. Many men began to be fired or laid-off, and there were not enough jobs for new graduates from the senior and junior high schools. Mr. P, who worked as a land surveyor at Kadena Air Base, was so incensed when he learned that many of his coworkers were going to be fired that he quit his job. "I was so angry, all I wanted at the time was to get out of Okinawa and just go anywhere." That was when he learned about the emigration plan to Bolivia. Mr. P was typical of the men who applied. Likewise, Mr. N described his state of mind at the time he learned about the plan: "I just couldn't stand the foreign occupation any more." Echoing Mr. P's and Mr. N's sentiments, Mr. V and Mr. L told me that they had actually wanted to go to Japan but could not get visas. All of these men jumped at the opportunity to leave Okinawa for Bolivia. They had no choice of destination. To them emigration to Bolivia simply promised them a way out of stifling Okinawa, where they had no bright prospect for their future, and a way to become an instant landowner of fifty hectares.

It was by no means a coincidence that the emigration to Bolivia was announced at that particular time. Given the labor unrest, the emigration plan was designed to "preserve the political stability" of Okinawa, as Tigner himself put it. The Americans were concerned that discontent would lead to communism:

> The Okinawan people are traditionally farmers, and ownership of land is one of their most cherished desires in life. Okinawa, with its rising population and decreasing areas of available land, will offer progressively less future for the farming population. Restiveness and dissatisfaction will inevitably accompany the waning prospects of land ownership and fading hopes for an adequate livelihood, particularly among the youth of Okinawa. Since Communists appeal to the youth of a nation, and with apparent success in many areas of the Communist-dominated world, the youth of Okinawa represents a potentially vulnerable element of the population. The prospects of obtaining

large tracts of free land in a distant community as afforded by an emigration program will give fresh hope to the youth and in this way serve to cope with their discontent and susceptibility to the Communists' false promises of reward.[6]

The early 1950s were indeed a volatile period in which anti-U.S.-occupation sentiment was spreading. With discontent building up among Okinawans, particularly the young and vigorous, emigration functioned as a safety valve. And it worked, I thought as I listened to Mr. C, still angry when he described how his family's farm had been posted with signs by the U.S. military reading "NATIVES OFF-LIMITS." Before leaving Okinawa, Mr. C had become an avid supporter of Senaga Kamejiro and, although not a member of the Okinawa People's Party, would go to the political rallies and applaud Senaga's speeches. (Senaga was chairman of the Okinawa People's Party and was elected mayor of Naha in 1956. The U.S. High Commissioner was so threatened by this he removed Senaga from office the following year.) What would Mr. C have done had he stayed in Okinawa? And what would have happened in Okinawa if he and men like him had not been given an opportunity to get out?

I see a parallel function in San Juan Yapacaní—another Japanese settlement located about 100 kilometers due west of Colonia Okinawa. Its immigrants came from all over Japan, but mostly from northern Kyushu. Immigration there started in 1957, when the violent labor disputes over the closing of the coal mines still raged. This topic also needs to be further explored.

THE IMMIGRANTS AND THEIR NEW LIVES

The Okinawan emigrants were divided into two groups for logistical reasons. The first group arrived in Bolivia in August of 1954. The second group arrived a month later. All but a few were shocked at and disappointed by the place they were going to make their home. It was covered with thick jungle, there were no adequate roads to the Uruma settlement from the railroad or anywhere else, and no bridge over the Rio Grande for access to Santa Cruz. The housing was not completed and, worst of all, there was no potable water nearby. Even the toughest men, who claim to have been so well prepared that they were neither shocked nor disappointed when they first arrived, remember the hardship of getting fresh water. They had to walk for miles to a pond to collect brackish water that was shared with wild animals. They even drank rainwater that collected in the furrows of wheel tracks. They dug a well by hand that was about eight meters deep, but the water was so salty it immediately caused diarrhea and burned the vegetables in their gardens.

The worst was yet to come. A mysterious disease spread, taking 15 lives and sending eighty-some others to their sickbeds between October 1954 and April 1955. The disease, its cause never determined, came to be called the "Uruma disease." So isolated from any outside help, barely connected with the nearest town of Santa Cruz by bad roads made worse with the onset of the rainy season, the immigrants felt abandoned. Medical help from Santa Cruz or the Ryukyu Government or the Americans was less than adequate. In March 1955, a group of physicians—three North Americans and two Bolivians—did arrive in the Uruma Settlement, but they were more interested in learning about the disease than in treating the sick. As soon as they took blood samples from the ill, they hurried back to Santa Cruz without offering any treatment.[7] Mr. S remembers that the sick whose blood samples were taken were not only left untreated but were deliberately denied treatment because the doctors wanted to observe and compare them with those who had been previously treated. Some of the former got worse. "You would have been better off not seeing those doctors," Mr. S says. His whole family except for his mother fell ill and one of his younger brothers died in December of 1954. "It devastated my parents," he remembers.

Many of the Okinawans started to wonder aloud whether the emigration to Bolivia was a government policy to dump them in the jungle. "I have never been rid of that suspicion," says Mr. E. Mr. C is more blunt: "I believe it was indeed a 'thinning policy' (*mabiki seisaku*)." (*Mabiki* refers to the thinning of young plants or fruits so that the remaining ones will grow big and healthy. It is also used to refer to infanticide for the purpose of reducing the number of mouths to feed.) Other immigrants told me they were so preoccupied at the time with simply surviving they could not afford to reflect on such things. Only later, when they started reading what others in Okinawa wrote about postwar Okinawan history did they begin to think, "Ah, yes, the Bolivia immigration policy intended to dump us in the jungle." Thus their perspective may be, to some extent, shaped by the reflection and reexamination that have been taking place in Okinawa during the last ten years or so.

To make matters worse, in February 1955, the Uruma settlement was attacked first by a terrible flood and then by a horde of rats, which spread disease even further. It turned out that the settlement site was actually located in the floodplain of the Rio Grande. The immigrants' spirits sank still further. "Every day people were fighting. Every day I heard men talking of nothing but escape," Mr. H said of the atmosphere in the settlement at that time.

Misfortunes struck harder at some than others. Mr. T lost his wife to the "Uruma disease" and was left to care for his four young children. "I don't want to remember those days," he said to me. Yet he clearly remembers the ages of his children when his wife died and tells me so without being asked: they were 1, 4, 6, and 9. The hardest part was looking after the infant, he added. Today he runs a small motorcycle parts and hardware shop that is attached to his livingroom, on whose wall pictures of his wife and of himself when young are hanging side by side. These are copies of their passport photos, he says. He never remarried.

Mrs. R's husband became the fifteenth victim of the "Uruma disease." She was heavily pregnant when she left Okinawa and had given birth to her fourth son on board ship. Caring for her infant as well as her other young children with water hard to get, food scarce, flooding that spoiled their bedding and belongings, and rats and mosquitoes by the hundreds was bad enough. Now she was left alone. What did she do? "I wished we could return to Okinawa, but I had no money. No one had that kind of money in those days. People helped me, though, in any way they could." Three years later she went to Santa Cruz with her youngest child and worked as a live-in maid for a Japanese family, leaving her older children in others' care. She lost one son to drowning. (In fact, more tragedies struck the immigrant families on the uncharted rivers and bad roads than would probably have been the case had they remained in Okinawa. Of the 14 women I spoke to, three had lost sons to drowning, one to a traffic accident, and still another had a severely disabled son due to another traffic accident.) In spite of all the tragedies in her life, Mrs. R remained incredibly cheerful. "It was my destiny and couldn't be helped (*unmei dakara shikataga nai*). How else could I take it?" she said with a ready smile.

The remaining immigrants decided to move from the Uruma settlement site and found an alternative site by themselves, to which they moved in August 1955. They did not, however, remain at the second site. It was too small and they had problems acquiring the land. About a year later they moved again to the current site, which became their permanent home, Colonia Okinawa. The further immigration, which had been placed on hold, resumed in 1957. However, this was not the end of the Okinawan immigrants' hardships due to unreliable rainfall, periodic floods (the one in 1968 was particularly devastating), unstable rice crops and prices, and so on. In the late 1960s there was a steady exodus of immigrants.

In 1967, the Japanese government assumed responsibility for Colonia Okinawa from the Americans, who held residual authority as the occupiers of Okinawa. Hence since 1968, Colonia Okinawa has received Japanese government aid through the Japan International Cooperation Agency (JICA), just as another Japanese community of immigrants, San Juan Yapacaní, has. In the early 1970s, on the advice of JICA, Colonia Okinawa began growing cotton on a large scale, using huge, expensive machinery bought with loans. It turned out to be a disaster, due to bad weather, poor harvests, crop diseases, and bad world prices. More immigrants left for Brazil and Argentina, and a few to Peru, where they had relatives, or else they returned to Okinawa or Japan.

Why, then, have some remained? Many of them explain it as a consequence of their own decision to come to Bolivia. It was their choice, they say. Some of the first arrivals boast of their "sense of mission" (*shimeikan*). For others going back to Okinawa was out of the question simply because they could not face the people at home as a failure. "How could I?" asked Mr. C. "Having been selected in the very first group of emigrants, the village office hosted a grand farewell party for me." A feisty woman, Mrs. Z, says, "It would have been too humiliating to go back without a success."

Have those men and women with the strong will either to satisfy their "sense of mission" or save face ever despaired? I asked Mr. C this while he drove me in his pickup on the bumpy, dusty road through Colonia Okinawa, along the wheat field he has given to one of his three sons. "Many times," he answered, glancing at the golden wheat his son will harvest in a few days with a huge combine harvester. Mr. C has given each of his sons a couple of hundred hectares of farmland along with the attendant big machinery, and he still has a large parcel left for himself and his wife. A man of eloquence but no frills, he is straightforward and wastes no time on pompous claims of a "sense of mission." Did he think about moving elsewhere? "Yes." When he could see no bright future, he sent his younger brother to Argentina to explore the possibility of moving the whole family there, as many others had done. His brother managed to set up a flower business and invited Mr. C and his family to join him. "But my wife wanted to go back to Japan. We couldn't agree on which country to move to. So we ended up staying here."

Many others did not have that kind of choice. They were strapped by heavy debts and simply had no money to buy plane or even train tickets to leave Bolivia, nor relatives in another country to help them move. So they stayed on, clinging to whatever little they had, and as a consequence saved face vis-à-vis people at home.

Their situation took a turn for the better in the early 1980s, when they began to grow soy beans. The cotton growing had ended in disaster, but it forced the Okinawan immigrants to mechanize, which was essential to success in soy bean production. Acquisition of land at low prices was relatively easy then since there were many available parcels owned by fellow settlers who had left or were leaving. Now those who have remained can say with no doubt in their minds that they are glad they emigrated to Bolivia.

TIES TO OKINAWA

What do these immigrants to Bolivia think of the current situation in Okinawa? Do they care about it at all? Most of them have made at least a trip or two back to Okinawa in the last twenty years. These homecoming trips started in the latter half of the 1970s, around the time when Okinawa hosted the Ocean Expo, which attracted a large amount of capital from the Japanese mainland. If the immigrants could not afford the fare themselves, someone in the family—usually sons and/or daughters who had gone to Japan to earn money—helped pay for the expenses. Most were surprised at the prosperity they saw in Okinawa. As Mr. Y put it, "I never dreamed Okinawa would develop that much." At the same time, many could not help but notice the impact of the U.S. military on the daily lives of Okinawans.

In addition, older immigrants listen to the NHK news daily on short wave and are fully informed of the political situation in Okinawa. They are sympathetic to their compatriots' demand, led by Governor Ota, to reduce the number and the impact of U.S. bases in Okinawa. While I was in Bolivia, the Japanese Supreme Court was about to decide whether Governor Ota had the right to refuse to sign the land leases for the U.S. bases on behalf of the landowners. The Colonia leaders often talked about it. No one expected Governor Ota to win; therefore, no one was surprised or overtly upset about the verdict in favor of the Japanese Government. "It's okay to lose," said Mr. C, who had his land taken for Kadena Air Base. "He [Governor Ota] stood up to make our case and fought courageously. That in itself is remarkable."

I don't know how the immigrants reacted to the result of the prefectural plebiscite on September 8, 1996, since I left Bolivia before then. I asked in the survey, "If you were living in Okinawa now, how would you vote in the referendum: 'in favor' or 'against' the reduction of the U.S. bases, or 'don't know?'" (The actual plebiscite asked voters only whether they were 'in favor' or 'against,' and did not provide the possibility of 'don't know.') The results of my survey were similar to those in Okinawa itself. The majority (73 out of 112, or 65.2 percent) were in favor, 10 respondents (8.9 percent) were against, 24 (21.5 percent) didn't know, and 5 (4.5 percent) did not answer the question. Among those who are in favor of base reduction, there is a wide range of opinions as to the role of the U.S. military in East Asia. A few think the presence of the U.S. military in Okinawa is utterly useless in protecting the security of either Okinawa or Japan, but most want to see the burden of having the U.S. bases spread out and shared by all of Japan. "After all, we lost the same war, didn't we?" says Mr. L. "So the mainland (*hondo*) should share the burden instead of making Okinawa bear all of it." The heavy presence of the U.S. military makes them feel that Okinawa is still under military occupation, and "Fifty years is too long under occupation."

Removed from their homeland, the immigrants (at least the first generation) seem to have retained certain old ways and ideas, which their compatriots in Okinawa no longer hold. The most pointed example is their attitude toward the national flag, the Rising Sun (*Hinomaru*). Since the Rising Sun flag was banned from any public place while they were still in Okinawa, the national flag is for the immigrants a symbol of their national unity against the American occupation. When they saw a Japanese ship with the Rising Sun displayed while they were en route to Bolivia they were overcome with emotion—they felt *natsukashii* (nostalgia for what they had lost). For Okinawans the 1972 reversion of Okinawa to Japan has changed what the Rising Sun flag symbolizes. But since the Bolivian immigrants left Okinawa before then, the symbolic meaning of the national flag has remained as if in a time capsule.

Their experiences with the Japanese government are also different from those of the Okinawans at home. The immigrants see the Japanese government as a benefactor of aid grants, which they appreciate since they received so little from the U.S. and Ryukyu governments. The new, modern Viru Viru airport, built with Japanese money and completed only in recent years, is an example of such largesse. The Bolivian immigrants believe they owe part of their current prosperity to Japanese aid.

I was invited to four parties, big and small, during my two-week stay in Bolivia. Men would consume large quantities of alcohol, although increasingly the older men would pour themselves Coca Cola under orders from their doctors. At one of those parties I sat next to Mr. P, the host and also one of the leaders of the community. He was in a gleeful mood.

"We've come a long way," he kept muttering as he poured Coca Cola into my glass, to which I responded by pouring more beer into his glass. "We used to fight at parties like this with lots to drink. Even at a wedding there were fist-fights. We were just boiling inside with anger and frustration and needed an outlet. Now that everyone's content, we don't fight any more. Yes, we've come a long way, and I'm very happy."

This does not mean that the Okinawan community in

Bolivia is trouble-free. Bolivia has just joined Mercosur, which could bring farm products duty-free from Brazil, Paraguay, and Argentina—a worrisome prospect for Bolivian agriculture. There have also been land disputes of many kinds, including Bolivians filing spurious claims to land that the Okinawans have made productive. Among the Okinawan immigrants themselves there is a growing tension between the Colonia and Santa Cruz residents over education and other issues. There is also conflict over whether the Okinawans should accept native Bolivians not just as their employees but also as neighbors and friends in their communities. These are serious issues. Nonetheless, for the first time in their lives, the Okinawan immigrants have control over their lives. They are now responsible for and have the means to decide their own destiny. Indeed, they have come a long way. As I poured beer into Mr. P's empty glass, and we toasted, over and over, the good life the Okinawans had at long last achieved I was pleased for them but also sad that this success was gained at the price of exile. What of those who have moved to Brazil, Argentina, and Peru? What has happened to them? How are they doing now and what do they think of the current situation in Okinawa? Our research continues.

NOTES

1. Kunimoto Iyo, *Boribia no "Nihonjinmura"* (The Japanese Village in Bolivia) (Tokyo: Chuo University Press, 1989), p. 66.

2. Oshiro Tatsuhiro, *Nanbei-zakura*, collected in *Noroesute tetsudo* (Northwest Railway) (Tokyo: Bungei Shunju, 1989), p. 45. This novella was first published in *Bungakukai* (August, 1987).

3. Kuniba Kotaro, *Okinawa no ayumi* (Steps Okinawa Has Taken) (1961), as quoted in Arasaki Moriteru, *Okinawa—Hansen jinushi* (Okinawa—Antiwar Landowners) (Tokyo: Kobunken, 1996), p. 65. Kuniba was an anti-U.S.-base activist in Okinawa in the 1950s.

4. *The 25th Anniversary of Colonia Okinawa* lists 3,218 immigrants, among whom several were born on the way to Bolivia. *Uruma kara no tabidachi: Koronia Okinawa nyushoku 40-shunen kinen shi (La historia de los 40 anos de la Colonia Okinawa)* (The 40-Year History of Colonia Okinawa) lists 806 names of residents, excluding Bolivians, in

Colonia as of February 1995.

5. James L. Tigner, *The Okinawans in Latin America: Investigation of Okinawan Communities in Latin America with Exploration of Settlement Possibilities* (Pacific Science Board, National Research Council, Washington, D.C., August 1954). This report was translated into Japanese and published as *Tigner Hokokusho* (Tigner Report) by the Ryukyu Government in 1957 and 1959. The journal of the Overseas Association of Okinawa, *Hiyu,* contains numerous articles on Okinawa's overpopulation.

6. Memorandum, 20 September 1952, by Paul H. Skuse (Chief, Public Safety Division, Government and Legal Department, USCAR) and James L. Tigner. Included in Tigner, *The Okinawans in Latin America*, p. 522.

7. Aniya Susumu, "A 40-Year History of Colonia Okinawa" in *Uruma kara no tabidachi* (The Departure from Uruma), pp. 84-85. This is a somewhat condensed version of a longer, handwritten manuscript. Mr. Aniya is one of the original immigrants, who was selected primarily because of his ability to record events. He has published a series of articles on the history of Colonia Okinawa in *Informativo Nikkei*, October 1995 through October 1996. I am currently in the process of transcribing his longer, handwritten manuscript about the history of Colonia Okinawa.

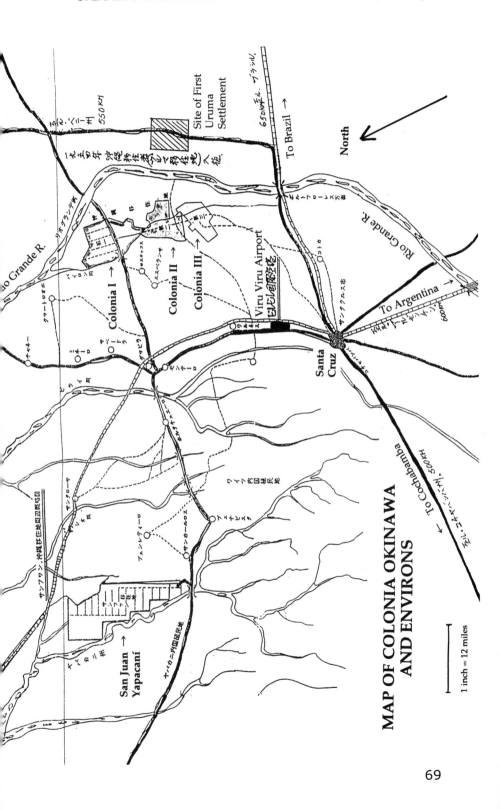

MAP OF COLONIA OKINAWA AND ENVIRONS

1 inch = 12 miles

North

To Brazil →

To Argentina

To Cochabamba

Rio Grande R.

Rio Grande R.

Site of First Uruma Settlement

Colonia I →

Colonia II →

Colonia III →

Viru Viru Airport

Santa Cruz

San Juan Yapacaní →

LIFE ON THE MAINLAND: AS PORTRAYED IN MODERN OKINAWAN LITERATURE

Steve Rabson

Two words that often recur in accounts of twentieth-century Okinawan history are *dekasegi,* "working away from home," and *yuugaku,* "studying away from home." Their frequency reflects the failure, until recently, of the Japanese central government to make needed economic and institutional investments in what is still the nation's poorest prefecture. Although more has been written outside Japan about the overseas emigrants who moved to places all over the world from South America to Eastern Europe, establishing what has become a large Okinawan diaspora, people who have left Okinawa to work or study on the Japanese mainland are, in fact, far more numerous. Before 1945 most went to do manual labor in factory districts, especially in the Osaka-Kobe area. Their numbers reached a peak of about 20,000 annually from the early 1920s through the early 1930s, a decade of severe economic hardship in Okinawa, which suffered most in Japan during the Great Depression. In 1925, for example, 19,926 Okinawa residents moved to the mainland seeking work, 8,994 of them to the Osaka-Kobe area.[1]

This decade was known as a time of "palm-tree hell" *(sotetsu jigoku)* in Okinawa because, during periods of extreme poverty, people ate plants that were unpalatable but provided some nutrition. It was also a time when emigration overseas, which had been continuous since the turn of the century, was now hindered by restrictive immigration policies abroad. The "Quota Law" enacted by the U.S. government in 1924, for example, discriminated severely against Asians. (This was not the only such anti-Asian measure, even in the U.S. There was also the "Gentlemen's Agreement" of 1908, specifically aimed at Japanese.) In Kushi Fusako's (1903-1986) story "Memoirs of a Declining Ryukyu Woman" *(Horobiyuku Ryukyu onna no shuki,* 1932), the narrator's close friend describes these circumstances.

At night it's pitch-black in S. City. I heard that all the rich folks there want desperately to move to N. to avoid high taxes. The stone walls in front of the houses are all crumbling now, and most of the yards inside have been turned into farm fields. Can you believe that S. is still Ryukyu's second largest city? To make matters worse, our immigrants are banned abroad. People can barely make a living these days by going to work on the mainland.[2]

The cities called "S" and "N" are almost certainly Shuri, capital of the former Ryukyu Kingdom, and Naha, the capital of Okinawa Prefecture.

Most of those who went to the mainland did unskilled labor in factories. And, as Kushi's story indicates, people did not necessarily migrate there by choice, but, in many cases, because poverty compelled them to leave home and earn money to support themselves, and frequently their families as well. Furthermore, wages and working conditions often fell far short of what employment agents had promised. Women from Okinawa who worked in mainland spinning factories suffered especially. Many were only thirteen and had just finished elementary school when their families contracted them, typically for between eighteen months and three years, to agents who often took exorbitant fees and sometimes mistreated the young women entrusted to them. Lodged in cramped, ill-equipped, and unheated "dormitories" where the food was described as "smelly rice" and "rotten fish," they were made to work extremely long hours in unhealthy and dangerous environments. As a result, besides serious injuries suffered in accidents involving high-speed loom machinery, many caught tuberculosis or other respiratory diseases and, unable to work, were sent home, sometimes to die.[3]

Despite the horrible conditions, a few women wrote that they were glad to have regular meals as well as a job that supported them and provided some money to send back to their families. Historians note that low wages and horrendous working conditions were common for unskilled factory workers from all over Japan during this period, but that people from Okinawa faced particular hardships. It was also a time when many impoverished farmers in northeastern Japan sold their daughters into prostitution for brothels in

Tokyo and other cities.

One woman published an essay anonymously in the October 21, 1934 *Osaka Mainichi Shimbun* describing conditions in the factory where she worked:

All of the 200 women here are from Okinawa. The bosses are cruel, making us work 12-hour shifts until the wee hours of the morning without even a minute's break. Many of us have fallen ill, and just the other day another one died. We have the highest rate of illness in Japan. But, if we run away, they'll just recruit other girls from Okinawa to suffer the same cruelty.

"Ballad of the Factory Girl" (*Joko ko-uta*), a standard among Okinawan folk songs, contains the following lines:

It's one or two a.m. when even the grass is sleeping.
But if I happen to doze off,
The boss will get angry,
Though he looks sleepy, too.
. . . .
I have parents, but they live in poverty.
When I'm homesick, I go down to the port.
But, watching the ships, I can only weep.

Besides atrocious labor conditions, Okinawans "working away from home" faced prejudice and blatant discrimination in mainland Japan. Largely because they came from a place where the culture differed from the rest of Japan in diet, religious practices, and regional dialects, Okinawans were viewed by many mainland Japanese as "strange," "rustic," or even "foreign." These attitudes resulted not only in painful personal insults, but also in discrimination so overt that signs were sometimes posted in front of employment offices and rooming houses announcing that "no Koreans or Okinawans need apply." As a result, many Okinawans settled in separate communities in large cities where a support system of friends, relatives, and Okinawan prefectural associations could help them secure lodging, find work, and feel less alienated.

Yet, Okinawan women in the spinning factories did not always accept these outrages passively. Regulations, such as censored mail and mandatory residence in dormitories that they could not leave even for short errands without special permission, were intended to discourage resistance by minimizing contact with the outside world. And factory managers pressured women from Okinawa to use "standard" Japanese, a language mainland supervisors could understand. But, although speaking Ryukyuan exposed them to reprimands from their bosses and discrimination on the mainland, Okinawan workers continued to use it for several reasons. First, it gave them a sense of camaraderie in factories where, as in the example above, they sometimes constituted a large proportion of the work force. And, second, it provided a secure means of communication for planning strikes and protests. Okinawan union organizers distributed leaflets in Ryukyuan to women in factories, and held meetings of workers at local Okinawa prefectural associations to discuss labor problems. These were attended, on occasion, by smiling company managers who thought they were spreading amity and harmony because they could not understand speeches that denounced company policies and urged job actions. The protagonist of "Shinzato Kanajo's Story from the Spinning Mill" (1988) by Higa Michiko describes the following episode:

> One day there was a power failure. And, for some reason, all the women from Okinawa gathered in one area of the factory and began speaking in Ryukyuan. Then some of us started singing Okinawan folk songs. At first our voices were soft and tentative,but gradually we got inspired and began to sing louder, clapping our hands and slapping the machines to keep time. Some women even started dancing and the other workers gathered around them. It really felt good. Then the manager came running over yelling for us to knock it off, stamping his foot to scare us. But I told him not to worry, that we were only singing Okinawa's version of "His Majesty's Reign" *(Kimi ga yo),* the Japanese national anthem.[4]

Yet, if factory workers found solace and solidarity in their ethnicity, some Okinawans in the business world and other walks of life considered it a handicap. The protagonist of Kushi Fusako's 1932 story "Memoirs of a Declining Ryukyu

Woman" is the narrator's uncle, who is a successful businessman living in Tokyo. Fearing discrimination and prejudice, he conceals from everyone he knows there that he was born and raised in Okinawa.

> [My uncle] was another of our people who could not reveal the truth about himself for all the twenty years he had lived in the middle of Tokyo. He managed several branches of a company, supervised university and technical school graduates, and lived in a spacious apartment with a bossy wife and a daughter in her prime who was soon to be married. Yet he had never disclosed the slightest hint to any of them that he was Ryukyuan.[5]

During a brief return visit to Okinawa, his first since leaving two decades earlier, he explains his reasons:

> I've already transferred my family register to X Prefecture on the mainland. . . . In fact, nobody in Tokyo knows I'm from Ryukyu. I do a good business with prestigious companies and have lots of university graduates working for me. You have to understand that if people found out I was Ryukyuan, it would cause me all kinds of trouble. To be honest, I even lied to my wife about coming here, telling her I was going to visit Beppu City in Kyushu.

Despite Kushi's not entirely unsympathetic portrayal of her protagonist, this story drew vehement protests from Okinawa prefectural and student associations in Tokyo. Both the student association's president and its former president denounced the story as "insulting" and "inciting discrimination." As a result, the editors of *Fujin Koron* (Women's Review) cancelled subsequent installments of this work, scheduled for serialization, in what came to be known as the "slip-of-the-pen incident" *(hikka jiken)*. Although banning the rest of the story, the magazine's editors allowed Kushi to publish a response to her detractors entitled "In Defense of 'Memoirs of a Declining Ryukyu Woman'" in the July 1932 issue, one month after the first (and last) installment of the story had appeared. It is a stirring essay that reads in part:

The current and former presidents of the Okinawa Student Association . . . demanded that I stop writing because they found my revealing portrayal of our homeland extremely embarrassing. In addition, they ordered me to apologize for my depiction of one character in the story . . . so that readers would not get the mistaken impression that all Okinawan men are like him. Yet in this story I [never made] any suggestion that all successful Okinawans are like him. . . All times and places in [it] have been changed to avoid embarrassing anyone who might be regarded as a model for its characters.

These men . . . were particularly upset by one phrase I used in the story: "the Okinawan people" *(Okinawa minzoku).* It annoyed them, they said, to have Okinawans put in the same category as "the Ainu people" or "the Korean people," minorities with which this word is often associated in Japan. Yet are we not living in modern times? I have no sympathy for their efforts to construct racial hierarchies of Ainu, Korean, and so-called "pure Japanese," or their desire to feel some kind of superiority by placing themselves in the "highest" category. . . Their outraged claims that what I wrote "demeans" and "discriminates against" Okinawans reveals, paradoxically, their own racial prejudice. . . . I certainly did not use the word "people" . . . to insult the Okinawan people of whom I myself am one.

[They also] claim my writing damages Okinawans' prospects for jobs and marriages on the mainland, but isn't it really their own servile attitude that is damaging our prospects? . . . These men should aim their protests at those capitalists who still discriminate against Okinawans instead of trying so hard to silence a voice from the heart of one uneducated woman.[6]

Kushi Fusako is certainly not the first and only writer to treat the touchy subject of "passing" by minority individuals who seek to assimilate and avoid prejudice in a hostile environment. In such American novels as *A Cycle in Manhattan*

(1923) by Saunter Winslow, *The Gold in Fish* (1925) by Fannie Hurst, and *The Godfather* (1969) by Mario Puzo, characters conceal their origins by "Anglicizing" their surnames in a country where white Anglo-Saxon Protestants are thought to be what Kushi might call "highest in the [social] hierarchy." Much as Irish, Italian and Jewish immigrants "Anglicized" their names in America, Okinawans and Koreans in mainland Japan chose to change their names, which are recognizably Okinawan or Korean, to something more typical of mainland Japanese.

For Okinawans, this might require changing the pronunciation, but not the writing, of Chinese characters in a surname so that, for example, the identifiably Okinawan name Kinjo (gold + castle) would be pronounced as Kaneshiro, its mainland equivalent; or Kabira (river + broad, flat) would be pronounced as Kawahira. Typically, Koreans whose names were Kim, written with the character for gold, might preserve this character, but change its pronunciation and add a second character to make a common Japanese name, such as Kaneda (gold + rice field). My father's family name had been Rabinowitz, a common Jewish surname meaning "rabbi's son," when his father immigrated to the U.S. from Russia at the turn of the century. It was changed to "Rabson" in the 1930s after the family opened a store in Manhattan. The reason given was "business purposes" because the "Anglicized" version would supposedly be easier for Americans to remember. Still, some family members objected and my father, who was a teenager at the time, never believed that this had been the only reason.

Despite literary portrayals elsewhere of efforts to "pass" and Kushi's persuasive defense of her story, she chose to stop writing for publication following the "slip-of-the-pen incident" in 1932 until after World War II. The war brought particular hardships for Okinawans on the mainland because many lived in the industrial areas of large cities that were the targets of intense fire-bombing. As for Okinawa itself, World War II brought a U.S. military occupation there that lasted twenty-seven years until 1972, twenty years longer than the Allied Occupation of mainland Japan.

Both the Battle of Okinawa and the prolonged occupation that followed are viewed by Okinawans as extreme manifestations of mainland prejudice. Despite advice in early 1945 from Prime Minister Konoe Fumimaro, the Showa Emperor is reported to have sided with those military leaders who wanted to continue the war, by now a hopeless cause, so they could wage "a decisive battle" for Okinawa. Thus Okinawa was sacrificed, and some 230,000 died in the worst battle of the Pacific War, in the mistaken hope that more favorable peace terms might be negotiated. The victims included some 147,000 Okinawans, with many killed by mainland soldiers seeking shelter from enemy fire or turning on local residents in their frustration of defeat. Okinawa is said to have been abandoned as a "throw-away stone" *(sute-ishi)*, a piece which is strategically sacrificed, like a pawn, in the game of go.[7]

Then, two years after the war, in 1947, the emperor sent a message through his counselor Terasaki Hidenari to General MacArthur's headquarters indicating that he would favor long-term U.S. military control of Okinawa. This proposal has been viewed as an effort to bargain, again with Okinawa as the "throw-away stone," for an early end to the Allied Occupation of the mainland. It has also been seen as an attempt to curry favor with Occupation authorities at a time when U.S. public opinion was for punishing the emperor as a war criminal and presiding judge William Webb of Australia at the Tokyo War Crimes Trials was calling for his indictment. A late-1945 Gallup Poll in the U.S. recorded 71 percent of the respondents advocating punishment of the Japanese emperor, including 33 percent who favored execution.[8]

Even after reversion to Japanese sovereignty in 1972, 75 percent of the U.S. military presence in all of Japan still occupies about one-sixth of this small island prefecture which represents only 0.6 percent of the nation's total land area. Again, mainland prejudice is cited to explain why the Japanese government broke repeated promises for a post-reversion Okinawa with a military presence "at mainland levels" *(hondo-nami)* and "free of nuclear weapons" *(kaku-nuki)*. Instead, the government acquiesced to continuing this vast occupation of bases without non-nuclear guarantees or limitations on the missions and deployments of troops. The resulting Reversion Agreement *(henkan kyotei)* of 1969 was sarcastically called the "prejudiced agreement" *(henken kyotei)* by Okinawans. Since then, despite some token transfers of a few missions after the abduction and rape of a 12-year-old girl by three U.S. servicemen in 1995, the Japanese government still refuses to equalize Okinawa's burden of bases throughout Japan.

During the prolonged occupation, U.S. government land seizures for base expansions in the early 1950s displaced thousands of farmers, and a military-service economy offered limited job prospects. So many Okinawans left, once again, for the mainland to find "work away from home." But now they needed special exit "passports" that were issued by American authorities only after conducting what were sometimes lengthy investigations. Procedural delays caused some to lose opportunities for employment and college admissions. This was also a time when accurate information about Okinawa, severed by American occupation from the rest of Japan, was hard to come by on the mainland, and misconceptions abounded. Japanese would often ask people from Okinawa if they spoke English at home or used knives and forks for their daily meals.

In his 1976 novel *Good Lookin' (Churakaagi)*, set in the early 1960s, Higashi Mineo presents a conversation between the protagonist, who has recently come to Tokyo from Okinawa, and one of his co-workers in a book-binding factory.

"Well, if it isn't a new face. Didn't you get here yesterday?"

"Yeah. Where're you from?"

"Fukagawa."

"Where's that?"

"Just outside Asakusa."

"Oh, then you're from Tokyo."

"Damn right. Lived here since I was a kid."

"You looked lonely, sitting all by yourself, so I thought you might be from somewhere far away."

"How 'bout you?"

"I'm from Okinawa."

"Okinawa? Wow, that's *really* far way. And you can't come and go freely from there, can you."

"No, you need a passport."

"A passport? Then it's a foreign country."

"I guess so."

"Well, then you're a foreigner. Strange kind of foreigner, though."

"Why strange?"

"'Cause your Japanese is so good. You speak English down there, right?"

"No way! I'm Japanese, and proud of it."
"Oh, really. I thought you might be Ezo."
"Ezo?"
"Yeah, like the people in Hokkaido. 'Cause your cheekbones poke out and you got lots of body hair. Are many people in Okinawa like that?"
"More on the average, I guess."[9]

Higashi's characters make exaggerated references here to physiological differences, owing to sources of early migrations, between many people in Okinawa and most mainland Japanese. Yet other Okinawans are physically indistinguishable from people on the mainland where there is also significant diversity. And individual variation in both places makes generalizations difficult.

Far more important are the above-mentioned cultural differences between Okinawa and other parts of Japan. Still, some Okinawans "working away from home" have found assimilation easier than people from rural areas on the mainland. In what Higashi himself has called "autobiographical fiction," his narrator discovers that he has less trouble speaking the standard Japanese language than another of his co-workers from northeastern Japan. The narrator was a high school drop-out in Okinawa where the local dialects are furthest from the "standard" (Tokyo) language. Yet he attributes his proficiency to the special efforts he made listening to the radio to learn Tokyo dialect as he looked forward to the day when he could leave his menial job on an American air base and move to the mainland.[10]

In these passages, Higashi conveys the kind of love-hate relationship many Okinawans have had with the mainland. On the one hand, since the turn of the twentieth century, it has held a strong attraction as a place for educational and employment opportunities, but, at the same time, it is a place where many have felt lonely and isolated. Since the reversion of sovereignty to Japan in 1972, Okinawans in large numbers continue to travel there for work. In recent years, with higher education more widely available in Okinawa, more people leave home for jobs in schools or in company and government offices. Many pursue successful careers, and settle permanently on the mainland. However, although overt discrimination is largely a thing of the past, prejudices and misunderstandings persist even a quarter century after reversion. Each year a number of people "working away from home" find themselves unable to adjust to life on the mainland, and go back to Okinawa. This "u-turn" phenomenon and a reluctance, especially among younger people, to take jobs in other prefectures have been cited as factors in Okinawa's unemployment rate which continues to be the highest by far in Japan (9 percent in Okinawa as compared to 4.5 percent nationwide in the recession year of 1999).

In contrast to the troubled history of many Okinawans "working away from home" on the mainland, those traveling there to study generally have had much better experiences. First of all, many more have gone because they wanted to, not because they were sent by their impoverished families out of economic necessity. From late-Meiji through Taisho (from 1895 to 1926) Okinawans who enjoyed periods of study on the mainland were leaders in the creation of a new Okinawan literature. Literary historian Okamoto Keitoku describes this period:

> After Japan's victory in the Sino-Japanese War of 1894-95, people came increasingly to admire Japan, and Tokyo culture spread rapidly in Okinawa. At the same time, young intellectuals who went to Tokyo for advanced, specialized programs of study found a culturally rich environment that stimulated many to write.[11]

There is a sharp contrast between portrayals of students from Okinawa who enjoyed the "rich" environment of Tokyo, a place associated with culture and education, and workers who toiled under grim conditions in the factories of Osaka and other cities in Kansai, places associated more with commerce and industry.

Okamoto explains how mainland influences spurred the beginnings of a new literature in Okinawa:

> At this time, the movement among the public at large to adopt the "common [Tokyo] language" was at a peak. This boosted the number of newspapers in Okinawa, providing more places for writers to publish, and establishing a vehicle for the new literature to reach a general readership. The earliest works to appear were *tanka* [poems in the mainland 31-sylla-

ble form], and the first fiction came later, in 1908. It was mainly young intellectuals who created and introduced this new literature, and, at first, it was modeled closely on the work of prominent writers in Tokyo. . . . . Furthermore, many of its earliest novels seemed to be based on the personal experiences of Okinawan writers who were studying in Tokyo.[12]

Yet not all Okinawans who left for Tokyo to "study away from home" had "rich" experiences, at least in the material sense. Particularly during economic hard times in the 1920s and early 1930s, many who were not from wealthy families, or lacked a steady income, barely managed to eke out a living. Among them was Yamanokuchi Baku (1903-1963), Okinawa's best-known poet in whose honor the Yamanokuchi Baku Prize is awarded annually to a promising poet. Still called with affection today by his pen-name "Baku," meaning tapir, he has also published fiction, essays, and wide-ranging memoirs from which the following account of his life on the mainland is drawn.

His best-known works on the forty years he lived in Tokyo describe prejudice, stereotyping, and pressures to assimilate. These writings, mostly in the first person, are poignant and revealing even if, as with all literary representations of reality, one cannot assume that a poet with a lively imagination and a keen sense of the dramatic is always chronicling actual incidents precisely. Yet Baku certainly does not portray all of his encounters with mainland Japanese as negative experiences. From his memoirs we learn that in Tokyo he rapidly earned the admiration of influential poets and critics, forming life-long friendships with several of them, most notably Kaneko Mitsuharu (1895-1975), his frequent companion during the tumultuous wartime and early postwar years. Baku's poetry also tells of Shizue, the woman from Ibaraki Prefecture he married in 1937, and their daughter Izumi, born in 1944. In addition, his early writings express a strong attraction for the language and culture of Tokyo that seems to have taken hold of him even before he got there.

Gaja, a classmate from elementary school, was then living in Tokyo. He also liked to write, and often sent me letters in an elegant style, closing with such lines as "the insects are chirping on this autumn night." More and more I was stirred with that Yamato feeling, and my heart overflowed with yearning for Tokyo.[13]

"That Yamato feeling" (*Yamato-teki jocho*) is evoked here by autumnal imagery typical of mainland Japanese poetry. His hopes realized, he traveled to Tokyo for the first time in 1922 to study at the Japan College of Art where he had gained admission. However, if Baku had sought aesthetic inspiration in Tokyo, he actually writes about the mundane troubles that dogged him from the day of his arrival. To start with, Gaja did not show up at Tokyo Station to meet him as promised, and he found himself alone in a big city for the first time in his life.

I didn't even know how to find his address, the only person I had to rely on. Lines of rickshas were parked in front of the station, and the drivers would glance over at me as I stood there wondering what to do. I should just have asked one of them directions, but I had no confidence speaking mainland Japanese (*Yamato-guchi*). I was afraid that, as soon as I opened my mouth, I would be marked as a country bumpkin. . . . Finally, one of the drivers asked where I was going. He warned me that, if I stayed much later, I would be thrown out of the station, and offered to take me where I wanted to go. There seemed to be no alternative, so I hired him. Pulling me along the late-night streets, he kindly stopped several times to ask the way, and at last I arrived at Gaja's lodging house (I:331).

Aside from language problems in Tokyo, Baku soon found himself facing poverty. Shortly after arriving, he learned that his father's business had failed, so he could expect none of the money promised for his tuition and expenses. For the next few months, he freeloaded off Okinawan acquaintances in Tokyo, moving from one lodging house to another, until he returned to Okinawa by free boat passage as a "refugee" after the Great Kanto Earthquake in September, 1923. Baku stayed with his family for a few months, but complains that he came under intense pressure from relatives to take a job right away to pay off some of his father's debts. Deciding instead to go back to Tokyo, he got as far as Naha only to discover that, with the house of his bankrupt family now owned by someone else, there was no place for him to stay and no money for the trip. At this point, he says he began his legendary wandering "lumpen" life style, sleeping outside in parks and on the beach. He describes chewing pine needles occasionally to alleviate his hunger, but writes about this with a light-hearted tone that might seem strange to Okinawans who have lived through times of the "palm-tree hell." Finally, a friend from his middle school days agreed to pay both their fares to Tokyo if Baku would accompany him there. And, arriving in the autumn of 1924, Baku resumed his freeloading where he had left off the year before, except that this time he quickly wore out his welcome. Shunned at friends' lodging houses for his lack of funds, he now began a series of menial jobs, such as janitor, night-soil collector, and barge crewman, that became the subjects for many of his best-known poems and stories in which, as he put it, "I sold my poverty" (II:149-59).

Yet, despite the hardships he describes, Baku continued to write poems that express his attraction for Tokyo's urban life-style, and its language. In the poem "Sketch on a Stroll" (*Sampo suketchi*, 1938), he writes admiringly of the free and easy way couples mingle openly in Tokyo, and regrets he has no girl-friend of his own.

> Young couples
> crouching in bristly thickets,
> young couples
> sitting on benches,
> young couples
> everywhere I look.
> Young couples must be in season now.
> And, my friend, that you are a boy and I, too—
> How unfortunate (I:120-21).

Baku also writes, in the poem "Blue Sky" *(Seiten,* 1938), of his attraction to Tokyo's spoken language, and his efforts to master it.

> Laughing, he said to me,
> *"Boku n toko e asobi ni oide yo."* "C'mon over to my

place."
I had picked up that Tokyo speech.
"*Kimi n toko wa doko nan da?*" "Where's your place?"
I liked its slightly nasal sound,
and even learned to dangle "*chatta*"
on the ends of works like "*komatchatta*" "I was in
trouble"
the way Tokyoites do.
Looking up at a clear blue sky,
I lingered outside for
a while in this city of sparkling speech (I:122-23).

While it reflects one kind of pressure to assimilate, Baku depicts his efforts to learn "sparkling" Tokyo dialect in this city of "blue skies" as a positive challenge. But, as critic Nakahodo Masanori has noted, if Baku was attracted by the "brightness" of Tokyo speech, within a year of his arrival in the city he encountered what Nakahodo calls the "dark side of its society" (II:359-60). Baku writes of his astonishment at hearing the false and vicious rumors that were spread about Koreans in the chaotic aftermath of the 1923 earthquake, resulting in vigilante massacres that took the lives of hundreds of Koreans, as well as many Japanese mistaken for Koreans.

There was a terrible commotion in the streets. I heard rumors one after another—that Enoshima had sunk to the ocean floor, that a tidal wave had swept away Kamakura, and, for what reason I had absolutely no idea, that a mob of Koreans was coming from Arakawa to attack Tokyo, and that they had thrown poison into the wells so no one should drink well water. Everybody was rushing around wildly, and, with some people carrying wooden clubs and Japanese swords, the mood on the street quickly grew bloodthirsty (II:360).

Baku has written fiction and poetry about the discrimination Koreans encounter in Japan, comparing it at times with his own experience as an Okinawan. In his memoirs he recalls the signs he saw on the mainland warning that "no Koreans or Okinawans need apply." His best known work on Koreans in Japan is the story "Mr. Saito of Heaven Building"

(Tengoku biru no Saito-san, 1939). Mr. Saito is an immigrant managing an acupuncture clinic in Tokyo who unsuccessfully tries to conceal his origins despite mistakes in his pronunciation of Japanese that are typical of native Korean speakers. He even mispronounces his own adopted Japanese name as "Saido." After Mr. Saito has been taunted for being a Korean by a salesman visiting the clinic, the narrator recalls that "living in Tokyo as a man from Ryukyu for the past sixteen years, I've run into people wherever I go who think like that salesman. They stare at me strangely, as if I'm not even human."[14]

Baku's most famous work depicting his own encounters with prejudice on the mainland is the poem "A Conversation" *(Kaiwa,* 1938). In his reminiscences he recalled what motivated him to write it.

> In the coffee shop where I used to hang out, one of the regular customers showed up one day after a long absence, his face deeply tanned. He announced in a loud voice to the woman who ran the shop and her daughter that he had been on a business trip to Okinawa. I'd been talking to some other people at the time, but, being from Okinawa, I was slightly irritated to hear him mention it. Most Okinawans feel uncomfortable at such times. Still, I could not suppress a certain interest in this man's impressions of my homeland. But hearing him talk about how he was invited to the home of a "chieftain," how he drank *awamori* [Okinawa's distinctive rice liquor] from a soup bowl, and how "the natives" do this and that, I felt as though he were conjuring up visions of a place I'd never seen. Although aware that this was simply a tourist's amusement, I was saddened, not only because I am Okinawan, but also because the manager's daughter was listening wide-eyed to this man's every word. I had been planning for some time to graduate from my lumpen life-style, and my relationship with this girl had progressed to the point where I was intending to ask her to marry me. I couldn't help wondering what she would think if she knew I was Okinawan. Sitting in a booth of that coffee shop, I concentrated all my energy on writing this poem (III:314-6).

"Where are you from?" she asked.

I thought about where I was from and lit a cigarette. That place associated with tattoos, the *jabisen* [three-string plucked musical instrument], and ways as strange as ornamental designs.

"Very far away," I answered.

"In what direction?" she asked.

That place of gloomy customs near the southern tip of Japan where women carry piglets on their heads and people walk bare foot. Was this where I was from?

"South," I answered.

"Where in the south?" she asked.

In the south, that zone of indigo seas where it's always summer and dragon orchids, sultan umbrellas, octopus pines and papayas all nestle together under the bright sunlight. It's a place, shrouded in misconceptions, where the people are thought not to be Japanese. . . , a place, viewed through stereotypes, that has become a synonym for "chieftains," "natives," and "karate. . . ."

"Somewhere near the equator," I answered (I:60-61).

Nakahodo Masanori has noted that, while Yamanokuchi Baku might have been reluctant to name his birthplace before World War II, the word "Okinawa" occurs frequently in his postwar writings. In a sense, Baku rediscovered his origins after the war. Not previously known as an advocate of any particular cause, he became a vigorous spokesman for Okinawan political and cultural concerns. He condemned the U.S. government for prolonging its "grasp of Okinawa," making the island into what Baku called an "unsinkable aircraft carrier" of concrete runways and barbed wire fences. And he chastised the Japanese government for its "weak-kneed" acquiescence in the continuing American occupation and militarization of the Ryukyus, asserting that "if Okinawans are to live in true equality, the military bases must be removed" (IV: 332-338).

Aside from protesting government policies, he published numerous articles in mainland newspapers and magazines, attacking widespread misconceptions and stereotypes about Okinawa. His subjects included music, classical poetry, language, religious observances and food. He reminded people who call Ryukyuan a "foreign" language that scholars have identified it as an ancient form of Japanese. He corrected a common confusion between Okinawan *awamori* and mainland *shochu,* a liquor distilled from potatoes and grains. And he chided those who say that *awamori* has a "strange smell," pointing out that mainland *sake* and European wines also have distinctive odors.

Dying in 1963, after a final visit to his homeland in late 1958, Yamanokuchi Baku never experienced post-reversion Okinawa, life on the mainland as someone from a now reinstated Okinawa Prefecture, or the recent "boom" of fascination throughout Japan with Okinawan music and popular culture. But much of his writing on his years in Tokyo remains fresh today.

Among those Okinawans who have experienced life on the mainland since reversion, many have expressed an ethnic pride in their "roots" that is a sharp contrast to earlier times when fear of discrimination caused some to conceal their origins and change their names. Such upbeat sentiments can be found in recent memoirs by residents of Taisho Ward in Osaka, where, of a total population of 80,000, 20,000 are migrants from Okinawa or, more commonly, their descendants. What have been called "ethnic communities" by Okinawan scholars originated during the 1920s and 1930s, when Okinawans who came to work in mainland factories faced severe discrimination. Such neighborhoods, which can also be found in Hyogo Prefecture, Yokohama, Nagoya, Kita-Kyushu, and other urban areas, provided needed support systems for new arrivals. From such troubled beginnings, these communities have developed steadily as people saved their money from factory wages, opened businesses, and bought property. And, while their economic resources are still somewhat below the average for mainland Japanese, the residents have enjoyed a relative prosperity in recent years. Although most Okinawans who come to the mainland today choose to live elsewhere, among the population at large, these communities continue to flourish. They are places where many of the stores have Okinawan names, where foodstuffs for Okinawan cuisine are sold in the markets, and where restaurants offer Okinawan food and drink as well as performances of Okinawan music and dance. Studios and culture centers teach the traditional performing and design arts to a large clientele, and Okinawa's local festivals are observed annually.

Born in Okinawa in 1951, Kinjo Isamu titles his memoir "Okinawa is Number One" (*Okinawa izu namba-wan*, 1996).

It was cold. That's the first thing I remember about coming to Osaka in late 1954 at the age of three. After we got our passports, the family—my parents and us five children—rode the boat over rough seas for three days and nights. . . Both my parents had already moved to Osaka at the start of the war. My father worked hauling military supplies, and my mother had a job in a spinning factory. It was a love marriage, and the war had just ended when my sister was born. But there wasn't enough to eat in the place where they had evacuated, and she died of malnutrition. After the war, my parents returned to Okinawa, but they couldn't make a living there, so they took us back to Osaka.

My parents maintained our Okinawan life-style so completely that sometimes we forgot we were in Osaka. We always spoke in Ryukyuan and, since we were among many other Okinawans in the Manzai-bashi area of Kita Okajima, it was easy to live this way. My father raised pigs and grew *goya* (bitter melon) in a vacant lot, and . . . made brown-sugar candy. My mother had her weaving implements sent from Okinawa, and made *kasuri* splash-patterned cloth.

We conducted all the annual observances strictly by the old lunar calendar, including the spring *shiimii* festival of feast and prayer honoring departed relatives, and the summer *o-bon* festival when spirits of the ancestors are said to return to this world for a brief visit. . . .

Far from feeling some kind of "inferiority complex" about Okinawa, we were like Okinawa patriots, convinced that it was the best place there was.[15]

As noted above, renewed ethnic pride has spawned more public performances of traditional music and dance in restaurants and at outdoor festivals, both on the mainland and in Okinawa. The Japanese media have focused on these events with particular intensity, creating a "boom" of public fascination that has made recordings of Okinawan music into best-sellers and Okinawan musicians into super-stars. On the one hand, this has been a welcome phenomenon, especially in communities where it has brought mainland tourist monies. But this trend has also produced a commercialized and exoticized "Okinawa," engendering new stereotypes and misconceptions that, once again, people have to deal with when they come to the mainland for work or study. It is a dilemma that might well be explored in the Okinawan literature of the future.

NOTES

1. Okinawa-ken Kyoiku-iinkai, *History of Okinawa Prefecture* (*Okinawa ken-shi*) (Tokyo: Kokusho Kanko-kai, 1989), I:655. All translations are by the author unless otherwise noted.

2. Kushi Fusako, "Memoirs of a Declining Ryukyu Woman" (*Horobiyuku Ryukyu onna no shuki*), *Fujin Koron* (Women's Review), June, 1932. Translation is by Kimiko Miyagi in Michael S. Molasky and Steve Rabson, eds., *Southern Exposure: Modern Japanese Literature from Okinawa* (Honolulu: University of Hawaii Press, forthcoming).

3. See the collection of memoirs in Fukuchi Hiroaki, ed., *The Tragic History of Okinawa's Women Factory Workers* (*Okinawa joko aishi*), (Naha, Okinawa: Naha Shuppan-sha, 1986).

4. *Jurin* (Grove), July and August, 1988, pp. 16-31.

5. See note 2.

6. Kushi Fusako, "In Defense of 'Memoirs of a Declining Ryukyu Woman'" ('*Horobiyuku Ryukyu onna no shuki*' *ni tsuite no shakumei-bun*), translated by Kimiko Miyagi (see note 2).

7. Aniya Masaaki, et al., eds., *Okinawa and the Emperor (Okinawa to tenno)* (Naha, Okinawa: Akebono Shuppan, 1988), pp. 14-15.

8. "Tokushu: Tenno to Okinawa" (Special Issue: The Emperor and Okinawa), *Bunka Hyoron* (Culture Review), November, 1987, p. 47.

9. From a collection of Higashi's fiction published by Bunshun Bunko press, Tokyo, in 1982, pp. 172-73. Its title work, "Child of Okinawa" (*Okinawa no shonen*), won the

Akutagawa Prize, Japan's most prestigious literary award, in 1972, and is translated in Steve Rabson, *Okinawa: Two Postwar Novellas* (Berkeley: Institute of East Asian Studies, University of California, 1989, reprinted 1996).

10. See *Good Lookin'* and "An Island Good-bye" (*Shima de no sayonara,* 1972) in the Bunshun Bunko collection cited above.

11. Okamoto Keitoku, "Literary Activity and Modern Okinawa" (*Kindai Okinawa ni okeru bungaku katsudo*), in *Anthology of Okinawan Literature* (*Okinawa bungaku zenshu*) (Tokyo: Kaifu-sha, 1991), XX:329-332.

12. *Ibid.,* p. 331-334.

13. *Yamanokuchi Baku zenshu* (Collected Works) (Tokyo: Shicho-sha, 1976, 4 vols.), III:330. All quotations from Yamanokuchi are from this edition.

14. II:149-161. Nakahodo Masanori notes that Baku had likely read Kushi Fusako's story "Memoirs of a Declining Ryukyu Woman," published seven years earlier in 1932, which might have influenced his writing of this work. II:362-363. "Mr. Saito of Heaven Building" is translated by Rie Takagi in *Southern Exposure*: *Modern Japanese Literature from Okinawa* (see n. 2).

15. In Ota Jun'ichi, *The Okinawans of Osaka (Osaka no Uchinaanchu)* (Osaka: Brein Senta, 1996), pp. 88-93.

©Steve Rabson, 1999.

OKINAWA, THEN AND NOW

Mike Millard

In 1967, I was shipped from Miramar Naval Air Station, in San Diego, California, to a small utility squadron based at Naha, Okinawa, then an American-run island with a Japanese culture that had been captured in bloody fighting during World War II. Okinawa had "good liberty," I was told by the old chief who processed my orders, by which he meant that it was a fine place for drinking and whoring, and better than months at sea launching bombing raids against Hanoi. Okinawa sounded all right to a teenage Navy aviation electronics technician enduring the final throes of an adolescence increasingly distorted by the distant thunder in Vietnam.

Not distant enough, at times. Following an auto accident, I had just spent three months in a Navy hospital ward with a broken jaw, lying next to a skinny, red-headed Marine whose lower jaw had been blown clean off by a Viet Cong bullet. Where his mouth should have been a clear plastic tube disappeared into bandages. A Navy cook whose gunboat was blown up beneath him was suffering through skin grafts to replace what had been burned away from his face. Guys sat on the porches of their wards with white-taped stubs for limbs, forever mutilated, nearly all of them under 20. My broken jaw didn't seem so bad in comparison. But a few months hidden away in the Oakland hills with warehouses of blown-to-hell kids changed my ideas about the projecting of U.S. military force, 25 years before the truth of the matter would occur to then Secretary of Defense Robert McNamara.

The next 18 months on Okinawa were a dark period of drinking to forget, of not caring whether I learned anything much about Japan, ending with a taste of bitterness as Americans were shipped back from Asia, confused like I was about the meaning of the war and not exactly welcomed home. My memories, therefore, are like puzzling shards of ancient pottery.

I recall, for example, a night of drinking in the "Ville," a bar district outside the air base at Naha, stumbling down an alley around midnight with a girl whose name I have long since forgotten, when she told me in broken English that it was New Year's and we ought to go to the shrine. I followed along and we joined in with thin streams of pilgrims that gradually thickened into thousands flowing up a hill above the East China Sea to the Naminoue Shrine atop a great jutting slab of rock. We slowly made our way upward with the oozing river of nighttime humanity to the front of the shrine, where amidst scented clouds of incense we threw money into a rectangular box overseen by several robed Shinto priests. She clasped her hands in a brief prayer. I had no idea what any of it signified, but she seemed to feel better for it. I did not even know, and perhaps neither did she, that Shinto had been imported into Okinawa by the Japanese and played no role in the indigenous Okinawan religion.

I remember piling into small taxis with my buddies Hickory and Oakes, going on liberty, racing down dusty oiled roads in the descending twilight to the glittering neighborhood that was our goal. The taxi would stop, the doors would swing open, and we would enter the warm night air where girls in sexy dresses stood in the neon glow at the entrances of clubs, enticing us, "Hey, GI, buy me a drink!" It was a rare evening that we managed to walk past more than two or three doorways.

Back home we weren't old enough to drink, but on Okinawa we could do whatever we wanted when we had money. Of course, we quickly learned that when we ran out of money, we lost our charm, so we played the game of trying to give up slowly what the bargirls wanted quickly. We would try to make drinks last through the evening, but it was difficult, and generally a paycheck didn't last more than two or three nights. Then it was the barracks for the remainder of the two weeks.

We would usually begin an evening at our squadron's hangout, the King Bar, where the girls knew us well and had little interest in us: we were E4 and below, and therefore not exactly rich. We would have a couple of serious drinks there, maybe whiskey, and set off on an adventure, bar-hopping our way around the Ville. Some nights we would stop at Jack's, an approved "A-sign" restaurant, for a steak and a beer. Then it was off to more exotic attractions. There was a bar, I recall, that featured a beautiful girl who danced naked with a huge python wrapped around her.

I remember one night when some army guy belted me in

the mouth after I said something, and I was so drunk I chased him out onto the street and flailed away at him as he punched me several more times. The next morning I found that my lip was split down the center and it took quite a few stitches to close it up.

Another night some black dudes came into the Ville instead of going to the Bush, "their" bar district in Koza, and beat up a white guy. There were rumors of race wars, and a guy from a P-3 squadron showed me a flare pistol concealed under his Hawaiian shirt. Fortunately, nothing ever came of it.

I met a girl from Waseda University, in Tokyo, who was walking around "observing" the GIs. We danced a bit and talked. We wrote to each other after I was transferred, and we even met in San Francisco after I got out of the Navy in the late 1960s. She liked to read Jean Paul Sartre and Herman Hesse and Yukio Mishima. One afternoon she and I came upon a march, Okinawans demanding that their island be given back to Japan, so we joined in. I was all for getting U.S. troops—including myself—back home, and it was a time to demonstrate your feelings openly.

But mostly we Americans just did our jobs, kept airplanes flying with radios that worked, and when we were off work we drank and bought sex from girls in short-time hotels behind the Ville near the beach. I didn't know anything then about yakuza gangsters who recruited the girls from families that were in their debt. It was just a wild place too far from home. What seemed at first like a paradise for young men quickly became a bore and then a jail for too many of us working to support a war that few of us thought was a good idea any more.

One afternoon Hickory, Oakes and I went to the place we called the Seawall, below Naminoue Shrine. It was a natural cove with several rickety wooden bridges reaching out over clear water to small shacks on pilings where you could buy beer and snacks. We sat at tables in the sun and kept the jukebox blaring. We were rockers who preferred Jimi Hendrix or the Beatles, as opposed to rednecks who favored Merle Haggard or Buck Owens. We were friends with a lot of rednecks. It was just a distinction that was observed during those war-polarized years.

Painted rowboats plied the water, children swam and laughed as their parents watched them from the platforms above. We drank tall, icy bottles of beer and talked about getting out of the Navy. Up the coast from Kadena, two sets of huge, dark aircraft, swept-wing B-52s, climbed at a sharp angle into the sky, on their way to lay waste to Southeast Asia. People glanced at us strangely. We were resented as intruders. We could feel it.

"War birds," Hickory called the planes. He was a tough, smart kid with a fondness for difficult novels. Later that night, we sat in the tropical evening outside our barracks on a soft grassy knoll, below a rusting Japanese gun emplacement left from the Battle of Okinawa. Hickory, leaning against a palm tree, broke down and began sobbing that "It wasn't supposed to be like this." Being betrayed is something you never forget. Our officers had told us that we were "protecting America," but it was on Okinawa that I realized we—all of the young, naive guys in the service then—had been sold out for greed, careers, ego, stupidity, whatever. Every few months I would get a letter from home telling me that another friend had been killed. It was then, on Okinawa, that I figured out that while governments might be composed of brilliant people, they didn't always perform intelligently.

REVISITING THE PAST

On September 4, 1995, three American GIs, not so dissimilar from myself thirty years ago, rented a car and prowled the backroads of Okinawa. Drinking heavily, they stopped at Kadena Air Base for more beer, condoms, and duct tape. They taunted each other about "the worst thing you ever did." They were Marine privates first class Kendrick Ledet and Rodrico Harp, both of Georgia, and Navy seaman Marcus Gill of Texas. After they abducted and raped a 12-year-old schoolgirl and were apprehended by military authorities, their pictures were splashed across the pages of Japanese mass-circulation newspapers with a glaring headline that translated roughly as "Devil Soldiers!" Their deeds would trigger a crisis in U.S.-Japan relations that continues today.

Although the commander of U.S. forces in Japan and the U.S. ambassador both apologized for the rape, by September 26 about 3,000 Okinawans took to the streets calling for the removal of U.S. bases from the island. On September

29, Gill, Harp, and Ledet were charged and turned over to Japanese authorities, but on October 21, about 85,000 Okinawans poured into the streets around the bases in the largest anti-military protest in the island's history. Then, incredibly, on November 17, the commander of U.S. military operations in the Pacific, Admiral Richard C. Macke, publicly commented that the three GIs were just stupid because for the price of their rental car, they "could have had a girl," outraging even mainland Japanese officials. Macke was forced into early retirement for his undiplomatic—even if true—remark, which illustrated how the U.S. military continues to view Okinawa and the Pacific region through neocolonial glasses.

Two years later I landed at the same airport on the outskirts of Naha where I had been stationed 30 years before, where C-130 cargo aircraft had taken off every day for Vietnam and returned the next day, empty and ready for the next load, and from which P-3 antisubmarine prop-jets had patrolled the waters off China and the Soviet Union. But there was no Soviet Union now. As we shuddered down toward the runway in the Japan Airlines jetliner, I could see the blue-green Okinawan sea where I used to snorkel along the shallow coral reefs just offshore. We touched down and taxied past the military hangars where I used to fix electronics gear in aircraft. There were still P-3s there, new models, marked with the red circle of the Japan Air Self-Defense Force.

Naha Air Base was returned to the Japanese in 1972, when the Ryukyu Islands reverted to Japanese rule. By that time, I was studying journalism on the GI Bill in Eugene, Oregon, and Okinawa had become a modest world news story. The United States kept the enormous Kadena Air Base and numerous other installations up north—40 of them, including facilities for nuclear submarines and a live artillery firing range. They cover about 20 percent of the island, much of the best land. And the odd thing is that of all the American military facilities in Japan, about 75 percent of them are on tiny Okinawa, less than one percent of the Japanese land mass. There are more than 50,000 U.S. personnel on the island today, and the 1995 rape of the schoolgirl was not the first serious crime committed by Americans. There has been a string of incidents. In 1955, an American military officer raped and killed a six-year-old girl; in 1959, a jet fighter crashed into an elementary school killing 17 children and injuring 121 others; in 1963, a high-school girl was killed by a U.S. military truck; in 1965, a fifth-grade schoolgirl playing in her garden was killed by a U.S. military trailer dropped from a helicopter; in 1968, a B-52 heading for Vietnam crashed just after takeoff, creating an anti-U.S.-military movement on the island; in 1970, a car driven by an American civilian struck an Okinawan pedestrian and military police fired shots to intimidate the crowd that gathered, setting off riots in which 73 vehicles were set afire. In the past twenty-five years since Okinawa's reversion to Japan, there have been 127 aircraft accidents, 137 brush fires caused by military exercises, and 12 cases of Okinawans killed by American personnel.

I arrived back in Naha in October, 1997, to interview Okinawa's controversial Governor Masahide Ota. Two well-groomed young men in dark suits from the governor's office met me. I asked to go first to Naha Airbase, where I had been stationed all those years before. Lieutenant Colonel Tateki Shinjo of the Japanese air force met me at the gate and we drove up a hill from where we could see the whole base—airstrip, hangars, buildings. We stood atop the old World War II-era gun emplacement, its barrel bent and rusty. Many of the sturdy cinder-block facilities from the U.S. days were still in use. I thought I recognized my old squadron area, but I wasn't quite sure. Only the hangars and flight line looked exactly as I remembered them. It seemed to me that we were standing directly behind where the old barracks once were: the pattern of the hills seemed the same, and the distance to the flight line and the placement of the golf links, which were now an obstacle course for Japanese servicemen. It seemed strange to me somehow that this should be a Japanese facility again, as it had been before the war.

My two guides were not allowed onto the base, perhaps, one of them suggested to me with a grin, because the troublesome prefectural government was not popular with the national government. He asked where else I would like to go, and I told him to Naminoue Shrine, on the hill at the edge of the sea.

As we drove down from the base toward Naha, it was quickly apparent that the changes in 30 years had been immense. I recognized only the contours of the land, the hills, the port before entering the city. The roads were now wide boulevards bordered by modern buildings. Naha no longer resembled Mexico, as I recalled it, but was indistinguishable from modern Tokyo. The squat, cinderblock typhoon-proof houses had been replaced by multi-story business structures, neon signs worthy of the Ginza, restaurants, retail stores, crosswalks, traffic signals, and well-dressed pedestrians. Naha seemed like simply another part of contemporary Japan. We skirted the seashore and pulled up alongside a hilly park-like area. "Here's the shrine," Iida, one of my guides, said, gesturing out the window.

I was lost.

We walked up a wide concrete roadway toward a small vermillion shrine that seemed smaller than I remembered it, not to mention that it was now imbedded in a dense urban area instead of perched on a great rock. But there it was, smoke rising from burning incense and the coin box in front, a few tourists milling around the grounds taking snapshots of their families in front of the Meiji-era structure. I wandered back down, to the side where I could look out over the sea. The Seawall, with its little piers that used to snake out over the cove, was gone, replaced by a bypass highway that carried traffic swiftly around the city. There was a white sand beach, however. Iida said the beach was artificial, and had been built about 20 years ago when the bypass was constructed. It was enormously popular in the summer, he said.

That night I called Toshio Hayashi, whose name I had gotten from an Okinawan journalist. Hayashi owns a small bar in Naha and also teaches college-level French and Latin on the U.S. airbase at Kadena. When I arrived at the Paradis du Lucia, located in a bustling modern entertainment district, I was greeted by a man with a wide, smiling face and a ponytail that hung nearly to his waist. He was dressed in a pastel tunic with an ornate rhinestone brooch pinned to it. Toshi, as he asked me to call him, is an unusual man with a classically trained tenor voice. His singing with karaoke accompaniment attracts a great many fans to his bar, including at least one black woman from a U.S. base who says that "Toshi's got soul." As I listened to him croon a popular Mariah Carey song, I saw her point.

Toshi took me for a stroll several blocks toward the beach, where the Ville used to be located. It had almost disappeared except for Jack's steakhouse, which still displayed its "A-sign," the official mark of U.S. government approval. I found only one old bar, dilapidated and obviously not used for many years. We walked toward the beach where the short-time hotels had been, and found instead their modern versions—"soapland" houses of prostitution, each one with a yakuza lounging in a chair or walking about in front. Business didn't seem to be very good. "It's still early," Toshi explained. I was gratified that the bar district was gone, but felt strangely nostalgic for my misspent youth. As we walked back to Toshi's bar, he told me that he had had a friend, a woman of about 50, who had recently died, but who had been a bargirl in the Ville back then. She was quite a character, he said, adding that I had probably met her.

Toshi had hired a young GI from Kadena, also named Mike, as a bartender. He was a kid in his early 20s from Chicago, a Bulls fan, and into the stock market. I asked Mike about the American bases and how the Okinawans felt about them. "We're here to protect them," he said genially, looking trim in an open-collar shirt, slacks, and a neat mustache. "And to protect America."

I had heard this before. "From whom?"

Mike hesitated for a moment to think. "Well, from China," he said.

"Are 20,000 Marines really going to stop the People's Liberation Army?" I asked.

He thought some more.

"Or North Korea," I offered. "What if there's trouble up there?"

Mike broke into a grin. "Hey, I just do what they tell me, man. I don't know why we're here. I'm just repeating what the officers say, that's all." It was the same line "the officers" had given us 30 years before, but they were referring to Vietnam at that time. And of course we had believed them too, at first.

Toshi was getting interested in the conversation now, from an Okinawan perspective. "Those bases aren't protecting anyone any more," he said as he moved behind the bar. "The Cold War is over. We all know that. We want the bases off Okinawa. They're just taking up all our best land." He paused. His thick brows knitted. "On the other hand, I make several thousand dollars a month teaching on the base. I need the money."

This is the dilemma that the whole island faces.

There really is no further rationale for maintaining the bases, not for Okinawa, not for the U.S., not even for the peace of the region, which could be secured just as well by Marines stationed in California. The bases are here because they have been for 50 years and continue to provide comfortable overseas facilities and command opportunities for senior officers. Okinawa is still "good liberty." Military bureaucrats are loathe to give up what is theirs, even if the training facilities are now too small on a too-crowded island, where occasional artillery shells are lobbed into backyards and sometimes airplanes fall from the sky.

The bottom line for Okinawans is that no matter how much they wish the bases would just go away and leave them in their gorgeous semi-tropical island, their average income is the lowest of any Japanese prefecture and unemployment is nearly double the national norm.

Okinawa still needs the American and Japanese money that the bases bring in, which in 1994 amounted to around 162.8 billion yen ($1.6 billion at the then prevailing exchange rate) according to Okinawan government reckoning. More than 8,000 Okinawans work on the U.S. bases, and many thousands more are employed in the entertainment and service industries around those installations.

MONEY AND POLITICS

The economic issue stood out in sharp relief on December 21, 1997, in Nago, where a non-binding referendum was held to determine whether the local residents supported the building of an offshore heliport so that the Marine Corps helicopter base at Futenma, in Ginowan, could be moved from its urban setting to the less-populated, safer location. One problem with this, of course, is that the base would not be removed from Okinawa, as promised by the Japanese and U.S. governments, but merely placed in a more remote location on the island. But the pattern for the past 50 years has been for the civilian population to build up around the bases, so that with the passage of time military installations are always located in dangerous places, surrounded by schools, hospitals, and residential areas, and ripe for disaster.

Leading up to the Nago referendum, therefore, a battle raged between the citizens who were in favor of the base and those who were not. It was opposed not only because of

the usual problems of drinking, brothels and violence associated with bar districts and military bases, but also because
the location proposed—a beautiful coastal area just off a
run-down section of Nago called Henoko—is home to rare
marine life. Henoko is adjacent to a Marine Corps ammunition depot that was scaled back after the Vietnam War, and
so it leaves the impression of a ghost-town with its dismal
blocks of abandoned bars, shuttered and broken windows,
and the occasional mangy dog darting up an empty street.
Henoko needs an economic infusion as badly as any place in
Japan.

Still, a newspaper poll two weeks before the voting
showed the heliport was losing. Japan's leading political
party, the LDP, pulled out all the stops, canvassing the area
and promising residents that their economic interests would
be served by the base, that its dangers and problems would
be few, and claiming that it was needed for the defense of
Japan by American forces. Chikako Yoshida, an Okinawan
activist who has a masters degree from Arizona State University, and who drove me around the area, said that the
central government should invest in Okinawa, but in a different way. "Instead of offering nice buildings and a community center, they should build a railway in Okinawa so that
people could live in Nago and commute to Naha. That would
help our unemployment problems. The bases are not the
answer."

Yoshida's view is shared by Robert Hamilton, a former
Marine Corps captain who was an artillery battery commander on Okinawa from 1986-88. One reason Hamilton has
come to oppose the U.S. basing policy is that "Currently on
Okinawa, serious and committed young Americans who have
volunteered to serve in their nation's armed forces are
increasingly being viewed as mercenaries to be isolated and
caged away from the local populace in peacetime, and only
to be let loose in times of military emergency." The proposal to move Marine Corps helicopter operations to an offshore
location certainly highlighted this and called into question
the Japanese commitment to the "alliance." Hamilton argues
that there is much more to being "a good and trusted ally"
than simply writing a check and keeping the troops out of
sight. However, Japan believes its partial financing of the
U.S. garrison constitutes an alliance and, according to
Hamilton, American "defense policy-makers are among the

worst offenders in reinforcing this mistaken belief."

Hamilton's arguments are powerful because he himself has trained troops in Okinawa. His unit had about 180 artillery pieces and consisted of about 4,000 Marines. "Firing live weapons is difficult. Twenty or 30 years ago you could fire a shell into a man's backyard, give him some money and tell him to keep quiet, and that was it. But today that's just not possible." Hamilton argues that the wide-open expanses of the western United States are much better training areas and that the Marines can live with their families and not feel like outcastes. "The argument that justified the American presence in Okinawa throughout the Cold War was that it was good to have a lot of Marines fairly close to Korea, so that in case of war there would be the potential of staging another Inchon landing." That mindset still seems to exist today, although there have been revolutionary advances in logistics in the intervening years.

Hamilton believes the real reason American troops remain in Okinawa is that the Japanese government wants them there. "It's a great deal for them. They don't have to recruit their own young kids and send them to boot camp and incur all the social disruption that goes with that. Especially in Japan, where they initially went off the deep end into imperialism, they've now gone clear in the other direction and try to stay away from establishing a military. Instead they just send several billion dollars down to Okinawa, and it's a great deal for Japan, however you look at it."

Hamilton says that as much as he dislikes conspiracy theories, he does believe that there is a very effective lobby on the Japanese side to maintain the American troops in Okinawa, both because they are convenient and because the are useful in bargaining to keep the U.S. markets open to Japanese export companies.

Nonetheless, the Nago referendum went against the heliport, creating a crisis for Prime Minister Ryutaro Hashimoto's government, which found itself in a bind between the wishes of its citizens and those of the U.S. government, its own powerful ministries, and business interests. Pressure was brought to bear, and within a week the mayor of Nago, Tetsuya Higa, announced that he would approve the heliport despite the wishes of the voters. He then resigned, as if to atone for what he had done.

GEOPOLITICAL WINDS OF CHANGE

Okinawa has not only had the geopolitical bad luck to become a military outpost for America and Japan off the shore of the emerging Chinese superpower. It is also simultaneously a cork in the bottle of a remilitarized Japan, as one U.S. general in a moment of rare candor publicly admitted, as well as a pawn in Japanese-American economic relations.

The American government would do well to reexamine the blurred policy concepts that led to its painful defeat in Vietnam. America's approach to Asia still seems based on the naive assumption that nations with heritages vastly different from the Western democracies will nonetheless evolve into "little Americas" if only they can participate in the joys of capitalism. But it doesn't take long on the ground in East Asia to realize that even with Kentucky Fried Chicken next door, Asians will remain culturally distinct, and that a one-size-fits-all foreign policy, oblivious of specific cultural and political realities, is critically deficient. In that sense, the error that was made regarding Vietnamese is being perpetuated with Okinawans and Japanese. We have failed to realize who they are, their motivations, and what is at stake for them.

Despite this, the U.S. Defense Department continues to insist that the Okinawan bases are crucial. The Japanese government is happy because foreign troops are kept far away from mainland Japan and, importantly, the U.S. garrison provides leverage that can be utilized in trade negotiations. Whenever Japan's trade surplus with America soars and trade friction heats up, the inevitable chorus of Japanese officials can be heard to wonder publicly whether U.S. bases are really in Japan's interest. Editorials suddenly appear in leading Japanese newspapers that question the security relationship, and U.S. officials hurry to calm the roiled waters. A trade agreement is produced that papers over yet another American sacrifice for "the greater relationship." Both sides declare victory to the press. It is a familiar scenario.

When I came to Japan in 1988 as a journalist, it was immediately apparent that the massive trade imbalance in Japan's favor was not a sign of a healthy mutual relationship. Yet Japan was doing everything it could, making every possible argument, and greasing every political wheel in

Washington to maintain the enormous trade asymmetry. Japan today enjoys an institutionalized trade surplus with the United States, and the security relationship is the glue that helps to keep it in place.

The Nye Initiative, named after former Assistant Secretary of Defense Joseph S. Nye, Jr., more officially known as the United States Security Strategy for the East Asia Pacific Region, published in 1995, declared that for the foreseeable future, U.S. troop levels in East Asia would remain at around 100,000, that the security alliance with Japan was the "linchpin of United States security policy in Asia," and that America must never allow trade friction to undermine that alliance. It even touted the U.S. defense capability as a wedge "to open foreign markets." Nonetheless, it doesn't require a great deal of common sense to understand that relying on an economic adversary to finance our nation's ability to maintain our military strength is not "a firm foundation." There is a measure of American self-reliance being lost, of self-determination disappearing, even of self-delusion.

The Nye Initiative, however, may not mean what it says, according to Ed Lincoln, former economic attache to the U.S. Embassy in Tokyo. When I interviewed him only days before his return in 1996 to the Brookings Institution in Washington, Lincoln asked me when his interview would be published. I assured him that it would be a couple of years, rather than a quick newspaper story, and on that basis he offered his opinion that Nye's document was not meant to last 20 years, but only until such time as the possibility of a North Korean nuclear threat could be discounted. If North Korea's leadership collapsed or if it ceased to threaten the stability of East Asia, that could provide an opportunity to reevaluate America's expensive forward-deployed defense posture.

OTA'S GRASSROOTS FEDERALISM

Okinawa's Governor Masahide Ota foresaw that possibility as well, when I spoke with him at his offices in Naha on October 31, 1997. Ota utilized a young woman translator for the first question, as if sizing up her abilities; then the former Fulbright scholar, Syracuse University graduate, professor and author, took over in fluent English.

In the Governor's calculation, the bases problem will solve itself over time. American forces will be pulled out as East Asia stabilizes. Over the next two decades, American taxpayers will lose interest in spending more than $30 billion a year to maintain an unnecessary and unwanted East Asian garrison. When that happens, Okinawa, like the Philippines, will lose an important source of income. Meanwhile, any political leverage that Okinawa enjoys today with Japan's central government because the bases are not wanted on the "Yamato" mainland will dissipate along with their gradual removal. Ota therefore believed he must obtain economic concessions from Tokyo quickly or Okinawa will remain as it is—small, beautiful, and poor.

Rather than watch Okinawa's fortunes dwindle, Ota decided to try to build up the economy while he had some clout in the form of public opposition to the bases. This, obviously, was a tricky maneuver. "There is a good chance that by 2015 the Korean problem will be solved and the relationship between China and America will be much better," Ota said. "In that case, there is no need for the U.S. military forces here. Even Joseph Nye has said as much."

Ota's government hoped to wring economic concessions from Tokyo in exchange for a gradual reduction or relocation of the bases through the year 2015, by which time they would all be returned to Okinawan jurisdiction. By receiving preferential treatment from the central government in terms of a large free-trade zone and tariff and tax concessions that would lure investment, Ota hoped to achieve economic parity with the rest of Japan.

"The Okinawan people would like to be more independent in a way. They would like to enjoy more autonomy," Ota said. "Okinawa used to be a kingdom that managed its own destiny. But since Okinawa became a part of Meiji Japan in 1879, the Japanese centralization system is so strong that you have to depend on them for everything. You cannot say anything, but simply follow whatever the central government asks."

Ota, struggling to secure from the central government the political power that Okinawans need to enhance their lives, saw not only historical precedent but also geographical reason to believe that Okinawa is a special case. "Although Kyoto, Hokkaido, and Nagano prefectures all have their own histories, Okinawa is different. Historically, they have evolved together since the Tokugawa consolidation in about 1600. But we were separate then, and after World War II as well."

The geographically remote Okinawans have long felt "outside" the inner circle of elites who govern from Tokyo. So perhaps the Ryukyu Islands have never fully embraced the emperor-based, centralized system of Japanese political and social rule that Ota says wields a tyranny of the majority over Okinawa today. "They ask us to serve the greater good, but could they say that they would do the same if the bases were in their hometowns?" Ota laughed, but without bitterness.

It is a measure of local control, a sort of federalism, that Ota and the Okinawans seek with their non-binding referendums and bargaining positions, much like that enjoyed today by the *lander* of Federal Germany. It is ironic that a system of Bismarckian authoritarianism continues today not in the land of its origin, but in Japan, where it was admired and emulated by Meiji samurai reformers such as Hirobumi Ito and Aritomo Yamagata.

The grassroots federalism espoused by Ota—signs of which have also emerged elsewhere in Japan in recent years in the form of civic referendums rejecting not only military bases but also nuclear power plants and garbage-incinerating facilities near population centers—seems to offer the prospect of a partial dispersion of political power from an authoritarian elite to the citizenry. Activist Chikako Yoshida said that since the 1995 rape incident in Okinawa, "More people have begun talking about Okinawan independence, about taking more autonomy from the central government. They are saying it's possible. We didn't think that way before."

Unfortunately, Ota himself was defeated in the gubernatorial election of November, 1998, by a candidate heavily supported by Tokyo's power structure.

Nonetheless, Okinawans are beginning to believe that they can be heard. Weary of their island's history of being used first as a battlefield and then as a military garrison while remaining the poorest of Japan's prefectures, this is perhaps their last, best hope—one for which they may be prepared to put up a political fight. And if this comes to pass, the American government may wake up surprised to find itself once again in a shameful position in Asia, from which it will be forced to make another embarrassing retreat.

THE 1995 RAPE INCIDENT AND THE REKINDLING OF OKINAWAN PROTEST AGAINST THE AMERICAN BASES

Chalmers Johnson

The Cold War in Europe ended in 1989 when the people of Berlin defied their overlords and began to dismantle the wall that divided their city. I believe that the Cold War in East Asia began to end six years later, on September 4, 1995, when three American servicemen abducted and raped a twelve-year-old schoolgirl in Okinawa. The reaction to that rape throughout Japan and also in South Korea mobilized otherwise inattentive people to the persistence of Cold War-type relationships in East Asia—particularly to the presence of 100,000 American troops—and started to end the artificial distinction between economics and security in relations between the United States and its trading partners in East Asia. It also caused some Japanese to begin to see Okinawa not simply as Japan's poorest prefecture but also as an American colony located on Japanese soil.

The U.S. and Japanese governments responded with a fierce reactionary campaign in order to protect the military bases and maintain the status quo. Nonetheless, the rape put the issue of Okinawa once again on the agenda of international politics. At the time of writing, the militarists of Washington and Tokyo are still withholding justice from the people of Okinawa. But the protest against the American presence in Okinawa has deepened and gained sophistication compared with the protests of the 1950s and 1960s.

In the October 21, 1969, issue of the now defunct *Look Magazine* the combat translator in the Battle of Okinawa and old Japan hand Frank B. Gibney wrote:

> Most of the 100 or so U.S. installations still on Japanese soil are of marginal value, but we cling to them. . . . The huge buildup of Okinawa into a nuclear-weaponed Gibraltar is an example of the development of U.S. Far Eastern security policy with scant regard to the people it was supposed to be making secure. . . .Now, on the eve of 1970, Okinawa is in

ferment. The new chief executive, voted in by a Communist-Socialist coalition, demands outright reversion. The first general strike in the island's history was staged against U.S. military installations, where some 50,000 Okinawans are employed. The discovery in July that the U.S. had stockpiled not only nuclear weapons but some form of nerve gas on Okinawa was enough to make the pot boil over. In Japan, the Okinawa question has become a matter of national honor. Newspapers sympathetically play up items like the recent prizewinning oration of Miss Setsuko Miyagi: "Okinawa's green mountains have been turned into ammunition dumps, nuclear submarines cruise in our beautiful coral sea. . . .Can't people on the mainland hear our Okinawan voice calling to them?"

Had the American Government considered Okinawa as a problem in political as well as military relations even a few years ago, this ferment could have been avoided. But the compromise and the reversion timetable that would have worked in 1966 or 1967 will not work today. . . . The ultimate American withdrawal from Okinawa and Vietnam presages a shift in the balance of power in East Asia.

The uncanny thing about these remarks is that they are completely applicable to the situation three decades later. East Asia is no longer underdeveloped, the Cold War has ended, the USSR has imploded, the United States has become the world's leading debtor nation, Mao Zedong has died, and elected presidents rule in Seoul and Taipei—but nothing has changed in Okinawa. The Pentagon and its spokesmen are still saying that the Okinawans must continue to bear the burdens of the bases because of possible "threats" from China, North Korea, Japan itself, or just "instability." The Japanese Government is still saying that it wants American troops based on "Japanese soil" but only so long as they are kept in Okinawa and no mainland Japanese need ever encounter them. And the Pentagon has become a leading component of the Japan Lobby in Washington, always arguing that American economic interests in trade with Japan and the Pacific must come secondary to the "broader relationship."

THE AMERICAN OCCUPATION

The Okinawan problem has a long and complex history following World War II. Nothing in this history reflects favorably on the governments of either the United States or Japan. The indifference of both American and Japanese officials to the civil and property rights of the people of Okinawa is a shameful legacy of the Cold War, a legacy that both sides today prefer to ignore or cover up rather than ameliorate.

In a sense it all began with the Battle of Okinawa of the spring of 1945. The U.S. military conquered Okinawa in the bloodiest battle of World War II well before Japan's final surrender. A third of the population of the Ryukyu Islands lost their lives in this battle. It is this history that makes the American occupation of Okinawa so different from the occupation of the Japanese mainland. Okinawa became an American base of operations. It was not a place that the Americans intended to "reform" or to make an ally as part of its grand strategy against the communist nations during the Cold War. It was treated as if it was American territory even though its inhabitants had none of the rights of Americans.

Between 1945 and 1950 the Americans occupied what Okinawan land they wanted, regardless of whether it had been publicly or privately owned. With the onset of the Korean War they expanded their bases into permanent American military facilities. There was never even a pretense of due process in the forcible seizure of land by the Americans. Nonetheless, the Okinawan farmers never gave up their titles to their land. When, in 1972, Okinawa reverted to Japanese sovereignty but the American bases remained undisturbed under the terms of the Japanese-American Security Treaty, the Japanese government had to deal with the claims of Okinawan landowners. It decided to treat the formerly privately owned land as if it had been taken over by the Japanese government in accordance with the terms of the Land Acquisition Law, a long-standing measure for forced lease or sale of land for public purposes. It then transferred the land to the Americans for their extended use under the terms of a newly enacted Special Measures Law for Land Used by U.S. Forces. Those provisions of the Land Acquisition Law that stipulate that public seizure of land be justified in terms of the public's welfare were simply ignored.

The Japanese government in effect forcibly leased the land and paid the owners rent. The government then sublet the land to the U.S. forces in Japan but with the Japanese government actually footing the bill.

Provisions of the Land Acquisition Law dictate that the leases be renewed every five years. They also require that documents be prepared identifying the land and that these documents be signed by the owners signifying the documents' accuracy and the owners' approval of their transfer to the state. If the owners refuse to sign, then the local mayor, or his designated substitute, must sign them. If the mayor refuses to sign or to name a substitute, this task is passed up to the prefectural governor. Since Okinawa's reversion to Japanese rule a number of landowners in Naha, Okinawa City, and Yomitan have refused to sign. From 1972 to 1995 the documents were always signed by the governor of Okinawa Prefecture. But after the rape of September 4, 1995, when the islands erupted in protest, Governor Masahide Ota refused to perform what the Japanese call "in-lieu signing" *(shomei daiko),* thereby precipitating a major crisis with the Japanese central government.

The prime minister of Japan sued Governor Ota under terms of the Local Autonomy Law to force him to sign the leases. The Naha branch of the Fukuoka High Court ruled in favor of Tokyo on March 25, 1996. Ota then appealed to the Supreme Court, which on August 28, 1996, again ruled in favor of the central government. It did so only a week before the people of Okinawa were scheduled to vote in a prefecture-wide plebiscite on the American bases, and both the speed with which the Supreme Court acted and the curtness of its one-sentence decision were widely interpreted as the government's attempt to intimidate the people of Okinawa before they went to the polls. It did not work. On September 8, 1996, by a ratio of 9 to 1, nearly 60 percent of Okinawan voters endorsed a reduction of the bases.

For a brief period in 1996 the lease expired on a piece of land that had been forcibly seized years earlier for an American communications and espionage facility, the Sobe Communications Center. The Japanese government was embarrassed by having to use its police to enforce the continued illegal American occupation of the land and by having to let the owner, Shoichi Chibana, hold a very well publicized family picnic on his property one afternoon. It was even more disturbed at the thought that during the spring of 1997, thousands more leases were scheduled to expire under many of the then 42 American bases. Hence the Hashimoto government pushed forward its revision of the Special Measures Law for Land Required by the U.S. Military Bases, cutting out the role of the prefectural governor in signing forced leases and putting that power squarely in the hands of the central government.

The new law was enacted on April 17, 1997, with 90 percent of the members of the Japanese National Diet voting in favor. It deprives Okinawan owners of their property rights and is also a clear violation of article 95 of the Japanese Constitution ("A special law, applicable to one local public entity, cannot be enacted by the Diet without the consent of the majority of voters of the local public entity concerned, obtained in accordance with law"). The Diet's rubber-stamping of de facto American colonial rule in Okinawa is comparable to the action of the Imperial Rule Assistance Association in 1940 in ratifying the Axis Alliance. It is inconceivable that the Japanese Diet would have agreed to such a law if it had affected mainland Japanese.

OKINAWAN PROTESTS

Tokyo has frustrated the Okinawans in seeking either a legal (through the courts) or a political (through the plebiscite) remedy for their plight. Conditions of these sorts in the past have elsewhere led to revolutionary violence. Many Japanese and Americans think that the Okinawan people are so even tempered and passive that they could not be aroused to direct action. The historic Ryukyu kingdom does have a legacy of pacifism that is in marked contrast to the feudalism and militarism that dominate Japan's past. However, such a view ignores the fact that Okinawans have twice before undertaken violent protests against their American and Japanese overlords—once in the mid-1950s over the land seizures and again in the late 1960s over the basing of atomic weapons and nerve gas in Okinawa and the use of Kadena Air Force Base as a launching pad for the B-52 raids against Vietnam. Both protest movements produced some reforms, even though the reforms actually adopted were chiefly intended to deceive the Okinawans rather than making real improvements in their lives.

The rape of 1995 ignited the third protest movement. Sexual assault is a fact of daily life in Okinawa. Shortly after the rape occurred, the *New York Times* (October 29, 1995) intoned editorially, "American military behavior in Japan has generally been good since the occupation in 1945." Given that in a period of only six months in 1949 Frank Gibney reported GIs killing 29 Okinawans and raping another 18 *(Time,* November 29, 1949) and that in late 1958 a fourth to a third of the Third Marine Division in Okinawa was infected with venereal disease, one has to wonder what the *New York Times* would regard as bad behavior. Similarly and predictably, Air Force Lt. Gen. Richard Myers, then commander of U. S. Forces in Japan, maintained that the 1995 rape was an isolated incident and not characteristic of "99.99 percent of U.S. Forces."

But General Myers is simply wrong. According to the conservative newspaper *Nihon Keizai Shimbun,* U.S. servicemen were implicated in 4,716 crimes between 1972 and 1995 based on bookings at the Okinawan Prefectural Police Headquarters. Thirteen years at 365 days per year adds up to 4,745 days. American servicemen thus committed just under a crime a day in Okinawa right through the period of General Myers's command.

Of course, not all of these crimes were sexual assaults. For sexual assaults, we must turn to research by the *Dayton Daily News* and a team of reporters led by Russell Carollo. *The Nation* (July 1, 1996) noted that it was not the *New York Times* or *60 Minutes* that went through 100,000 court martial records going back to 1988 to find out how many American servicemen had actually been brought before a military court charged with rape and how they had been treated. It was instead the staff reporters of the hometown newspaper of Wright-Patterson Air Force Base in Ohio who did the work. What did Carollo and his associates find?

Since 1988, Navy and Marine Corps bases in Japan have had the highest number (169) of courts-martial for sexual assaults of all U.S. military bases worldwide. Since there is a big Navy base at White Beach and a Navy contingent at Kadena and the Marines have twenty different bases spread all over Okinawa, Japan for all intents and purposes here refers to Okinawa. This rate was 66 percent more cases than the number two location, San Diego, with 102 cases but more than twice the personnel. Getting this information on actual courts martial required months of filing Freedom of Information Act requests, and the Army agreed to release its records only after being sued in court by the *Dayton Daily News*. Hence the statistics cited in their stories of October 1-5, 1995, do not include Army figures, which would only increase their magnitude.

The incidence of reported rape in the United States is forty-one for every 100,000 people, but at the American military bases in Okinawa it is eighty-two per 100,000. And that is only counting reported rapes. In Okinawan culture it is unbearably difficult and humiliating for an adult woman to bring a charge of rape, something that the Marine Corps has often relied on in covering up its record. Thus the numbers undoubtedly understate the actual occurrence of rape. More disturbingly, the *Dayton Daily News* articles revealed that the U.S. military had allowed hundreds of accused sex offenders in its ranks to go free despite their being convicted in courts-martial. *The Nation* concluded that "Covering up sexual assault is Pentagon policy."

But the Pentagon may have met its match in a group that has no interest in covering up military assaults on women, Okinawa Women Act Against Military Violence. Led by Suzuyo Takazato, a member of the Naha City Assembly, and Carolyn Francis, an American Methodist missionary in Okinawa, the group sent a delegation of 71 women to the Fourth U.N. Forum on Women held in Beijing. On September 7, 1995, they presented to the forum a revealing report and chronology of what Okinawan women have experienced under the American military occupation of their country. They returned to Okinawa on September 10 to be met with the news that on September 4 three American servicemen had gang-raped a twelve-year-old girl and injured her so badly that she required two weeks in the hospital. This group then became the spearhead that mobilized the Okinawa people and government. Their efforts led to the largest protest demonstration in Okinawa's history, the rally of 85,000 people at Ginowan on October 21, 1995, to demand that the American and Japanese governments pay some attention to their grievances. Without any sense of irony, the Okinawan Women have repeatedly quoted from the speech of Hillary Rodham Clinton, honorary chairwoman of the U.S. delegation to the Beijing women's forum, that "women's rights are human rights" and that military rape is a war crime.

Before the trial of the three Americans had even begun, the commander of American forces in the Pacific, Admiral Richard C. Macke, seriously worsened the situation by commenting that "For the price they [the confessed rapists under his command] paid to rent the car, they could have had a girl [i.e., a prostitute]." He was forced into early retirement for this remark, but it nonetheless signalled to the Japanese that the problems lay not just with lowly enlisted men but also with their commanders. A week after Macke's blunder the Okinawan police were once again asking for American military help in identifying yet another American who had raped a Japanese woman at knifepoint near a Marine Corps base. Macke himself stayed on as Pacific forces commander for some three months after being asked to leave and then took a job as a vice-president of Wheat International Communications Corp. of Vienna, Virginia, but with Macke still based in Honolulu. In announcing the appointment, the president of Wheat made no mention of Macke's trivialization of the rape but did say that "Dick Macke has a tremendous reputation for having the best interests of the region at heart" (*San Diego Union Tribune,* March 16, 1996).

THE 1995 RAPE INCIDENT

The three confessed American rapists, Seaman Marcus Gill, 22, of Woodville, Texas; Marine Pfc. Rodrico Harp, 21, of Griffin, Georgia; and Marine Pfc. Kendrick Ledet, 20, of Waycross, Georgia, are, unfortunately, typical American servicemen. Harp is the father of a nine-months-old (at the time of his arrest) daughter and a graduate of the ROTC program in Griffin, Georgia. Ledet was a Boy Scout and church usher. Gill had a college football scholarship. All were based at Camp Hansen. Gill told the court that "It was just for fun" that they decided to kidnap and rape an anonymous Okinawan woman picked out at random.

They seized the girl at around 8 PM after she had just left a stationery store. Harp and Gill confessed they violently beat her while Gill bound her mouth, eyes, hands, and legs with duct tape. Gill, described in court by an acquaintance as a "tank," is 6 feet tall and weighs 260-270 pounds. He confessed to raping the girl, while the other two claimed that they had merely abducted and beaten but not raped her.

According to the Associated Press, "The court interpreter broke down upon hearing his [Gill's] account of lewd jokes he and his companions made about their unconscious and bleeding victim" (*Los Angeles Times,* December 28, 1995). Police introduced into their trial a plastic bag they found in a trash can. It contained three sets of bloodstained men's underwear, a school notebook, and duct tape.

The rape took place on September 4. By September 8 the Okinawan police had identified the perpetrators on the basis of rental car records and had issued warrants for their arrest, but the Americans did not turn them over to local authorities until September 29. Whether true or not, it was widely reported in the Japanese press that the three had the run of their base and were spending their time "eating hamburgers." This is not just a matter of American delays but of "extraterritoriality," one of the most offensive aspects of Western imperialism in East Asia. From the time the United States got it written into its treaty with China following the Opium War of 1839 to 1842 (yes, it was an American invention), "extra'lity," as it was called, meant that if a European, American, or Japanese committed a crime in China (or today in Japan or South Korea if he or she is a member of the American armed forces, or married to or the child of someone who is), the foreigner was turned over to his or her own consular officials, rather than being tried under the law of the country in which the crime occurred or that of the victim.

It is not an exaggeration to say that the Chinese revolution was in part fought to be rid of this demeaning provision. It lasted in China (except for the Germans, who lost their extra'lity as a result of losing World War I) until 1943. It reflected the Western belief that Asian law was barbaric and that no "civilized" person should be subjected to it. It actually meant that criminals of all sorts hid behind Christian conversion or some other attempt to ingratiate themselves with one or all of the imperialist powers in order to place themselves beyond the reach of local laws.

Article 17, section 5, of the Japan-U.S. Status of Forces Agreement (SOFA) stipulates: "When U.S. servicemen and their families commit crimes, they shall be detained by U.S. authorities until Japanese law enforcement agencies file complaints with the prosecutors' office based on clear suspicion." It gives U.S. authorities the right to refuse Japanese investigators' requests to hand over suspects when they are attached to the military. The delays in the system have often been used to transfer American suspects back to the United States, where they usually just disappear. They are, in any case, beyond the reach of Japanese authorities.

As a result of the protest movement following the Okinawan rape, the U.S. and Japan signed a "side letter" to the SOFA allowing GI's suspected of rape or murder to be placed in Japanese custody before they are indicted if Japanese investigators request it. In Korea, American suspects get handed over to local authorities only if they have been convicted by a U.S. military court. It is of course unimaginable that Americans would accept such special treatment for foreign military personnel visiting or training in their country. And that is precisely what breeds the deep sense of injustice among Okinawans every day that their "uninvited guests" remain there.

The rape caused the greatest crisis in Japanese-American relations since the anti-Security Treaty struggle of 1960. It did not, however, halt the endless series of sexual offenses that plague Okinawans. Ben Takara, an Okinawan poet and chemistry teacher at Futenma Senior High School, told *Newsweek* (October 14, 1996), "We once surveyed our girl students, asking if they had had any scary experiences with U.S. soldiers on their way to school or back home. One third to one half of the students answered yes. . . . The rape case a year ago was just the tip of the iceberg. I must say that the Japan-U.S. security treaty has not protected the safety of Okinawans."

In 1992, in connection with the 20th anniversary of the reversion of Okinawa to Japanese rule, public opinion polls revealed that 85 percent of the people of Okinawa wanted the Americans to go home *(Asian Survey,* September 1994, pp. 828-840). After the rape that percentage rose to around ninety percent in all of Japan and close to unanimous in Okinawa (FBIS, *East Asia,* November 16, 1995, p. 17). Today the massive American bases still occupy some 20 percent of the main island of Okinawa, or about 10.5 percent of all of Okinawa Prefecture. Some 75 percent of all American facilities in Japan are located in Okinawa. Okinawans are convinced that this military presence explains why Okinawa is Japan's poorest prefecture, with a per capita income only 70 percent of the national average.

In 1990 Okinawans elected retired university professor Masahide Ota as governor on a platform of getting the bases back from the Americans. Ota was partly educated in the United States and has published many books on Japanese and American discrimination against Okinawa. He emerged as the only Japanese politician in living memory who both paid attention to what the people had elected him to do and who did not betray them when faced with bureaucratic resistance. His governorship, 1990 to 1998, marked the high point of the third Okinawan protest movement. It ended with a concerted drive by the Liberal Democratic Party, the American Embassy, and the Pentagon to defeat Ota and replace him with a more docile politician, one more typical of other Japanese prefectural governors. The background to Governor Ota's defeat is the Japanese-American plan to build an artificial, "floating" military airport near Nago in northern Okinawa and the decisive rejection of the plan by the people of Nago. The Marine heliport, the Nago plebiscite, and the defeat of Governor Ota are treated in detail in another chapter in this volume.

Meanwhile Okinawans continue to wait—for the next rape, or the next helicopter to crash into a schoolyard, or until some new event arouses the government in Tokyo to listen to what some of its own former members are now suggesting. Former Prime Minister Morihiro Hosokawa has proposed in no less a forum than the prestigious U.S. journal *Foreign Affairs* (July-August 1998) that the U.S.-Japan Security Treaty be renegotiated on a more equal basis, and that U.S. troops be withdrawn altogether from Japan. The United States government remains adamantly opposed to this idea. Its military likes living in Japan in bases it has occupied continuously since 1945, with the Japanese government paying most of the maintenance costs.

AMERICAN POLICY

What is the American rationale for clinging so tenaciously to a treaty that seems to have outlived its Cold War relevance? Where did the Defense Department's commitment to keeping 100,000 troops in Japan and South Korea indefinitely come from and why has it not been more widely discussed in both the United States and Japan? These are critically important questions but the answers are not easy to come by. The United States has been anything but candid on the subject. Some answers clearly belong to the Japanese category of *tatemae* (public pretense), whereas others seem to bring us closer to what the Japanese call the *honne* (or the true motives) of the matter. The fundamental reason for obfuscation appears to be nervousness about change on the part of both governments.

In February 1995, the Department of Defense reversed its previous policy started by President Bush of gradually drawing down American forces stationed in East Asia and committed the United States to the continued "forward deployment" of some 100,000 troops in Japan and South Korea until at least the year 2015. The author of this new policy was Joseph Nye, Assistant Secretary of Defense for International Security Affairs until December 1995, when he returned to Harvard. He is a professor of international relations and the author of the textbook *Understanding International Conflicts: An Introduction to Theory and History* (1993). His so-called "Nye Report" was enthusiastically welcomed in Japan when it was issued, since it perpetuated Japan's leverage over the United States, and it played an important role in stiffening the position of Japan's negotiators in the auto trade talks of the summer of 1995. Thanks to Nye, the trade negotiators knew that the United States had unilaterally given up its most important bargaining chip—namely, its Cold War treaty commitment to continue defending Japan.

In the July-August (1995) issue of *Foreign Affairs,* my colleague Barry Keehn and I warned that the Nye Report and the policy it enunciated were misconceived. We wrote that the attempt to freeze the Pacific in a Cold War framework amounted among other things to the most profound expression of American lack of trust in Japan since the end of the war. In response to this article, we were attacked by the American establishment as "isolationists" (even though it is isolationism in reaction to the end of the Cold War that we were trying to head off) and by the Japanese establishment as "Japan bashers" (even though we were more ready to see Japan emerge as a normal country than some members of its Ministry of Foreign Affairs). Our intent was to put on the agenda for discussion American trade and security policies toward the Asia-Pacific region, subjects that had been neglected for too long. We also hoped to prevent what actually has happened—namely, an emotional incident intervening and taking matters out of the hands of policy specialists—although we did not predict that the festering grievances of the Okinawans would be the source of the incident. In retrospect, we might have guessed that.

On September 4, 1995, the same day that two Marines and a sailor in Okinawa were abducting and raping an Okinawan girl on her way home from shopping, Assistant Secretary of Defense Nye was speaking to the Foreign Correspondents' Club in Tokyo, where among other things he said, "This [so-called Nye Initiative] puts a halt to the planned reductions of the early 1990s, and reflects our assessment of the realities of the region." What are these realities? Primarily Korea and China, he said. During his visit to Japan in November 1995, just before the APEC summit, Nye said again to the press that 100,000 troops were needed in Northeast Asia because of the "clear and present danger" posed by North Korea (*Japan Digest*, 11/28/95). His boss, Secretary of Defense William Perry, in an interview with the *Nihon Keizai Shimbun* on November 13, 1995, said "The Japan-U.S. security alliance is most important for deterring the PRC's [People's Republic of China] military expansion." These, then, are the two most important *tatemae* reasons for keeping the Security Treaty essentially as it has been since 1952.

In addition to mentioning China and Korea, Nye at the Foreign Correspondents' Club gave two further reasons for the forward deployment of 100,000 Americans. He said, "Alliances can be adopted for a post-Cold War era, not against a particular enemy but as a guarantor of security. . . . The U.S.-Japan alliance is not against a particular adversary but against a situation where countries in the region might feel pushed to arm themselves against each other and against uncertainty, were it not for a stabilizing and reassuring U.S. presence." To make such an open-ended commitment more attractive to the American taxpayer, he also added that, "It costs us less to station troops in Japan than it would to keep them at home" (since Japanese taxpayers support them more generously than any other U.S. ally). In the Nye Report itself, he also claimed that American troops helped to keep Asian markets open, thus suggesting that if we did not have troops in Asia our annual trade deficits of several hundred billion dollars might be even larger.

CHINA AS A THREAT

These are the *tatemae,* or formal, reasons for the new policy. None of them should be taken seriously except the issue of China, and it is so serious as to make the stated policy look ridiculous. Since the United States has no coherent, well-thought-out policy toward China, it actually has innumerable policies reflecting many diverse interests in the United States. Some Americans continually harangue the Chinese to keep their hands off Taiwan, liberate Tibet, continue respecting non-Communist norms in Hong Kong and Macau, and negotiate over the Spratly islands, even though China has claims to all of these places that are older than the United States' existence as a country. Other Americans criticize China for its dictatorial government, its building of a dam on the Yangtze, its contribution to global warming because of rapid development and coal-burning, its alleged shipments or arms to countries we disapprove of, its human rights record, and its insensitivity (by Western standards) to the U.N.-sponsored women's convention. We also acknowledge that China is, like us, a thermonuclear superpower and entitled to create some international norms on its own, although in practice we seem to forget this.

It seems clear to me that we need a serious national policy for adjusting to the reemergence of the world's oldest continuously extant civilization on the world scene. The talk of "containing" China is merely a desperate attempt by the military-industrial complex to find a new excuse for selling ever more ingenious and deadly weapons to all the parties concerned. It refuses to recognize that China today is developing through commerce, not through threats to its neighbors, and that the main war-mongers in East Asia at the end of the century are the United States and its allies.

In any case, the United States is certainly not going to deter China militarily by keeping an understrength Marine division in Okinawa, one that former Defense Secretaries Carlucci and Aspen had scheduled for demobilization until Nye intervened. Equally important, the so-called Weinberger Doctrine stills exists as American military policy. It says that the United States will not use force in international relations without specifying the endgame and how we get out of the engagement. In dealing with the world's largest social system, the Weinberger Doctrine essentially means that we are never going to use ground forces against China.

The only credible military force that might deter China is the carrier task forces of the Seventh Fleet. A logical policy would be to withdraw all ground forces from East Asia, since they are both a source of instability in relations with the host nations (as the Okinawan rape demonstrated) and a provocation to the Chinese, and instead strengthen American sea power in the Pacific. The United States is the only Pacific nation with the capacity to project power across great distances; that is our defining competence and we should preserve and rely on it, at least so long as some nations in East Asia invite us to do so. It should not be endangered by inappropriate deployments of American troops, which could in any case be easily transported from Hawaii or Guam or the U.S. mainland in times of crisis.

NORTH KOREA

North Korea poses a lesser and very different problem. The United States, South Korea, and Japan have an agreement with Pyongyang to replace its plutonium producing capacity with safe reactors. This agreement, based on the initiative of former President Jimmy Carter, opens the way towards a peaceful defusing of the 1994 Korean confrontation. But whatever transpires, the situation on the Korean peninsula today is totally unlike that of 1950, when the Korean War broke out. South Korea currently has a 650,000-man army of its own that can handle any threat from the North other than one in which China or Russia joins or a nuclear threat. South Korea is twice as populous and has at least twenty times the per capita income of the North. In November, 1995, Chinese President Jiang Zemin made a state visit to Seoul, thereby offering much greater security to the south than the presence of token U.S. forces.

More seriously, North Korea is an isolated and failing communist country. In June 1994, well before the Nye Report, the Japanese military analyst Shunji Taoka concluded that North Korea was producing only 60 percent of the grain it needed and that there was a high probability it would collapse because of its economic contradictions and isolation following the end of the Cold War. He believes that the troops of the Third Marine Expeditionary Force in Okinawa, the 54 F-15s of the 18th Tactical Fighter Wing at Kadena Air

Force Base also in Okinawa, and the amphibious vessels at Sasebo, which are all explicitly deployed to meet an emergency in Korea, are no longer needed. North Korea today is being demonized as a "rogue regime" primarily in order to justify these American military deployments.

In thinking about the alleged American military contribution to stability in East Asia, it is necessary to ask what the sources of instability are in the region, whether military force is an appropriate response to any of them, and whether American ground forces are an appropriate military response. Needless to say, none of this type of analysis has been done by the Pentagon. Most of the threats to stability in the region are non-military. They range from the economic crisis that began in 1997 because of irresponsible investments by American, Japanese, and European speculators, to potentially uncontrolled population movements, the exploitation of cheap labor, and ethnic tensions. "Stability" is in any case too nebulous a concept to form the basis for a military strategy or as an explanation to the American people for our defense of a very rich and populous region.

To the extent that there has been stability in the region, it was caused by high-speed economic growth on the pattern pioneered by Japan. Nye argued that this economic growth was made possible by the American security umbrella (or, in his favorite phrase, "security is like oxygen; you never miss it until it is gone"). This may have been partly true during the early postwar years, when the main security problems in East Asia were revolutionary wars against colonialism, often under Communist leadership, in China, Vietnam, Cambodia, Indonesia, Malaya, and the Philippines. Whether or not the United States should ever have gotten involved in any of these wars, they are now over and only a few embers still smoulder concerning the unification of Korea and the status of Taiwan. The situations that remain no longer have any relevance to the Cold War struggle between communism and democracy and are today at worst potential civil wars. Economic mismanagement and irresponsible American pressures for small countries to open their borders to international investors brought instability to East Asia. The presence of American forces made no difference whatsoever.

Perry and Nye also argued that it is cheaper to keep American forces in Asia than in the United States, something they must know to be false. The actual costs of America's

East Asian security commitments vary from just under $40 billion, in the estimate of the Cato Institute, to William Tow's calculation that "U. S. forces in Asia presently account for US$43 billion, or about 15 percent of the overall US defense budget" (*Contemporary Security Policy,* August 1994, p. 15).

Tokyo contributes over $4 billion each year toward the upkeep of American forces in Japan, in what the Japanese government has dubbed its *omoiyari yosan,* or "sympathy budget" (meaning sympathy for the poor Americans who cannot afford their foreign policy). The total cost of the Japanese bases is said to be $6.2 billion; hence this is what Perry and Nye are referring to when they repeatedly say, as Secretary Perry did at the annual banquet of the New York Japan Society in September 1995, "The most tangible measure of this support is Japan's commitment to provide 70 percent of the cost of keeping our troops on its soil." The problem with this figure is that the Japanese funds actually go for the salaries of some 23,000 Japanese employees of the Americans (including translators of Japanese magazines and newspapers hired by the CIA), local construction costs, utilities, and rents for confiscated land. None of the Japanese funds ever goes into an American account.

ORIGINS OF THE NYE REPORT

Since the Nye Report affects them more than anyone else, the Japanese have naturally devoted more attention than the American press to investigating its intellectual genesis and finding out who were its actual authors. Two of the more important Japanese studies are by the investigative journalist Takao Toshikawa, writing in his *Tokyo Insideline* (April 30, 1995), before the rape; and the distinguished defense intellectual, Tadae Takubo, writing in the October 1995 issue of *Seiron,* after the rape. Both agree that the ideas behind the Nye Report derive from a paper by Patrick Cronin and Michael Green, two young staff members of the National Defense University, a subcontractor to the Pentagon. In this paper Cronin and Green were reacting to a Japanese report of August 12, 1994, delivered to the Boei Mondai Kondankai (Defense Problems Deliberation Council), which is a private advisory body to the prime minister. Known as the "Higuchi Report" after its chairman Kotaro

Higuchi, this document rather hesitantly advocates that Japan be more aggressive in making international contributions other than just the monetary kind. In his September 1995 speech to the Foreign Corespondents' Club, Nye himself referred to the Higuchi Report in a favorable light.

But according to Takubo and Toshikawa, Cronin and Green wildly overreacted to it, concluding that Japan was about to slip the U.S. leash. They in turn influenced their young friend Kurt Campbell (b. 1957), Assistant Secretary of Defense for East Asia, and he then sold their story to Joseph Nye and his adviser on Japan, Ezra Vogel. The story they bought was that Japan was just about to step forth on its own, although the only evidence of this was Japan's decision to continue trading with Iran despite the American boycott. Tadakazu Kimura, an *Asahi* correspondent in Washington, wrote for his newspaper shortly after the Nye report was released, "The Pentagon is worried that with the Cold War over, the mutual security pact is considered in Japan less essential or even unnecessary, and that this mood may encourage a drift away from the U.S." *(Asahi Shimbun,* February 28, 1995).

According to Toshikawa, the State Department demurred and argued that Cronin and Green were exaggerating threats to the alliance. Toshikawa concludes, "Policy was hijacked by a bunch of dilettantes." Takubo is also scathing on the subject. He writes that although many Asian leaders claim to fear Japanese rearmament, they also know that Japan could not even agree to send medical personnel during the Gulf War and that its troops in the Cambodian peacekeeping operation broke and ran when confronted with any form of danger. In his view, there is no evidence whatsoever of a Japanese impulse toward aggression or militarism, and the aim of the Nye Report is simply to prevent Japan from competing with the United States in the international security arena.

The United States is also motivated by economic interests. The Pentagon in one of its lesser known roles—namely that of lucrative trade agency—is one of the U.S.'s most important sources of commercial policy. The United States is by far the biggest munitions merchant in the world today, with total annual sales of around $12 billion. Its closest competitor is one or another of its European allies with sales of a third of that amount. The "rogue state" of North Korea hardly even figures in this league, with $40 million. Japan is one of America's biggest customers for weapons. The United States sells to the Japanese Self-Defense Forces Airborne Warning and Control Systems (so-called AWACS aircraft), AEGIS missile systems for destroyers, and Patriot air defense batteries. It is also doing everything in its power to get the Japanese to buy the Theater Missile Defense system, a spin-off from the Star Wars program. There are many people at the Pentagon who have ample incentive to want to perpetuate the Japanese-American security relationship unchanged for as long as possible, regardless of whether there are credible threats to security in the area.

Meanwhile, despite (or perhaps because of) the serious and sustained efforts of Perry, Nye, and, more recently, William Cohen to think of good reasons to keep American ground forces in Japan, the Japanese government has decided to cut its own forces. The new National Defense Program Outline, adopted by the Murayama government in November 1995, replacing the old one dating from 1976, cut Japan's overall troop levels by 20,000 men, demobilized four army divisions, eliminated 300 tanks from authorized armor strength and ten surface ships from the navy. It also abandoned any claim to repel a "limited and small-scale invasion," which the 1976 Outline had as an objective. In the future, the Japanese government merely proposes to "cooperate" with the United States if an invasion of its own country should occur. It should be noted that public opinion polls reveal that few Japanese actually believe the U.S. would come to their defense if the nation were threatened.

In a letter to the editor of the *Japan Times* (Feb. 16, 1997), Ralph Cossa, an American military theorist and defender of the Pentagon, denounced Governor Ota of Okinawa for his "inability (or refusal) to understand the geopolitical environment in which he lives." Cossa further chided Ota for being insensitive to "the fact that U.S. service members are putting their own lives at risk to protect Japan's (and America's) national security interests."

But Cossa himself seems woefully ignorant of the Asian geopolitical environment. Newt Gingrich, former speaker of the U.S. House of Representatives and once the third most senior American political leader, said in a July 1995 speech: "You do not need today's defense budget to defend the United States. You need today's defense budget to lead the world. If you are prepared to give up leading the world [actually American hegemony], you can have a much smaller defense budget."

Even if the American troops are not in Okinawa to defend the U.S., they are there to defend Japan, according to Cossa. But the senior military correspondent of the *Asahi Shimbun,* Shunji Taoka, writes elsewhere in this volume that except for the nuclear area, since the late 1950s, Japan has been responsible for its own air defense. According to Taoka, withdrawal of American forces would not require Japan to spend any more on defense.

Other supporters of the American presence in Okinawa say that the troops and aircraft are "forward-deployed" to be ready for any emergency. But Okinawa itself is not likely to be the scene of any future conflict. American troops based in Okinawa would have to be transported to an actual war zone in, say, the Middle East. The American amphibious assault ships based at Sasebo are not big enough to move the huge American forces on Okinawa. In times of a genuine crisis, the American troops on Okinawa are most likely to be stranded there.

COLONIAL OUTPOST

Why then are they there? I believe they are military colonialists—representatives of an American empire that came into being in East Asia as a result of World War II. Just as the United States's earlier colonial outpost in East Asia, the Philippines, was a result of the Battle of Manila Bay of 1898 so the current American colonial outpost in East Asia, Okinawa, was a result of the Battle of Okinawa of 1945. For the past half century, Okinawa has had an international status similar to that of Korea when it was a Japanese colony from 1910 to 1945.

Okinawa and Korea resemble each other in four particular ways. First, in terms of formal legal structures, the Japanese always claimed that the Koreans acquiesced in Japanese rule, just as the Americans and Japanese both claim that the Japanese government has merely leased part of its territory to the Americans. This, of course, ignores Japan's military occupation of Korea in the course of the Russo-Japanese War and the United States's military occupation of Okinawa in the course of World War II.

Second, the Japanese in Korea tried (even though ultimately without success) to destroy the national identity of the local people. They did this through education, enforced name changes, and suppression of the Korean language. During the 1950s and 1960s, the Americans tried to do the same thing to the Okinawans. By broadcasting the news in Okinawan dialect and calling the people Ryukyuans, the Americans tried to weaken Okinawan loyalties to Japan.

Third, the Japanese in Korea and the Americans in Okinawa contend that their respective occupations contributed to the economic development of the two regions. But only after South Korea was liberated from Japanese rule did it became one of the world's richest countries, even though divided by the Cold War. Okinawa is also likely to prosper only after the American bases have been removed.

Fourth, the Japanese claimed that their occupation of Korea was required for Japan's "security." Korea was said to be like "a dagger pointed at the heart of Japan." But as former prime minister Shigeru Yoshida often pointed out, if Japan had not occupied Korea, it would not have gotten involved on the continent of Asia and would have avoided its disastrous war with China of the 1930s and 1940s. The United States's claim that its presence is required to maintain security and stability in East Asia is equally doubtful. Peace and stability exist in Asia because of high-speed economic growth, not foreign troops.

The difference between Korea and Okinawa is that Korea was liberated from colonial rule fifty years ago, but Okinawa, even at the end of the 20th century, is still a semi-colonial enclave.

III.

OKINAWAN IDENTITY

ASSIMILATION POLICY IN OKINAWA: PROMOTION, RESISTANCE, AND "RECONSTRUCTION"

Steve Rabson

The Japanese phrase *doka seisaku* is defined in dictionaries as a policy in which a nation endeavors to make the life-styles and ideologies of the people in its colonies the same as its own. Among the Japanese, and those who study Japan, *doka seisaku* is often associated with Japan's colonial rule of Korea between 1910 and 1945. At its most repressive, this policy was one of forced assimilation (*kyoseiteki doka*). During the last ten years of this period, it included elimination of Korean language study in the schools, compulsory use of Japanese, shutting down of all civilian Korean language newspapers, forced attendance at Shinto ceremonies, and the notorious 1939 "Name Order" requiring that all Koreans change their family and given names to Japanese readings. Some Koreans cooperated with the Japanese colonial administration, working usually in the lower echelons as police and local officials who enforced these edicts. On the other hand, there was also resistance in the form of protest against specific policies and criticism aimed particularly at those Koreans who were helping to carry them out.

The term *doka seisaku* has also been applied to Okinawa during the Meiji period; and coercion, cooperation, and resistance characterized Japan's assimilation policy and its effects there. But while Okinawa during the Meiji era is sometimes called "the first victim of Japanese imperialism"—suggesting that it was acquired and governed more like a colony than a prefecture—the circumstances were really quite different from those in Korea.

CHINESE CONTACTS

To understand how these circumstances developed, some background is helpful. As with much in prehistory, a certain amount of conjecture remains over the precise sources of early migrations that populated the Ryukyu Islands, the largest of which is now called Okinawa. But people are known to have come at various times from South China, Southeast Asia, Polynesia, and what is now mainland Japan. The physical features of many Okinawans differ even today from those of most mainland Japanese; yet others are indistinguishable in appearance from people in mainland Japan, where there is also significant variation. The geographical sources of Okinawa's population have been surmised from early methods of rice cultivation, kilning, and navigation. Early cultural sources are said to be perceptible today in traditional music, dance, village festivals, religious observances, and diet. But, as with imported skills and artifacts everywhere, adaptations have occurred that make it difficult to locate origins precisely.

The most often-cited origin for various aspects of Okinawan culture is China, to the extent that a popular notion in mainland Japan has persisted to this day that Okinawans are somehow more Chinese than Japanese. To be sure, there are Chinese influences in the diet, architecture, and burial customs of Okinawa that have not been seen in Japan, at least in recent times. But since China has also been the largest source of imported Japanese culture, some things often identified as quintessentially Japanese actually came from China via Okinawa. These include certain words, place-names, pottery styles, and religious rituals.

Chinese influence in Okinawa was also political. Early political organization in Okinawa centered around regional lords, called *aji* or *anji.* After years of rivalries, wars, and consolidations, three separate kingdoms emerged in the twelfth century—Nanzan, Chuzan, and Hokuzan—South, Central, and North. In 1372, emissaries arrived from the Ming Court and mildly pressured King Satto of Chuzan to establish a tributary relationship with China as other countries in East Asia had done. In 1429, when a single Ryukyuan Kingdom was unified under Chuzan, the continuing tributary relationship with China turned out to be non-threatening as well as enriching, culturally and economically. The Kingdom of Ryukyu, called Liu-ch'iu in Chinese, was required to send envoys to the Ming Court, but China did not interfere in its politics and trade, as Japan did with increasing frequency starting in the early seventeenth century.

The relationship between China and Ryukyu had profound and lasting effects. Starting in the fourteenth century, students were sent annually to Peking as *ryugakusei* (students studying abroad). The kingdom's leaders also learned China's language, literature, arts, and philosophy from teachers who resided along with Chinese artisans and traders in a special section of Naha called Kume, which remains as a tourist attraction today. The architecture of public and private buildings came to be based on Chinese models, as were court ranks and rituals, a trend also observable in Nara-era Japan. And, as in Japan, Confucianism became influential in Ryukyu, where indigenous ancestor worship made it particularly adaptable. Chinese laws, such as those banning firearms and regulating land ownership, were adopted, as were Chinese dietary customs, particularly the use of chopsticks and the raising of livestock. The raising of pigs and eating of pork continues today to be much more common than in the rest of Japan, causing mainlanders to perceive Okinawa as "Chinese" or "foreign."

The period between 1400 and 1550 is often called the Golden Age of the Ryukyu Kingdom. A highly developed merchant marine maintained a flourishing international trade with China, Japan, Korea, and Southeast Asia. Some of its most profitable exports were textiles, dyes, lacquer ware, fans, colored silks, paper, porcelains, gold, copper, grains, fruits, and vegetables. Ryukyuan vessels and crews also trans-shipped cargoes between countries, like Panamanian and Greek freighters of today. Problems during the "Golden Age" included Chinese customs officials who extorted bribes from Ryukyuan traders, and occasional misbehavior by Ryukyuan visitors to China. But Ryukyu-Chinese relations were, on the whole, mutually beneficial.

Meanwhile, relations between Japan and China worsened during the fifteenth and sixteenth centuries. Japanese pirate fleets *(wako)* conducted devastating raids against China, and in 1415 the Ashikaga shogunate, ironically following Chinese custom, declared the Ryukyu Kingdom to be a tributary of Japan. Matters came to a crisis in 1590 when Toyotomi Hideyoshi ordered King Sho Nei to provide troops and supplies for Hideyoshi's planned invasion of China through Korea. After initially hesitating, the king reluctantly shipped food supplies to the Japanese troops, which foundered in Korea and withdrew after Hideyoshi's death in 1598.

Although avoiding entanglement in a war between its neighbors, the Ryukyu Kingdom now became an object in the conflict over Hideyoshi's succession. Shortly after Tokugawa Ieyasu prevailed in the decisive battle at Sekigahara in 1600, he placed Okinawa under the domain of Shimazu Iehisa, the daimyo of Satsuma province in southernmost Kyushu. Shimazu was given the title "Lord of the Southern Islands," and in 1609, he sent an army of samurai to assert his control over Okinawa. For 250 years, Satsuma imposed severe restrictions and high taxes but allowed the Ryukyu Kingdom to maintain at least an appearance of independence as well as its tributary relationship with China so that the Shimazu daimyo could profit from the still-flourishing trade.[1] This was a way for Satsuma to get around the closed-country *(sakoku)* policy imposed by the Tokugawa shogunate after the 1630s. Despite Satsuma's repressive and exploitative policies, contacts between Okinawans and Japanese culturally enriched both. The popular entertainments of Edo and Osaka became fashionable in the Ryukyu Kingdom, where the traditional *kumi-odori* theater borrowed aspects of *no* and *kabuki*, and the world of Japanese theater welcomed Okinawan costumes, dances, and folk songs.

THE MEIJI PERIOD

In contrast to the Shimazu daimyo, who had tried to maintain the appearance of Ryukyuan independence, the Meiji government pursued a campaign to consolidate and extend its authority. From the early 1870s Japan tried to eliminate all political vestiges of the kingdom, real and symbolic. The government turned Okinawa into a prefecture partly out of concern that the kingdom posed a security problem. As an unassimilated territory on Japan's southern frontier, it could be used as a stop-over point for outside forces threatening Japan, as Commodore Perry had already demonstrated when his fleet of "black ships" made an uninvited call at Naha in 1853 on their way to Edo Bay.

Tokyo's assimilationist policy drew protests not only from the people of the former Ryukyu Kingdom, but also from China, which still claimed it as a tributary state. Fearing Japanese annexation, Okinawan aristocrats asked the Ch'ing government to intercede on the kingdom's behalf, and also asked former U.S. president Ulysses S. Grant to mediate the dispute during his visit to East Asia in 1879. The Meiji government had already used a massacre of Ryukyuan sailors by Taiwanese aborigines in 1871 as a diplomatic pretext to claim that Ryukyuans were "subjects of Japan" in need of protection, and it organized a punitive "expedition" to Formosa in 1873. (This Formosa expedition was largely comprised of Kyushu samurai led by Saigo Takamori's brother Tsugumichi and was partly designed to distract them from attacking the Meiji government itself, as in fact they did four years later in the Satsuma Rebellion.)

In 1872, Tokyo announced publicly that it was abolishing the Ryukyu Kingdom. This unilateral act, coming exactly five hundred years after King Satto's 1372 treaty of suzerainty with China, was euphemistically called the Ryukyu Disposition *(Ryukyu shobun).* Protracted negotiations of the issue between Japan and China, also involving Britain and the United States, dragged on for more than twenty years, until rivalry between the two countries in Korea finally led to the Sino-Japanese War of 1894-95.

Meanwhile, the last Okinawan king, Sho Tai, was forcibly exiled to Tokyo in May of 1879, and Okinawa was made a Japanese prefecture. Despite initial efforts in Tokyo to send highly educated and able officials to the new prefecture, Okinawans deeply resented the placing of outsiders in positions of leadership, especially when these "replacements" were carried out in some cases by physical coercion, including imprisonment of Okinawan officials. As time went on, the quality of Tokyo's appointees declined, especially in the lower echelons, where a high percentage of the police force and low-level bureaucrats were men from Kagoshima who had failed to find employment after the abortive Satsuma Rebellion of 1877. To make matters worse, the men appointed as governors of Okinawa prefecture in the Meiji era were often resentful of being assigned to a "remote" post, and sometimes took out their frustrations on the very people whose welfare had been entrusted to them.

It was during this period that prejudices developed which became widespread and enduring in Japan. As George Kerr notes in *Okinawa: The History of an Island People:* "Japanese who visited Okinawa on business or in fulfillment of official duties tended to carry back to other prefectures stories of . . . bizarre and unfamiliar things. . . . The government asserted that Okinawa prefecture was an integral part of the Japanese empire, but to unsophisticated Japanese eyes the . . .ways and speech of the Okinawans set them apart as rustic, second-class cousins within the Japanese nation-family" (pp. 398-99).

Yet, even in the face of such Japanese attitudes and policies, opinions among the people of the former Ryukyu Kingdom about their future political status grew increasingly divided as Tokyo's dispute with Peking over sovereignty in the Ryukyus dragged on. The local intelligentsia were split between the pro-Chinese "stubborn faction" *(ganko-to)* and the pro-Japanese "enlightenment faction" *(kaika-to).* Though clearly favoring the *kaika-to* the Meiji government was initially reluctant to antagonize the *ganko-to* which still held considerable economic and political influence and had a strong vested interest in the status quo.

One negative consequence of this reluctance was that land and tax reforms undertaken in other prefectures as critical elements in the so-called modernization program were delayed in Okinawa. As linguistic historian Shinzato Rumiko has pointed out, this had the effect of widening the political and economic gap between Okinawa and the mainland. Taxes in Okinawa were proportionately much higher than elsewhere in Japan; yet the Okinawans could not send representatives to the national diet, established under the Meiji Constitution of 1890, until twenty-two years later, in 1912. The situation in Meiji-era Okinawa is often contrasted with that in Hokkaido, where the government poured money and energy into developing a vast territory sparsely inhabited by a more easily manipulated population of Ainu hunters and fishermen. By contrast, Okinawa had limited natural resources and a population whose loyalty to the Meiji state was seen as problematic.

ASSIMILATION, TOP-DOWN

While the Meiji government withheld economic reforms and political representation for Okinawa, one realm in which assimilation was promoted early and vigorously was education, particularly in the realm of language. Linguists Shinzato and Hokama Shuzen have divided the implementation of this policy into two phases: a top-down period that lasted from 1879 to 1895, and a bottom-up consolidation period lasting from 1895 to 1937—twenty-five years beyond Meiji.[2]

The dividing year of 1895 marks Japan's unexpected victory in the Sino-Japanese War, which led to rapid decline of the pro-Chinese faction in Okinawa. At that point, more Okinawans came to see Japan as a nation on the rise, offering them the best hope for the future.

Before 1895, the policy of assimilation was imposed almost entirely by mainland administrators and educators, as the term "top-down" suggests. It included efforts to discourage tattoos, suppress *yuta* spiritual healers, reduce the influence of local *nuru* priestesses, consign local deities into the hierarchical pantheon of mainland state Shinto, and censor *kumi-odori* dance dramas thought to contain material "dangerous to the national polity" or "injurious to public morals." But language was the crucial issue. The dialects of mainland Japan and the Ryukyus are closely related structurally but became mutually unintelligible after they split from a single "mother dialect" sometime around 700 A.D. The Meiji government considered language "standardization" *(gengo doitsu)* an important policy that it later applied to the whole country. But the situation was seen as urgent in Okinawa because the population was almost entirely monolingual in a Ryukyuan dialect.

The early language "standardization" program in the Okinawan public schools was not a rousing success partly because sending children to school at all placed a heavy burden on farmers dependent on family labor in the fields. Second, Okinawans initially viewed Japanese as the language of outsiders, of a ruling class of government officials hostile to them and their culture. Children were frightened of mainland teachers who often seemed alien, harsh, and condescending. Also, at this time the Okinawan aristocracy and gentry, who had been raised on Chinese classics, saw no value in learning Japanese. The early "standardization" program sparked student strikes and angry newspaper editorials because it was seen as focusing too narrowly on language-learning and indoctrination in imperial ideology, ignoring other subjects thought to be important, including English. Mainland administrators consistently rejected these complaints, insisting that mastery of "standard" Japanese was essential for successful assimilation and to insure the loyalty of Okinawans as "imperial subjects."

That the promotion of assimilation in education, starting with language, had wider political and ideological goals is affirmed by Ichiki Kitokuro, an official of the Home Ministry: "We have no other recourse but education in breaking the stubborn thought of Okinawans and assimilating them to the civilization of the home islands [*naichi*]."[3]

Portraits of the Meiji Emperor and Empress *(goshin'ei)* were introduced into the schools of Okinawa in 1873, earlier than in any other prefecture. Japanese military leaders, who saw Okinawa as a vulnerable defense perimeter, also saw Okinawans as potential traitors because of the Ryukyu Kingdom's past association with China. Yamagata Aritomo and other high-ranking military officers came to inspect Okinawan schools to be sure that education was doing everything possible to turn Okinawans away from China and toward Japan. In this effort, as later, there was often confusion about what was Chinese and what was Okinawan, which contributed to the government's zeal for eradicating what were said to be "harmful local customs" through a heavy-handed campaign called *akushu haishi* (bad habit elimination). As for the dichotomy between China and Japan in the Meiji era, it was the Okinawans themselves who, on their own initiative, turned toward the latter.

ASSIMILATION, BOTTOM-UP

The Sino-Japanese War convinced many Okinawans that closer identification with the victorious nation, rising in wealth and status, was not such a bad idea after all. An early effect of the war was the decline of the pro-Chinese faction among Okinawan intellectuals. But among the population at large there was a broad, if not deep, effort to identify with Japan. Boys changed their hair-styles from the traditional topknot and pin to the crew cut popular on the mainland. Women began adding the *-ko* suffix to their given names, and men adopted *kun* pronunciations for their names which previously had readings that were closer to *on.* In Okinawa, unlike in Korea four decades later, such renaming was voluntary.

In the field of journalism, the newspaper *Ryukyu Shimpo,* founded in 1893 and still one of two major-circulation dailies in Okinawa today, advocated in its early editorials that Okinawa could advance materially and socially only by fully assimilating with Japan. One writer insisted that "We must even sneeze as the Japanese do." The *Shimpo* also published articles on Okinawan history and culture in an effort to inform mainland readers, especially those residing in Okinawa, and to dispel prejudices and stereotypes. By this time Okinawans were enthusiastically taking up the cause of language "standardization" in the period linguists now call "bottom-up consolidation." Basil Hall Chamberlain's influential 1895 *Grammar and Dictionary of the Luchuan Language*, showing a genealogical relationship between the Japanese and Okinawan languages, was embraced as evidence of shared ethnicity. A year later scholar Nakamoto Masaya published *Okinawa goten* (Okinawan Language and Dictionary) with the stated aim of helping Okinawans overcome the "interference" their first language imposed on their efforts to learn Japanese. Nakamoto wrote in his introduction that speaking a language intelligible throughout Japan was essential to building a powerful nation.

A resolution to promote the Japanese language was passed at the All-Okinawa Teachers Convention of 1916 which recommended that teachers commit themselves not only to speaking correct Japanese, but also to punishing students who spoke Ryukyuan at school. Anticipating their teachers, students at Shuri Middle School had already volunteered six years earlier, in 1910, to banish Ryukyuan from the school grounds. And, in the same year, students at Naha Middle School agreed to adopt the notorious punishment placard *(batsu fuda)*, also called the dialect placard *(hogen fuda)*, to be hung around the neck of students caught speaking Ryukyuan on the school premises. Wearing the wooden placard was considered a disgrace and resulted in a lowered grade. And, according to the rules, the only way a student could get rid of it was to catch another student using Ryukyuan to whom it could be passed on. This Okinawan version of "hot-potato" was later criticized for making children spy on each other, damaging their social development and self-esteem.

Despite these efforts, initiated in large part after 1895 from Okinawa itself, Okinawans continued to experience prejudice and discrimination in mainland Japan. The situation was exacerbated because Okinawans seeking education and employment were moving in large numbers to the mainland where their labor was often welcome, but their somewhat differing customs and tendency to use the Ryukyuan language among themselves was said to make them harder for supervisors to control. Also, when economic conditions worsened in other prefectures around the turn of the century, Okinawans were hard-pressed to find jobs anywhere in Japan. It was during this period that they first began emigrating abroad in large numbers to Hawaii and to South and North America. Nevertheless, a number of Okinawans were welcomed into mainland artistic and literary circles where their work was praised for its distinctive style and, in the case of literature, for its illuminating perspectives on late-Meiji Japan.

Another source of tension was the conscription of young Okinawan men into the Japanese military. They were exempted for some two decades from the Conscription Law of 1873 because of lingering doubts about their loyalty to the Meiji state. But as a result of Japan's victory in the Sino-Japanese War, some Okinawans began to pursue distinguished military careers, attaining high ranks. It was a source of considerable local pride when a warship commanded by Imperial Navy Captain Kanna Kenwa, a native of Okinawa, brought Crown Prince Hirohito to Naha for a celebrated one-day visit in 1921 on the first stop of the prince's historic voyage to Europe. Unfortunately, there was also prejudice among the imperial forces, and Okinawans who spoke their language to each other were on occasion mistaken for the enemy during the Sino-Japanese War. Imperial soldiers accusing Okinawans as spies, in part because of their local language, also had tragic consequences fifty years later during the devastating battle of 1945.

EFFECTS OF PREWAR ASSIMILATION

How was the assimilation policy of the Meiji period viewed in retrospect during the decades that followed? Perhaps the most frequently stated view among Okinawans in Taisho and early Showa was that it had succeeded, and that they should now be accepted as full-fledged members of the Japanese nation-family. Okinawans especially resented being continuously compared to the people in Japan's colonies, such as Taiwan and Korea, and to other minorities in Japan who had been the object of assimilation policies. Their indignation sometimes led to a kind of *yatsuatari* (indiscriminate rage or scapegoating) in which those who are the object of prejudice seek to raise their status by aiming prejudice at others. As the *Ryukyu Shimpo* insisted in April 1903: "To line up Okinawans with Taiwanese barbarians [*seiban*] and Hokkaido Ainu is to view Okinawans, who are truly Japanese, as one of these. No matter how insensitive Okinawans may be, we can never put up with this kind of humiliation."[4]

This angry editorial was sparked by a 1903 exhibition in Osaka that featured what was called a Human Museum *(jin-ruikan)*. As widely advertised, this "museum" displayed "live specimens of exotic peoples" who were Taiwanese, Ainu, and Okinawan women wearing their traditional dress. Newspaper reports in Okinawa did not object to this dehumanizing exhibit in itself, but to its inclusion of Okinawans, whom the writers insisted were fully assimilated Japanese. Likewise, Okinawan intellectuals protested vigorously when news broke of a plan to include Okinawa under the jurisdiction of the Taiwan governor-generalship. Again, it was not colonialism in itself that they objected to, but the idea of being placed in the same category as those who were not "true Japanese."

The effects of assimilation policy and ideology were also evident in ethnographic research on Okinawa, by both Okinawans and mainlanders. A central theme in the research of Iha Fuyu, the founder of Okinawan ethnography, and mainland anthropologists Yanagita Kunio and Orikuchi Shinobu, was that Okinawan culture, especially in it ancient forms, is of central importance to the culture of Japan. The remnants of ancient Japanese words and place names in modern Ryukyuan dialects, local religious practices thought to originate in Micronesia, and Okinawan pottery techniques were all identified as examples of "pure Japanese culture" that had survived in Okinawa, but had regrettably disappeared in the cultural mishmash of modern Japan. There was, of course, a downside to this worship of the archaic. Okinawa's portrayal as a storehouse for relics of the Japanese past also implied a certain backwardness.

THE PACIFIC WAR AND AFTER

The cruelest of the many ironies of the Pacific War was that, after years of discrimination on the mainland where Okinawans were sometimes denied employment and lodging, they saw the Battle of Okinawa as an opportunity to prove, once and for all, their loyalty to Japan and their full assimilation as Japanese. Diaries written just before the battle by teenage Okinawan boys in the local defense corps *(boeitai)* express joy at the chance to demonstrate "the Yamato spirit" and to honor the emperor by repulsing the invasion of "savage" Americans. The *boeitai* fought tenaciously against advancing American forces, and high school girls, conscripted as combat nurses into such units as the legendary Himeyuri Student Corps *(gakuto tai),* gave their lives caring for battlefield wounded. But such sacrifices only swelled the numbers of victims in a tragically misguided cause. Japanese soldiers ordered mass suicides of Okinawan civilians to stretch dwindling food supplies, and forced others out of overcrowded caves and tunnels into heavy enemy fire. In perhaps the most outrageous betrayal of the Okinawans' determination to assimilate, Japanese soldiers shot thousands at point-blank range in their anger over defeat, accusing the Okinawans, sometimes on the basis of a few words uttered in dialect, of being spies. This worst battle of the Pacific War took the lives of more than two-hundred thousand local residents.

The end of that war did not, of course, end the controversy over assimilation. It only brought a new party into the discourse—the United States. The American military prolonged its occupation rule of Okinawa until 1972, twenty years beyond the occupation of mainland Japan, and continues to "occupy" vast areas with its bases to this day in what is, unfortunately for Okinawa, a convenient staging area for weapons and troops to virtually all of Asia. To maintain unrestricted use of this bastion, Pentagon policymakers insisted for almost a quarter of a century that they must retain administrative control over most of the Ryukyu Islands which entailed forcible land seizures, denials of legal rights, and numerous inconveniences and indignities. Finally, local opposition, in the form of mostly peaceful but occasionally violent demonstrations, became so disruptive during the Vietnam War that even the U.S. military was forced to concede that American administration had become detrimental to their mission, risking utility of the bases it was supposed to ensure.

But so long as the Pentagon was still trying to prolong its occupation, military intelligence and propaganda agencies, such as the Army's Counter-Intelligence Corps and Public

Relations Section, embarked on a vigorous campaign to convince Okinawans that they were *not* Japanese. The American government was thus endeavoring to undo the effects of *doka seisaku,* which had also initially been imposed "top-down" by the Meiji government. The difference was that no "bottom-up consolidation" response was forthcoming among Okinawans to this misguided undertaking, which expended millions of American taxpayer dollars.

The American campaign for "disassimilation" was pursued in large part out of fear that the movement for reversion to Japanese sovereignty, having gained considerable momentum by the early 1950s, would succeed and force the military to deal with more restrictive Japanese policies toward American bases, or even to withdraw altogether if the opposition parties came to power in Tokyo. American occupation authorities in Okinawa officially adopted the word "Ryukyuan," widely mispronounced and misspelled as "Ree-*yoo*-kian," "Ryoo-*kyoo*-ian," or "*Rye* (as in bread)-yoo-kian" for all references to the local population. For ideological support of the disassimilation campaign, the United States Army funded the research and writing of officially approved histories emphasizing Satsuma's invasion and exploitation of the Ryukyu Kingdom, as well as Japan's later discriminatory policies and attitudes toward Okinawa after it became a prefecture. The campaign also entailed occasional censoring of the press and denunciations of opposition leaders, especially those advocating reversion, as "Communists"—a label that carried more stigma among local Americans than it did among Okinawans.

Okinawans complained that they were often told by Americans how lucky they were to have been liberated from the oppression of Imperial Japan. But when they objected to occupation policies such as seizures of land and denials of legal rights, they were reminded that they were the people of a defeated country, and that the United States was, after all, protecting them and the rest of "free" Asia from Communism.[5] In psychology, this is known as putting someone in a double-bind.

There was, however, at least one nominally positive aspect to this American campaign—the funding of museums, libraries, and exhibitions of cultural artifacts from the Ryukyu Kingdom with American taxpayer dollars. The Pentagon even paid for a radio station that was supposed to broadcast exclusively in a main-island Okinawan dialect and to avoid the use of "standard" Japanese. Unfortunately, announcers and copywriters were hard-pressed to find, in this now-disappearing language, modern theoretical and technological terms with which to report the daily news. As a practical necessity, they resorted occasionally to words from English or even—horror of horrors—Japanese.

During the period of American military rule, the local opposition, especially school teachers, resisted the "Ryukyu-ization" campaign, insisting, as school teachers had since Meiji, that Okinawans were Japanese. The *hi no maru* (white field, red sun) flag, banned from display under American occupation law except on certain holidays, became a poignant symbol of this resistance at countless rallies and protest demonstrations in support of reversion. In a double-edged irony, the *hogen fuda,* or punishment placards, were brought back into the schools to hang around the necks of children caught speaking local dialect. The majority of Oki-nawans supported, at some level, the long struggle for return to the motherland (*bokoku fukki).* And even those who did not actively join the movement insisted that they were Japanese, easily seeing through the "Ryukyu-ization" campaign as a propaganda ploy to prolong the American military occupation.

"REASSIMILATED" ONCE MORE

The movement finally bore fruit on May 15, 1972, when Okinawa was "reassimilated" into the Japanese polity. Yet assimilation persists as an issue today. On the one hand, it is seen as insufficient to have boosted Okinawa to a level of material prosperity equal to the rest of Japan. Local eco-nomic conditions have improved markedly since reversion, but Okinawa's per capita income is still only seventy percent of the mainland's. Furthermore, the prefecture is still forced disproportionately to sacrifice its land and quality of life to the maintenance of vast American military bases. Three-quarters of the American military presence in all of Japan remains on the island thanks to the *henkan kyotei,* the 1969 "reversion agreement" that in Okinawa was sarcastically called *henken kyotei*—the "discriminatory agreement."

Moreover, in what is sometimes called a "secondary occupation," Japanese corporations have bought up choice ocean-front properties for luxury hotels and golf courses, where Okinawans are employed as service workers for mainland managers and customers, with the profits being removed to the mainland. With ubiquitous resort construction now threatening to destroy the coral-based ocean environment that attracts tourists, this economic marginalization is seen as a kind of cannibalism, rather than assimilation.

On the other hand, post-reversion assimilation is also criticized as being too thorough in demanding political, cultural, and ideological conformity with the mainland. The Ministry of Education's efforts to promote patriotism in the schools by ordering display of the Japanese flag and singing of the national anthem have, like the occupation's prohibition of flag displays before reversion, sparked angry protests from teachers and others who resent what they see as a renewal of Meiji assimilation policies designed to "make imperial subjects" *(kominka)* of Okinawans.[6] This resentment is exacerbated by the national government's reluctance to acknowledge wartime atrocities, especially those committed in Okinawa. Teachers have also requested that Okinawa's history and culture be more fully taught in the curriculum, even as they are frustrated by an educational system geared relentlessly toward college entrance examinations on which there are very few, if any, questions about Okinawa.

More than two decades after reversion, local disillusionment with mainland policies and attitudes has radically transformed the image of *hi no maru*. Before 1972, the flag was a cherished symbol of liberation from American military rule and re-assimilation with Japanese compatriots. Today, for many Okinawans, it is a despised symbol of past aggression and continuing domination by Tokyo. Thus, assimilation—promotion, resistance, and "reconstruction"—continues to spark debates in Okinawa that swirl around such familiar dichotomies as ethnic versus national, homogeneity versus diversity, and local versus central. And because these debates are played out in ways that are particularly concentrated and conspicuous, Okinawa is fruitful ground to study these issues.

NOTES

1. George Kerr, *Okinawa: The History of an Island People* (Rutland, VT: Tuttle, 1958), pp. 157-69; and Steve Rabson, *Okinawa: Two Postwar Novellas* (Berkeley: Institute of East Asian Studies, University of California, 1989 and 1996), pp. 5-6.

2. Hokama Shuzen, "Okinawa ni okeru gengo kyoiku no rekishi," in Tanikawa Ken'ichi, ed., *Waga Okinawa hogen ronso* (Tokyo: Kijisha, 1970), pp. 186-216; and Rumiko Shinzato, "The Standardization Movement in Okinawa: A Sociolinguistic Perspective," paper presented at the symposium of the International Society for Ryukyuan Studies, Naha, August 1991, p. 13.

3. Quoted in Ota Masahide, *Okinawa no minshu ishiki* (Tokyo: Shinsensha, 1976), p. 346; trans. in Alan S. Christy, "The Making of Imperial Subjects in Okinawa," *Positions* 1:3 (Duke University Press, 1993), p. 615.

4. Editorial from April 1903, quoted in Matayoshi Sekiyo, *Nihon shokuminchika no Taiwan to Okinawa* (Ginowan, Okinawa: Aki Shobo, 1990), p. 264. Translated in Christy, "The Making of Imperial Subjects," p. 616.

5. Miyagi Etsujiro, *Senrosha no me* (In the Eyes of the Occupiers) (Naha: Naha Shuppansha, 1982), pp. 89-103.

6. For an analysis of an important Okinawan flag-burning incident, see Norma Field, *In the Realm of a Dying Emperor* (New York: Pantheon, 1991), pp. 33-104.

[Note: This article is a revised and updated version of a chapter in Helen Hardacre, ed., *New Directions in the Study of Meiji Japan: Proceedings of the Meiji Studies Conference* (Leiden: Brill, 1997) and is reprinted with permission.]

BEING "JAPANESE" IN BRAZIL AND OKINAWA

Kozy K. Amemiya

On August 15, 1945, Japan surrendered unconditionally to the Allied Powers, thus concluding World War II. Given such a solid fact, it seems strange that a large number of Japanese refused to believe that Japan had been defeated even a decade after it had happened. These Japanese were not cut off from the outside world and lacking all access to information, like those few former Japanese soldiers left behind and hiding in the jungles of the Philippines and Guam. They had even seen the photograph of the signing of Japan's surrender on the U.S.S. Missouri. Yet, nothing convinced them. They believed in Japan's victory so doggedly they looked with suspicion at what was normally considered a piece of hard evidence of Japan's defeat and interpreted it as an image fabricated by the United States. These believers in Japan's victory were Japanese immigrants in Brazil, who came to be called the *kachigumi* (victory faction).

The *kachigumi* ideology held sway over a majority of the Japanese community in Brazil for several years after 1945. Not only did those who believed keep their faith in Japan's invincibility; they also did not tolerate those who acknowledged Japan's defeat, who were called *makegumi* (defeat faction). As far as the *kachigumi* people were concerned, the denial of Japan's defeat indicated that one was a "true Japanese." The *makegumi* were a bunch of traitors and "non-Japanese" *(hikokumin)*. The *kachigumi* terrorized the *makegumi,* culminating in more than a dozen assassinations.

Why did some Japanese immigrants in Brazil (and also some in Peru) adopt such an extreme attitude and become fanatics while other immigrants in similar situations did not? German immigrants to Brazil, for example, initially doubted the defeat of their homeland, but it did not take them long to recognize it as a fact and resume a normal life. How did the *kachigumi* idea about the Japanese develop halfway around the world from Japan and remain alive for so long?

In part, it was due to the geographical and social isolation of the Japanese immigrants. Other factors were the imperial education the first generation of immigrants had received in Japan and the propaganda they were fed in Brazil by the Japanese government and retired veterans of the Japanese Imperial Army. These factors interacted with one another to shape the *kachigumi* mentality. If that were all, then the problem would be a peculiar phenomenon of prewar Japanese immigrants in Brazil. But there is also the issue of identity—the individual immigrant's effort to become and remain a "true Japanese" in a situation in which that identity was automatically regarded with suspicion.

To explore the problems of "Japanese" identity with which the immigrants in Brazil grappled, I will compare the identity issue of the Okinawans, specifically, the Life Reform Movement (*seikatsu kaizen undo*) in the 1930s and early 1940s. The Okinawans were at the periphery of Japan, although they were not considered an ethnic minority like the Koreans or Chinese living in Japan. The Okinawans, encouraged by the Life Reform Movement, tried to transform themselves from "peripheral Japanese" into "Japanese," just as the immigrants in Brazil did via the *kachigumi* ideology. Both of these groups had to grapple with the socially constructed model of what a Japanese should be in the early 20th century, as they tried to reproduce this model within themselves in places either geographically or socially quite distant from Japan.

IMMIGRATING TO BRAZIL

The first group of immigrants from Japan, 791 in all, arrived in Santos, Brazil in 1908. Most were so-called "contract immigrants" (*keiyaku imin*), who had signed a contract to work on the coffee plantations. A small number of immigrants were so-called "free immigrants" (*jiyu imin*) or "called immigrants" (*yobiyose imin*), who were invited to Brazil by families or friends. By 1941, over 180,000 more had followed them, pushed out of Japan by the collapse of the agricultural economy and the failure of burgeoning modern industrial sectors to absorb all the excess labor from the rural regions, pulled by the expansion of the coffee plantations and an acute labor shortage in Brazil, and also lured by the immigration agents' sweet promises of making a great deal of money in a few years by picking coffee beans. Three quarters of all the prewar immigrants to Brazil arrived between 1925 and 1935, when Japan was preparing for its military and territorial expansion in East Asia.

Most of those emigrating to Brazil, like those going to other countries, had no intention of spending the rest of their lives in their host country. They went to Brazil hoping to return home when they had made enough money to start over in Japan. In a 1938 survey of 12,000 immigrant households, 85 percent of all the respondents answered that they hoped to return home, only 10 percent responded they would remain in Brazil permanently, and the remaining 5 percent were not sure. Even those who intended to stay in the host country wanted to retain their Japanese nationality.

It did not take the new arrivals long to realize that the immigration agents had made false promises and that it would be impossible to achieve their original monetary goals while employed as plantation workers. Often, they were not paid the wages agreed upon in the contract. Living and working conditions were far worse than they had expected, and they were forced to buy their food and other supplies at exorbitant prices at stores owned by plantation owners. In a harsher environment than they had imagined in Japan, they began to think of themselves as abandoned by the Japanese government *(kimin,* i.e., "thrown-away people") rather than as immigrants *(imin).* Quite a few broke their contracts before they were completed, moving into the undeveloped lands of remote and isolated areas of the northwest, where they settled as independent farmers and set up self-contained communities. Later arrivals joined them in the northwest, moving further and further out into the frontier, and repeating the resettlement process of the first groups.

In these new settlements, the immigrants formed associations for protecting their common interests. The associations built and maintained schools, provided translators, gave directions and advice, shared information on the workings of Brazilian society, and helped the immigrants in dealing with the government offices of Brazil. As the immigrants began to settle down and their welfare needs lessened, the associations also became a pipeline between the immigrant community and the Japanese government. The Japanese government exploited these associations for nationalistic purposes and used the immigrants to disseminate propagandistic materials. These materials included textbooks, magazines, and films designed to perpetuate the spirit of Japan.

Japanese language schools played a major role in instilling and reinforcing Japanese nationalism among the immigrants and their progeny. Commonly called "Japanese Schools" *(Nippon gakko)*, they had direct ties with the Japanese government through the associations. In 1936 the Japanese Ministry of Education gave financial support to establish the Association of Japanese Education Dissemination in Brazil (Burajiru Nihonjin Kyoiku Fukyukai) through which it funneled guidance and instructions to the schools. These schools were not merely Japanese-language schools for the immigrants' offspring; they were also centers of emperor worship, where all Japanese immigrants' children were educated to become real "Japanese." There, all imperial holidays were observed by both children and parents with ceremonies in which the photograph of the emperor and empress was displayed, the Imperial Rescript on Education was read, and other rituals of respect and obedience to the emperor were conducted. In 1938, there were 187 such schools with about 10,000 students altogether in Brazil.

The Japanese schools symbolized the status of Japanese immigrants' settlements as Japan's virtual colonies. While each settlement was organized and run by the immigrant associations and there were regional leaders, no leaders for the entire immigrant community emerged out of the associations because the administrative structure encompassing the entire immigrant community was supplied by the Japanese government. At its pinnacle sat the Japanese Consulate General in Sao Paulo. The Ministry of Colonization (Takumusho) and the Ministry of Foreign Affairs supported a semi-private Overseas Enterprise Company (Kaigai Takushoku Kabushikigaisha) that controlled immigration, and the Development Union of Brazil (Burajiru Takushoku Kumiai) as its local affiliate, to help the immigrants in economic activities.

The romanticization of Japan began as soon as the immigrants left Japan. An immigrant wrote his relatives in 1926 on the boat near Singapore on his way to Brazil:

Every morning, I pray silently to the easterly sky. Not to God, nor to Buddha, but to Japan itself. The farther away I move from my homeland, the stronger my appreciation and respect with awe for the emperor's country *(kokoku)* have become.

In this immigrant's mind, "Japan" was already becoming transformed from a place he knew by living there into an ideal image. Such an image of "Japan" paved the way for an image of what it meant to be "Japanese."

In addition to their national identity, the immigrants (particularly those from mainland Japan) developed in Brazil a new consciousness of their ethnic identity—something they had never had at home. In Japan they had no experiences in their daily lives that made them conscious of their ethnicity. They had identities in their immediate and extended families, hamlets and villages. When they thought of themselves as Japanese, it was their national identity. In Brazil, they were exposed to other ethnic groups, against whom they defined themselves, and were defined by others, as Japanese. In the course of their movement into the hinterland and the reorganization of their community, the old unities of families, villages and prefectures of origin in Japan also weakened. In this process, their shared experiences and a sense of common ethnicity became a unifying force beyond the boundaries of their former communities. Only the Okinawans succeeded in keeping their prefectural identity reasonably well intact. Still, the Okinawans, too, were regarded, and regarded themselves, as "Japanese" vis-à-vis other ethnic groups in Brazil. They referred to themselves as *kenjin* (literally, "prefectural person") vis-à-vis the mainland Japanese, indicating they were a group from a distinct prefecture.

For Japanese immigrants in Brazil their ethnic identity became entwined with their national identity. Since they had no intention of staying in their host country permanently, but hoped to return to their original homes with a fortune as a banner of success, Japanese immigrants in South America in the prewar era remained Japanese subjects. Even as their hopes grew dimmer, they still dreamed of a return journey home. Ironically, now that immigration is flowing from Brazil to Japan, these "reimmigrant" Japanese Brazilians also hope to return home, namely to Brazil, after they have made sufficient money.

The Japanese government did not encourage the immigrants to return, but neither did it encourage them to cut their emotional and moral ties with Japan. Japanese government officials gave conflicting messages in their instructions to immigrants, prior to their departure for South America. The immigrants were lectured, usually at the port of embarkation, about working diligently and settling permanently in the host countries as law-abiding, loyal, model citizens. At the same time, they were also told "to retain their identity as Japanese and always to fulfill their obligation as subjects of Japan." For the immigrants, the latter message resonated more loudly and was easier to follow, particularly given their imperial education in Japan. The other part of the instructions (to work diligently as law-abiding, model citizens of their new country) impressed the immigrants less, but it was not that difficult to follow, until the homeland and the host country set out on a collision course and loyalty to both became impossible.

BETWEEN TWO NATIONALISMS

Japanese immigrants were first confronted with Brazilian political opposition to Japanese immigration in the 1930s. It was prompted by a surge in Japanese immigration, Japan's invasion of China, and also the rise of Brazilian nationalism. Under such conditions, the immigrants reinforced their unity and identity as "Japanese."

A large increase in Japanese immigration had begun in 1924, when the number of immigrants jumped from the previous year's 895 to 2,673, as a result of the shut-down of immigration into the United States. The number again more than doubled in 1925 to 6,330, and continued to climb. In 1933, new immigrants from Japan numbered 24,494 and accounted for 53.2 percent of all immigrants entering Brazil in that year. Such large waves of Japanese immigrants, against the backdrop of Japan's invasion of northeast China in 1931, stirred concern among Brazilians, who were stimulated by nationalism of their own, and evolved into an anti-Japanese campaign in 1933-34. The advocates of this campaign argued that the Japanese were not an ideal racial component for Brazil because their culture was too different and they tended to be clannish and self-contained and were unwilling to assimilate into Brazilian society. "The Japanese are insoluble like sulfur," claimed Oliveira Vianna, Brazil's leading social scientist, in 1932. "Insoluble like sulfur" came to be a frequently used phrase by anti-Japanese advocates. They were also suspicious about the Japanese being militaristic. The most radical among the anti-Japanese advocates, Congressman Xavier de Oliveira, called the Japanese immigration into Latin America an "immigration for conquest," and argued that each immigrant was a soldier in disguise. "Brazil is a Manchuria in South America," he declared. In such an atmosphere, a law to limit immigration was passed in 1934, with the Japanese as its specific target.

This law was never implemented, since Brazil was still in need of farm labor. But the number of Japanese immigrants to Brazil sharply declined anyway, as Japanese emigration headed more to Manchuria, China, and Korea. Instead of limiting the number of Japanese immigrants, the Immigration Law placed detailed controls over immigrants' lives, and in 1938 and 1939 various Brazilian states passed and enforced a series of laws to keep the immigrants' activities further in check. They were aimed at controlling immigrants' organizations, prohibiting publications in languages other than Portuguese, and promoting the assimilation of foreign-born Brazilians.

Under such circumstances, the Japanese immigrants' anxiety grew. At first, it was due to their isolation in Brazilian society resulting from the decline in new immigration from Japan, rather than the anti-Japanese campaign. At the same time, Japan's expansion into China and Manchuria inspired hopes among the Brazilian immigrants that they might be needed on the new frontier in East Asia. In that case, they began to think, they would rather contribute to building the Greater East Asia Co-prosperity Sphere instead of lingering in Brazil. The more despairing they were in Brazil, the more attractive became the image of themselves working under the Rising Sun flag for the Greater East Asia Co-prosperity Sphere.

Their hopeful imaginings were put on abrupt hold, however, when the Pacific War broke out. Diplomatic relations between Brazil and Japan were severed in January, 1942, although Brazil did not declare war against Japan until June 1945, while it did so against Germany and Italy in August 1942. But the diplomatic break resulted in the pullout of Japanese officials from the Japanese Embassy and Consulate General. Japanese immigrants were left with no protection in the midst of tightening control over their activities. Their assets were frozen, their bank withdrawals were limited to a small amount each month, and the titles of their real properties were seized. All these things led to a number of bankruptcies and closures of factories, stores and farms, and a loss of many jobs for Japanese. That was not all. The use of and education in the Japanese language were forbidden, Japanese schools were closed and organizations disbanded, listening to shortwave radio programs from Japan was prohibited, Japanese publications were forbidden, and any sort of literature in Japanese was confiscated. Japanese newspapers, on which almost ninety-percent of the immigrants relied for information, were shut down.

The closure of the Japanese Embassy and Consulate General also left the immigrants with a large vacuum in the moral and social center of their community, in which "the old Japanese way" was honored and maintained. They had felt abandoned when they first encountered the harsh living and working conditions in Brazil. With the pullout of Japanese diplomats and representatives, they felt abandoned by the Japanese elite in a wilderness of enemies, victimized by the Brazilian government, and surrounded by hostile people.

There were incidents that made them feel vulnerable and helpless. In early 1942, fifty Japanese immigrant families were driven from land in Sao Paulo that they were leasing and had developed into vegetable fields. American and British companies refused to sell the Japanese immigrants oil, machinery, automobiles, and certain types of food. A retired sergeant from the Japanese Imperial Army was suspected of being a spy and tortured to death by the Brazilian police, and the investigation of his death was obstructed. Some farmers in a town three hundred kilometers from Sao Paulo had their homes searched by the police and not only were their radios and Japanese publications confiscated, but they were also robbed of their money. One such family protested and ended up with the husband and son shot to death. In another state, thirty Japanese and German families were raided and robbed and the women raped by ordinary Brazilians.

Similar cases occurred in other areas as well. To make the immigrants feel even more powerless, about 350 Japanese families living in the heart of Sao Paulo and forming a Japanese commercial section, were evicted in September

1942, and told to get out within ten days. In July 1943, all the Japanese families along with Germans living in Santos and its vicinity, about 10,000 individuals in all, were ordered to leave.

Information on such incidents traveled fast among the immigrants by word of mouth, since they had no newspapers or radio programs of their own. Under such circumstances of increasing violence and repression, all the immigrants could do was to lie low. They clandestinely listened to news on shortwave radio and believed every glorious word the Imperial Headquarters *(Daihon'ei)* told them about how Japan was winning every battle. While victorious news from their homeland comforted them on the one hand, it also emphasized their sense of isolation.

What eased their anxiety was the hope of reemigration back to Asia as Japan expanded its control in China and Southeast Asia. The prerequisite for their dream to come true was, of course, Japan's victory. In other words, for the immigrants, with their identity as Japanese, their background of imperial education, and their hopes of returning to Asia, there was no other course but to help their homeland win the war. Amid the emotional and social turmoil, arguments about so-called "enemy industries" began to circulate among the Japanese immigrants—namely, that production of certain export items would benefit the enemy, the United States, and therefore engaging in such an industry was an act of treason to Japan. These items were, oddly enough, peppermint and silk. Peppermint, it was argued, was used as the coolant for airplane engines and silk was the material for parachutes. Such an argument was, of course, totally baseless. Peppermint had no industrial use, and Americans already had nylon with which to manufacture parachutes.

It is not clear exactly when and who started the "enemy industry" argument, under what circumstances, and how it spread. What is more important is that it persuaded a majority of Japanese immigrants to act accordingly. In late January 1944, when the "enemy industry" argument really began to take hold, farmers who were engaged in the production of these items were thrown into a terrible dilemma. By hard work, they had survived their initial hardships and managed to establish an economic foundation. To work hard was also to live up to their reputation, and therefore, to prove they were true Japanese. Now, it was argued that working hard could damage their own homeland. Still, some farmers were reluctant to comply since peppermint production and sericulture were bringing in a good income. They were accused of wanting Japan's defeat. Pressure was applied on farmers who continued to produce peppermint and silk, with other Japanese calling them names, snubbing them or, finally, ostracizing them from the community. Soon, the accusations escalated into sanctions against the farmers, resulting in the burning of fields and silkworm houses.

There was also internal pressure on the entire immigrant community to think and act like "true Japanese" and adhere to the "old Japanese spirit." There was no room for negotiation as to the definition of a "true Japanese." To be "Japanese" meant to remain loyal to the Emperor and to have no doubt about Japan's victory in the war. Around the time when the "enemy industry" argument was spreading, numerous nationalist secret societies and informal organizations sprang up in various parts of the immigrant community. Among them were Shindo Renmei (League of the Way of the Emperor's Subjects), Aikoku Rengo Nipponjinkai (Japanese Association of the Patriotic League), Hakuryukai (White Dragon Society), and others. It was these nationalist groups, often led by former officers of the Imperial Japanese Army, that moved into the vacuum left by the Japanese government, and that provided the immigrant community with a sense of unity and affirmation of their identity. Their influence grew rapidly and became the core of the *kachigumi* (victory faction) in the postwar period.

KACHIGUMI

Japanese immigrants in Brazil were in the dark as to accurate information on the war, with no newspapers to read (most of them could not read Portuguese), and few radios at hand (most had been confiscated). Fabricated "news" of Japan's winning battles escalated, ironically, as the major cities in Japan suffered air-raids and particularly after the battle in Okinawa ended with a disastrous loss for Japan. Such false information was circulated through word of mouth and mysterious leaflets. Pressure on Japanese immigrants to remain loyal subjects of the emperor created a frame of mind that caused the immigrants to "interpret" the news from Brazilian media (hence on the U.S. side) and to sift the "truth" out of it. Maeyama Takashi, one of Japan's leading scholars of Brazilian Japanese, observes that the Japanese immigrants selectively accepted the information that suited their symbolic structure and rejected as false that which did not. In this process, the falsehood was accepted as "news" and news was cast out as being "false," involving each immigrant as a coauthor of the falsehood. The report on Japan's surrender to the Allied Powers on radio and in Brazilian newspapers of August 15, 1945, was thus "interpreted" as Americans manipulating the fact of Japan's victory into Japan's defeat. An avalanche of "news" followed that "confirmed Japan's victory." By August 17, however, news from Brazilian newspapers and radios convinced some Japanese of their homeland's defeat. These Japanese made rational judgments of the information they received, but their judgment did not prevail over the emotional responses of other immigrants. Those who acknowledged Japan's defeat came to be called the *makegumi* (defeat faction) or *ninshikiha* (acknowledging school).   Diametrically opposed to them were the *kachigumi* (victory faction) or *kyokoha* (hardheaded school).

Numerous *kachigumi* groups were formed, many of which were led by Shindo Renmei. They spread more false reports, allegedly from Japan, on the postwar situation after Japan's victory. The source of such "reports" was often the shortwave radio of a member of Shindo Renmei. But the shortwave radio "had bad reception" and some people doubted the credibility of any news received by it. To such skeptics, Shindo Renmei retorted, "Only the true Japanese with Japanese spirit can hear the correct messages from Japan" or "You can hear it if you listen with Japanese spirit." The aim of such arguments is clear: to purge any opposition by manipulating the shared identity based on the same value system. Soon, Shindo Renmei turned to exploiting the anxiety of the immigrants to reap financial gain. They solicited donations for their activities, sold fraudulent tickets for the return journey to Japan, and also sold fictitious real estate in the Philippines and Java as sites of reemigration. By telling immigrants what they wanted to hear, Shindo Renmei rapidly gained influence over them. In April 1946, Shindo Renmei was at its peak, with about 80 branches, claiming over a hundred thousand members. Its influence reportedly reached 90 percent of Japanese immigrants. It also carried out terrorist activities against their opposition, namely the *makegumi*, resulting in sixteen assassinations and ultimately leading to the arrest of Shindo Renmei leaders and the disbanding of the organization.

The dissolution of Shindo Renmei did not invalidate the *kachigumi* people's faith in Japan, although their faith no longer included a belief in Japan's victory. Most *kachigumi* people gradually accepted Japan's defeat as fact, although it took many almost a decade to do so. It took some even longer to come to terms with the fact. Halfway around the world from home, scattered in the Brazilian hinterland, living and working among themselves with little communication with the world outside their self-contained communities, Japanese immigrants held onto any thin thread that made them feel connected with the homeland to which they hoped to return some day. Rumors, particularly those that were favorable to Japan, were easily believed under those conditions. Many immigrants continued to believe in the perpetuation of the Japanese spirit, and even though Shindo Renmei was disbanded, *kachigumi* followers observed rituals as the emperor's subjects at home or within themselves.

The *kachigumi* followers were led to believe that they would receive free tickets home to Japan as long as they remained "true Japanese"—that is, as long as they adhered to and maintained the "Japanese spirit." One case, almost too bizarre for words, is described by Takagi Toshiro, who stumbled across the legacy of the *kachigumi* during his visit in Brazil in the 1960s and has written the most vivid account of this group. In the postscript of his book, *Kyoshin—Burajiru Nikkei-imin no soran* (Fanatics—Disturbances by Japanese-Brazilians), Takagi describes the November 1972 Japanese homecoming of the Hamahiga, Higa, and Maeda families, all *kachigumi* members. No sooner had they landed in Tokyo than the oldest, Hamahiga Ryoki, age 81, took his hat off, threw his arms up in the air, and exclaimed, "Long Live His Majesty! Long Live Japan!" ("*Tennoheika banzai! Nippon banzai!*"). It was his first return trip to Japan since he had left his home in Okinawa in 1920. He was so completely convinced of Japan's victory in the war that everything he saw in Japan—the new prosperity, the emperor still living in the Imperial Palace, and so on—appeared to him as proof of Japan's victory. He was accompanied by his wife, age 71, and their grandson, age 37. The other two families, Higa and

Maeda, had eleven members in all, ranging in age from 13 to 65. At Yasukuni Shrine, they were overcome with emotion and wept.

These three families had lived close together in Brazil. Every morning all the members would gather at the Higa family's home and conduct a daily ceremony. They would stand in neat rows in front of the family altar shelf with a purple curtain, bow to the picture of the emperor and the empress on the altar, and sing *Kimigayo,* the Japanese national anthem. Then, Hamahiga's grandson would recite the Imperial Rescript on Education, not knowing that it had been abolished in 1948. Takagi points out that public schools in Japan had conducted a similar ceremony since the Meiji era, but only on imperial holidays. The three families kept up this ceremony together every day for almost thirty years in Brazil. There were other family groups at the time that were conducting similar ceremonies every day. They believed that by doing so, they would prove themselves to be "true Japanese" and be rewarded with a free return journey home.

The Hamahiga and Higa families did get their airfare paid by the Japanese government, but not as a reward for being loyal subjects of the Japanese empire. It was, instead, government aid to impoverished Japanese families overseas. Since such aid was not forthcoming to the Maeda family, they sold their land in order to raise money for the trip home. It is ironic that these families' home, Okinawa, had been occupied by the United States, the victor of the Pacific War, until May 1972, and that only after Okinawa's reversion to Japan could they return there. It is particularly ironic for the Maeda family, whose family house in Kin stands directly in front of the United States Marine Corps Base, Camp Hansen.

OKINAWANS' LIFE REFORM MOVEMENT

Okinawans have a culture of their own, distinct from that of the Japanese. Yet their national and ethnic identities as distinct from their identities as Japanese have been ambiguous. Since Okinawa lost its political independence and was incorporated into Japan in 1879, Japanese have considered Okinawans to be Japanese nationals. They have not been recognized as a separate people as Koreans and Chinese are. Yet, as a people they have never been fully accepted into the Japanese mainstream, but have been kept at the periphery—in terms not only of geography, but in politics, the economy and social life as well. I call them, therefore, "peripheral Japanese," and their Life Reform Movement was an effort (at least as far as the Okinawans involved were concerned) to transform Okinawans from "peripheral Japanese" into mainstream "Japanese."

The motive for promoting the Life Reform Movement evolved out of a concern about the many Okinawans leaving their homes for the mainland due to the breakdown of their economic base. Prewar rapid modernization devastated Japan's rural economy and brought about a large-scale exodus of rural people as migrant workers to the urban, industrial regions. Okinawa was particularly hard hit. As of the mid-1920s, a large proportion (70-75 percent) of the households in Okinawa were engaged in agriculture, of which the majority were destitute farmers with less than 5 *tan* (1.225 acres) of land. The main items they produced were yams and sugar cane, which occupied three quarters of the arable land. The production output of Okinawan farmers in terms of yen was less than half the national average, both per household and per capita. Okinawa had become unable to feed itself and imported from the mainland *(hondo)* essential food, such as rice and soy beans, as well as fertilizers and hardware for farming.

The deficit became enormous and irreversible by the mid-1920s. Compounding the difficulty, Okinawa was burdened by taxation. During the ten-year period 1919-28, Okinawa paid the state 68,000,000 yen in taxes and received from the state 23,000,000 yen. Upon such a fragile Okinawan economy descended the avalanche of the post-World-War-I recession, the financial crisis and finally the Great Depression. The rural regions were driven to near starvation, a condition commonly known as "palm-tree hell" *(sotetsu jigoku),* during which people resorted to eating sago palms, which are quite poisonous without elaborate preparation. The Tokyo government provided Okinawa with no policy to absorb the excess rural labor force and feed the population. Thus, the excess population poured out of Okinawa as cheap labor to the mainland or overseas, and Okinawa became the number one emigration prefecture.

The migrant workers from Okinawa to the mainland were mostly young and unskilled, and concentrated in the Osaka area. Most of them lived and worked closely together when they first arrived. In their new environment where these ordinary Okinawans came into contact with other Japanese for the first time, they became conscious of themselves speaking a different language from others surrounding them. They began to be sensitive to their distinctiveness and their identity as Okinawans. The development of Okinawan ethnic identity parallels that of Japanese immigrants in Brazil discussed earlier. But unlike the immigrants in Brazil, Okinawans in mainland Japan shared the Japanese national identity with others surrounding them, while developing their ethnic identity. Also, while the ethnic and national identities merged into being "Japanese" for Japanese immigrants into Brazil, for Okinawans to become "Japanese" was to discard their ethnic identity and traits (including their language). There was pressure on the Okinawans to become "Japanese." Now dependent on Japan for their economic and political survival, Okinawans themselves took up the task of assimilating into Japan.

Their effort manifested itself in the Life Reform Movement in the latter half of the 1930s through the 1940s. It was promoted by Governor Fuchigami (himself a mainland Japanese) and targeted as objects of "reform" the Okinawan language, traditional dress, surnames, plays in Okinawan, female shamans called *yuta,* and other distinctively Okinawan cultural traits. This movement is generally understood as a campaign to translate the top-down assimilation policy into practice, just like the campaigns to wipe out the traditional culture in Korea and Taiwan and transform the peoples into Japanese imperial subjects *(kominka undo).* Both campaigns were a step toward the National Mobilization System of wartime Japan. Indeed, Governor Fuchigami insisted that all local Okinawan characteristics should be wiped out in order to unify the entire nation.

However, the Life Reform Movement was enthusiastically supported and promoted in Okinawa and in Osaka by Okinawans themselves. Their enthusiasm resulted from the negative image of "Okinawans" vis-à-vis the "Japanese" that had emerged in the course of modernization. Tomiyama Ichiro argues that the two images were juxtaposed, respectively, as "non-hygienic" vs. "hygienic," "affective" vs. "rational," "lazy" vs. "diligent," "backward" vs. "modern," "disorderly" vs. "orderly," and so on. The elements in this image of the "Japanese" are not cultural traits but markers of ideal workers in modern capitalist Japan and characteristics that were expected of or desired in modern Japanese society. The negative imagery of the "Okinawans" was also translated in the real world as the basis for discriminating against them.

By the 1920s, the stereotype of Okinawans was firmly fixed in the minds of many employers in Osaka—that they spoke the language in such a different form from standard Japanese that they could neither communicate well nor learn new job skills, and that they would change jobs frequently. It was true that Okinawan workers tended to move from one job to another, instead of staying in the same job. Tomiyama argues that it was their attempt to get out of the "Okinawan-style" low-wage labor market. Indeed, there were employers who sought out Okinawan workers because they worked hard for low wages, while others shut them out because they perceived the Okinawan dialect as a problem, as well as due to their lack of technical skills.

The promoters of the Life Reform Movement were well-intentioned insofar as they wanted to help Okinawans lift themselves from the bottom of Japanese society. They were deeply concerned about securing acceptance for the vast number of fellow Okinawans emigrating overseas or to the mainland to work or enter military service. Tomiyama refers to many of the advocates of this movement in Osaka as a "pseudo-elite." They were able or had opportunities to climb the social ladder, in spite of their lack of secondary or higher education, by means of on-site training and hard work. They knew what it would take for Okinawans to gain upward mobility in Japanese society. They insisted that fellow Okinawans strive to reach the same level as other "Japanese" in terms of the language, habits and customs, hobbies, and so forth, so as not to appear inferior. Their goal was not just personal. They believed that their homeland, Okinawa, would be the ultimate beneficiary because the emigrants, either to the mainland or overseas, would bring Okinawa prosperity and thus modernize their homeland.

The primary target of "reform" in this movement was the language. When Okinawans spoke their language with one another among mainland Japanese, they were not considered as merely speaking their home dialect, but looked at with suspicion as non-Japanese. The language they spoke thus became a litmus test of whether they were "true Japanese." Okinawans were placed in the situation in which they needed to learn so-called standard Japanese *(hyojungo).* Their "need" matched the central government's policy of using it to force the cultural assimilation of Okinawans.

The campaign to encourage the use of standard Japanese began as soon as Okinawa was incorporated into Japan, and was pushed more vigorously in the 1930s as part of the National Spiritual Mobilization Movement *(kokumin seishin sodoin undo)* to promote loyalty of the "Japanese" to imperial Japan. While the movement was imposed upon them from Tokyo, Okinawans in leadership positions embraced it and promoted it with a vigor that had no parallel in any other prefecture. In fact, the movement evolved into the Okinawan Dialect Eradication Movement *(Okinawago haizetsu undo).* This was carried out to such an extent that the folk scholar Yanagi Soetsu publicly criticized it as excessive when he visited the island in 1940. Yanagi's public criticism sparked a major debate in Okinawa, which spread as far as Tokyo.

The campaign to impose the use of standard Japanese has often been regarded as having been implemented only in Okinawa and nowhere else in the mainland. Yanagi himself thought so. Many others who studied the campaign and modern Okinawan history have failed to check whether similar campaigns were carried out elsewhere. This may be due to the intensity of the campaign in Okinawa or due to the uniqueness of the Okinawan language. However, according to author Shiba Ryotaro, the standardization campaign was not unique to Okinawa. Shiba notes that he personally knows of similar campaigns that took place at elementary schools in Kagoshima and Kochi Prefectures before and after World War II. He witnessed more than once in the fourth decade of Showa (1955-1965) elementary school children wearing tags on their chests that said, "Speak the common language (i.e., standard Japanese)." He further claims that there still was, at the time of his writing (1978), some kind of punishment at school for speaking in dialect.

Why then is the Okinawan experience regarded as different from others by Okinawans and mainland Japanese alike? It is because Okinawans faced a reality different from other mainland dialect speakers who acquired and spoke standard Japanese. Since "standard Japanese" was considered at the time "superior" to dialects, all dialect speakers were made to feel somewhat inferior or at least awkward—probably with the exception of Kyoto and, to a lesser degree, Osaka dialect speakers. Perhaps mainland dialect speakers took on different personae, as Okinawans did, when they spoke standard Japanese. Still, they were able to speak it without giving up the identity of who they were, and when they spoke their home dialect they did not have to worry about being suspected as non-Japanese.

It was a different story for Okinawans. Their dialect, with its sounds and vocabulary so different from any others, made the speaker suspect as a non-Japanese, or at best, it would give away the speaker's identity as Okinawan. With the stereotype already established about the "Okinawan" as "non-hygienic," "affective," "lazy," "backward," and "disorderly," Okinawan speakers were instantly suspected of not being good workers in "hygienic," "rational," "diligent," "modern," "orderly" industrial Japan. In other words, Okinawans had to erase their Okinawan-ness in order to become "Japanese." This difference in the reality between mainland Japanese and Okinawans concerning the imposition of standard Japanese is important—particularly in understanding why the Okinawans initially reacted to the standardization campaign with such enthusiasm and why they later came to regard it as a peculiarly painful experience.

The Okinawans supported and promoted the standardization campaign to the fullest extent as a strategy of self-defense. No doubt their strategy also suited the government's goal to wipe out Okinawan culture, but that was a secondary consideration. The Okinawans' primary goal was to push all Okinawans forward to modernity by shedding their Okinawan-ness and becoming "Japanese," since that seemed to be the only way for Okinawa to achieve prosperity. Forsaking their own language was a price they were willing to pay at the time.

However, no matter how hard they tried, the Okinawans were not fully accepted as "Japanese." They were kept at the periphery and silently deepened their awareness of it. In 1945, their tie with Japan was abruptly severed as Okinawa was placed under occupation by the United States military. This parting from Japan did not encourage the Okinawans to seek their independence. Having become "Japanese," albeit peripheral ones, the Okinawans did not have a symbol of their own with which to unify themselves and fight against the foreign occupation. Instead, the Okinawans pursued reversion to Japan as a way to free themselves from the American occupation, demanding equal treatment with mainland "Japanese."

So powerful and firm was the value of being "Japanese" instilled in Okinawans, even postwar Okinawan immigrants, who often had more grievances against the Japanese government than prewar Okinawans, that they failed to shake off the value system that had been inculcated in them before the war. One of the leaders of Okinawan immigrants in Bolivia, who immigrated there in 1954, felt that his people were abandoned by the Japanese government after the war, and he was angry with the United States for occupying his island and driving him and his family from their family land. He had become a supporter of Senaga Kamejiro, leader of Okinawa People's Party (Okinawa Jinminto) before he emigrated to Bolivia against the backdrop of land appropriations forced by the United States for the purpose of constructing military bases. Yet, he recalls that when he saw a Rising Sun on a Japanese ship in port somewhere on his way to South America, he was overcome with nostalgia mixed with joy and sadness. It was then forbidden by the United States to display the Rising Sun flag in public. This immigrant admits that he still pays due respect to the Rising Sun as he was taught before the war even though he is critical of the Japanese government's treatment of Okinawa.

NEW IDENTITIES AFTER THE "JAPANESE"

Even today, *kachigumi* behavior seems bizarre, just as it struck Brazilians at the time. The Okinawans' Life Reform Movement, particularly its Okinawan Dialect Eradication Movement, seems excessive, as it did to some artists and intellectuals in Japan at the time. Yet, neither was deviant from the "Japanese," or at least from what they believed "Japanese" ought to be. For that matter, mainland Japanese themselves did not escape the forces pushing them to be "Japanese." The basic framework of the ideal model of "Japanese" was forged by the Meiji state for modern nation-building. It was reinforced in the 1930s with a strong emphasis on loyalty to the emperor for the purpose of mobilizing the nation for Japan's overseas expansion. A large body of literature in both Japanese and English is dedicated to analyzing how the state installed the machinery for producing "Japaneseness," how organizations at every level of society contributed to maintaining and reinforcing this, and what price all ordinary people caught up in this process ultimately paid—the suppression of individualism, the loss of traditional communities and of particularism, and more.

However, the price of becoming "Japanese" away from home seems to have been a particularly painful one that mainland Japanese who did not have to deal with the split of ethnic and national identities could not truly understand. For mainland citizens, conforming to the "Japanese" mold was a question of national imperatives. For those at the periphery or geographically removed from Japan, the issue of becoming "Japanese" involved both national and ethnic identities, touching each individual's inner world about who he or she was.

For the Japanese immigrants in Brazil, national and ethnic identities merged into a moral model around which they tried to unify their community. They watched each other to see if they were "true Japanese," which led to a moral, and literal, purge. In addition to experiencing inner turmoil, many individuals paid a high price in other ways. The first generation of immigrants, victims of discrimination in the country to which they had moved, reacted by adopting an ultraorthodox version of the Japanese stereotype. Ultimately forced to give that up, they came to terms with staying in Brazil permanently and resolved to "become ancestors of future Japanese-Brazilians." The following generations are developing their identity as an ethnic minority in Brazilian society. Although some are now in Japan as reimmigrants to earn money, most want to return to Brazil.

For Okinawans, to become "Japanese" was to discard their ethnic identity and characteristics. Victims of discrimination within Japan, they reacted at first like the Japanese immigrants in Brazil by becoming "more royalist than the king." Then, separated from Japan and under American occupation, they awoke to their own distinct identity. Yet, they were not free from the legacy of being "Japanese," and had to assert their Japanese identity in order to free themselves from foreign occupation. Since its reversion to Japan, Okinawa has received a cascade of big capital and commercialism from the mainland, along with rigid bureaucratic control by the central government designed to wipe out regional characteristics. Okinawans now have lost their own language. Its use in everyday life is forever gone and with the onslaught of mass media from the mainland, the standardization of the language has accelerated. Only in recent years is an effort being made to revive the Okinawan language in literature and the performing arts. Okinawans have been struggling to reestablish their identity and searching for a system of ideas with which to help determine their own destiny. They are reclaiming their ethnic identity as "Okinawans"—or "Ryukyuans" as some prefer—more strongly than ever.

All ordinary people caught up in Japan's forced development from above suffered the loss of their individualism and particularism in the homogenization of creating the perfect citizen of the *kokutai,* Japan's concept of a mystical national polity. But those outside the mainstream suffered more than those inside. In becoming "Japanese," the immigrants in Brazil and the Okinawans, as both groups and individuals, paid enormous prices. Critical reflection on their experiences as "Japanese" has given rise to new identities. The Japanese immigrants in Brazil and everywhere else overseas are creating new hyphenated identities of their own. The Okinawans seem to be moving in recent years toward embracing their ethnic identity within Japan. The construction of such new identities will create a more diverse model of being Japanese than the monolithic model that was at one time imposed from above.

OKINAWA'S CHOICE: INDEPENDENCE OR SUBORDINATION

Koji Taira

Okinawans do not agree among themselves on what to make of Okinawa's 1972 reversion to Japan as Okinawa Prefecture. The Japanese government has been manipulating the Okinawan psyche with an adroit policy that combines economic paternalism (the "carrot") and political/administrative oppression (the "stick").

Economic paternalism has brought prosperity to Okinawa with a per capita income roughly 70 percent of Japan's. Through a cabinet-level agency for Okinawa's development, the Japanese government has invested in the prefecture's infrastructure a 25-year total of 5 trillion yen, creating an economy dependent on public works. Contrary to the economic planners' expectations, agriculture and manufacturing (the goods-producing sector) have been performing poorly, while the tertiary sector (trade, utilities, finance, services, government, etc.) has grown to unhealthy proportions employing more than 70 percent of Okinawa's labor force.

The domination of local governments by the central government is, of course, a well-known characteristic of overly centralized Japan. Okinawans consider their relationship with Tokyo particularly onerous partly because of a lack of experience—for 27 years they were under U.S. control and forced to fight a different kind of political warfare. A more important reason is the abysmal level of autonomy they have experienced since reversion. This experience has utterly contradicted the expectations they formed, based on the Japanese Constitution, during the period when they were fighting for more self-government under the U.S. occupation.

Okinawans' political and administrative disappointments occurred even before reversion, when Japan failed to secure an agreement with the U.S. for a substantial reduction of the areas occupied by the U.S. military bases. Japan's post-reversion policy of economic paternalism and political and administrative oppression of Okinawa is a product of the high-priority defense policy built around the U.S.-Japan mutual security alliance, which requires, at least in the two governments' perceptions, a continued U.S. military presence in Okinawa.

Nonetheless, life at 70 percent of one of the world's highest per capita incomes is not bad. Okinawans' love of the carrot and their hatred of the stick show up as political vacillation between a prefectural government supported by the Japanese government and one representing indigenous forces for reform. In November 1998, Okinawans elected a new governor favored by the Japanese government over the two-term reformist incumbent.

Okinawa's independence from Japan in the context of its economic dependence on it may sound utopian. However, many considerations make it a reasonable topic for discussion, at least on a hypothetical level. A major reason for taking it up is that Okinawans' desire for independence seems always to be latent in their minds, becoming visible from time to time in various forms. For example, 1997 was a banner year for the demonstration of Okinawans' desire for independence from Japan. In February, on the Diet floor, an elected member of the House of Representatives from Okinawa asked the government "What would the government do if Okinawa wanted independence?" In March, a former reversion leader, Ouyama Choujo published an instant bestseller entitled *A Declaration of Okinawan Independence*. Several books by others with the independence theme quickly followed suit. In May and June meetings and symposia cropped up in many places with emotions running high for Okinawan independence. Books and articles critical of independence also appeared. Forums to air competing views were popular events in Okinawa.

THE CONSTITUTIONALITY OF OKINAWAN INDEPENDENCE

To the question about Okinawan independence raised by Representative Uehara, the government replied that the Constitution had no provision for such an event and that independence of any area within Japan could not be legal (*The Ryukyuanist*, No. 38, Autumn 1997, p. 1). Uehara did not pursue the issue, but the fact that an Okinawa-elected member of the House of Representatives went on record

with the idea of Okinawan independence might well be considered a historic milestone in the evolution of the Okinawan-Japanese relationship.

Whether there are constitutionally proper or valid ways
to achieve Okinawan independence is a tantalizing question.
In *general,* no country would constitutionally provide for its
own break-up. In Japan, however, Okinawa has always been
a *special* case. Historically, it was not part of Japan. After
some decades "in" Japan, it was taken out of Japan and later
taken back by Japan. Therefore, why could it not be taken
out again? Instead of accepting external decisions, Okinawans might well consider taking the matter into their own
hands and settling Okinawa's international status once and
for all via their own initiative.

The Japanese constitution allows for "a special law,
applicable only to one local public entity," such as a prefecture, city, town, or village, subject to one condition. Article
95 states: "A special law, applicable only to one local public
entity, cannot be enacted by the Diet without the consent of
the majority of the voters of the local public entity concerned, obtained in accordance with law." This provision is
generally understood to mean that a referendum or
plebiscite is required for the passing of a special law applicable only to one prefecture, city, town, or village.

Article 95 implies that the Japanese Diet can enact a special law to permit Okinawan independence, provided a
majority of the residents of Okinawa approve it in a referendum. Passing any law, of course, requires the support of a
majority of Diet members. This in turn requires a nationwide political campaign to elect politicians sympathetic
toward Okinawan independence. Nor is it a foregone conclusion that a majority of Okinawans would support independence. Clearly, Okinawans' overwhelming desire and support
for independence must precede all other political processes.
Popular support for independence in Okinawa has not yet
reached such a level.

There are many laws for special measures "applicable
only to Okinawa Prefecture" that have never been tested by
a referendum. These laws therefore violate Article 95 and
other articles of the constitution. Okinawans' property rights
have been particularly vulnerable despite Article 29: "The
right to own or to hold property is inviolable." Property rights
and the principles of local self-government were central to

Okinawa governor Ota's defense against the government's charge that he neglected his duties when he refused to sign authorizations to allow the government to expropriate private land for military use.

Once we begin counting how the Japanese government has violated the postwar constitution in relation to Okinawa, the dubious honor of the first violation goes to the Showa emperor (Hirohito). In September 1947 (four months after the constitution went into effect), Hirohito overstepped the boundary of acts permitted to him as the "symbol of the State and of the unity of the people" (Articles 1-8). He suggested to General MacArthur that the United States might indefinitely occupy Okinawa under the subterfuge of "a long-term lease" while letting Japan retain sovereignty over it (for details, see Irokawa Daikichi, *The Age of Hirohito*, New York: Free Press, 1995, pp. 99-101). This amounted to a territorial negotiation clearly not permitted to a "symbolic emperor." Furthermore, by this act, the emperor became a symbol of the "disunity" of the people, although perhaps in the emperor's view, Okinawans were never part of the Japanese people whose unity he symbolized. This opens up the issue of the ethnicity or nationality of Okinawans, which I shall discuss below.

Okinawans were under U.S. administration until May 15, 1972. During these years of American occupation, Okinawans were subjected to many actions by U.S. government authorities that were questionable if judged by the human and civil rights guaranteed under the Japanese constitution. Prominent among these injustices were cases of forced expropriation of privately owned land by the U.S. military. In the few years prior to 1972, as the reversion approached, the question arose of what to do with the private land seized by the U.S. military. Okinawans hoped that the seizures would be judged unconstitutional and illegal and that the land so taken away would be returned to its rightful owners. Their hopes were dashed because the thinking of the Japanese government was totally different. Shortly before reversion, the Japanese government passed a special law meant only for the land used by U.S. military bases in Okinawa to permit the perpetuation of these bases. After reversion, Okinawans argued that the special land law, which was clearly applicable only to Okinawa, should be put to the test of a referendum according to Article 95 of the constitution. The

Japanese government replied that Okinawa was still under U.S. administration and outside the jurisdiction of the Japanese constitution when the law in question was enacted.

Perhaps the Japanese government was technically correct, but the suspected motivation for enacting such a law just before reversion and the cold technical correctness that followed it greatly reduced the Japanese government's credibility in Okinawa. In this way the U.S. bases were permitted to remain undisturbed in post-reversion Okinawa and many other questionable practices of the U.S. administration in Okinawa were similarly "legalized" in Okinawa's transition from a U.S.-administered area to a Japanese prefecture. Subsequently, however, the Japanese government has been using its economic "carrot" to prevent Okinawan dissatisfaction from rising. For example, it has repeatedly raised the payments for rent on the land seized for the bases by a factor that far exceeds the level and trends of Okinawan land rents generally.

The latest reckless political/legal maneuver by the Japanese government occurred in April 1997. Both houses of the Diet passed a revision of the Special Measures Law for Land Required by the U.S. Military Bases by majorities close to unanimity. This law, originally enacted in the 1950s, was a general law applicable to any area in Japan, but the 1997 revision was special legislation instigated by and addressing problems that had developed only in Okinawa. The usual procedure for expropriation of land for public use requires the consent of the owners affected and the approval of a Land Expropriation Committee. At the time, the Land Expropriation Committee was still investigating some cases of owners who had refused to renew leases with no prospect of completing the investigations before the expiration of the leases. To avoid the awkward legal consequence that the land might be illegally held against the owners' wishes, the Japanese government wanted to make it lawful to occupy and use the land without leases until the Land Expropriation Committee finished its investigations. Thus a bill to revise the existing land law, so the U.S. military bases could legally occupy what was otherwise illegal, was proposed and the Diet gave it overwhelming support.

This nearly unanimous Diet vote suppressing the rights of owners to recover their land upon the expiration of the leases surprised and saddened many Okinawans as well as mainland Japanese. Clearly, this was not meant to be a general rule by which the government intended to handle military land cases in all parts of Japan. The lawmakers shared a tacit understanding that it was a special rule meant only for Okinawa with no general, dangerous implications for the safety of private property in other areas of Japan. Okinawans interpreted the incident as an assault by the Japanese government on the property rights of Okinawans. They recalled how the U.S. military had expropriated their land with bayonets and bulldozers. They saw no difference between that and the legislative violence the Japanese government inflicted on them. The landowners have sued the government for violating the constitution, and court proceedings began during 1999.

Okinawans are unusually conscious of their constitutional rights, although the remedies they have won on constitutional grounds are few compared with the legal remedies they have been denied. Okinawans' "irrational" confidence in the constitution has made them a laughing stock among mainland Japanese who, secure in their rights, seldom think about the constitution or even the Japanese state. What they care about is politics, which in Japan has come to turn almost exclusively on economic interests. However, some perceptive Japanese who visit Okinawa suddenly discover the heavy hand of the state everywhere, of which they were completely unaware back home. A common saying has thus arisen: "In Okinawa, the Japanese state is very visible" (*Okinawa de wa kokka ga yoku mieru*). That is also a description of the Okinawans' predicament: they have to cope with the impact of the powers of the state on many aspects of their everyday life. In Okinawa, the Japanese state unjustly condones the expropriation of 20 percent of Okinawa's land for military use and has been playing all the legal, political, economic, and other tricks it knows to defend that basic injustice. Although Okinawans have been patiently pursuing the constitutional route in seeking justice, it is a good question how much longer their patience will last. Independence via Article 95 may offer Okinawans one last chance to use the Japanese constitution to do away with all the disappointments they have suffered at the hands of the Japanese state.

Some Japanese are perceptive supporters of the idea of Okinawan independence. They are already disappointed with the Japanese legal and political environment in which, in their evaluation, the constitution has almost diminished to the equivalent of a dead letter. In this kind of constitutional climate, they suggest, it would be a waste of time to rely on the constitution for anything. Thus, by a different line of reasoning, they have reached the same conclusion as the government's response to Representative Uehara: "There is no constitutional way for Okinawa to gain independence."

NATIONAL SELF-DETERMINATION FOR OKINAWANS?

National self-determination, which successfully created many nation-states in Eastern and Central Europe after World War I and again after the Cold War, is a simple formula that Okinawans may find convenient. But "nationhood" and the "nation-state" are difficult concepts for the Japanese to comprehend. In their understanding, the state is a sovereign institution and the principal player in international relations (actually interstate relations), whereas nation refers to the people governed by a state. (The same semantic confusion exists in English.) What is crucial for the problem at hand is the understanding of a nation without a state, a nation submerged in a state another nation has established. It is these distinctions that the Japanese generally do not understand.

In Meiji Japan, somebody erroneously translated "nation" as *kokumin*. When the idea of "national" self-determination became popular in Taisho Japan, it was called *"minzoku" jiketsu*. But *minzoku* was already used for "ethnicity" or "ethnic group" with the implication of some powerless human group somewhere in some country. In due course, *minzoku* was hijacked by "nationalists" *(minzoku-shugisha)* obsessed with the power and glory of Japan as a nation-state *(minzoku kokka)*. After the war, "nation-state" again became an ambiguous *kokumin-kokka*. An individual national is also called *kokumin,* so the confusion continues.

Most Japanese naively believe that Japan is a unitary state as well as a single nation *(tan-itsu minzoku)*. This belief rejects individuals other than those issuing from that single national stock as bona fide nationals of Japan. How two or more "nations" can live together in one state (good-naturedly deluding themselves that they are one nation-state) is largely a mystery to most Japanese. For example, many Japanese are not aware that the United Kingdom, which they admire very much, actually consists of four "nations" in their respective domains (English in England, Scottish in Scotland, Welsh in Wales, and Irish in Ireland, now only in its Northern Counties). Many Japanese assume that the United Kingdom is a synonym for England and that its people are all called English.

In trying to explain to Japanese that Okinawans constitute a nation and that Okinawa is not merely a place name but the home of the Okinawan nation, I often use the U.K. example. After my Japanese audience accepts the fact that, for example, the English nation resides in England and the Scottish nation calls Scotland its home, I say that in Japan, the "Uchinanchu" nation is in Okinawa and the "Yamatunchu" nation exists elsewhere in Japan. (These are Okinawan words best not translated into "Okinawans" and "Japanese.") I then explain the theory and practice of "devolution," through which Scottish nationalists have lately brought Scotland to the brink of independence from the United Kingdom. By analogy, I suggest that a similar division and transfer of sovereignty might be made from Japan to Okinawa. The mention of sovereignty always spoils the whole show. The Japanese suddenly become aware that they are hearing what they should not. They believe in the unitary nation-state of Japan with its undivided sovereignty.

Even in the U.K., "devolution" officially is not a "division of sovereignty." But the establishment of a Scottish parliament with exclusive powers to govern, with no interference from Westminster, in all matters of domestic scope and concern—and with only a few well-defined broader matters such as defense, foreign diplomacy, and macroeconomic policy retained by the U.K. government—does indeed appear to be the creation of a quasi-independent state, which may well become a full-fledged state in the future. Okinawan independence could be modeled on the U.K. example. Clearly, the prerequisite for this type of devolution is recognition of the nationality or nationhood of Okinawans, as in the case of the four nations of the U.K. Such an Okinawan nation, whose self-governing powers are severely restricted under the current system of government in Japan, could then acquire a large part of state sovereignty with respect to internal government while certain powers of a national scope were retained by the Japanese government. More radically, one might argue that if a Japanese emperor could give Okinawa to the U.S. and retain only "residual sovereignty," as the Showa emperor did, Okinawans should analogously be able to take Okinawa into their own hands while conceding the historically tested "residual sovereignty" to Japan.

A "division of sovereignty" between a central and local governments raises no eyebrows in a federal state. But the idea is anathema to most Japanese. Since 1995, the Japanese government has been promoting a concept it calls *chihou bunken*, which literally and conceptually means a "division of powers between the central and local governments." But the Japanese law which gave rise to this activity curiously leaves the term *chihou bunken* undefined. The law only demands action to "promote" *(suishin) chihou bunken* by finding out what roles the state should take on itself and what roles should be assigned to local public entities. It has to do with sharing roles *(yakuwari buntan)*. Starting with the overly centralized unitary state, the law intends that *chihou bunken* should leave the state only those roles of national scope, transferring other roles to local governments. In other words, the law demands new job descriptions for the state and local governments and undermines the proper meaning of *bunken,* to divide or devolve *power.*

The *"power"* to be divided by *bunken* is the "power to govern," that is, sovereignty, which is surely a far larger concept than mere job descriptions. The "power to govern" creates its own job descriptions. The Committee for the Promotion of Chihou Bunken created by the *bunken* law has been engaged in inventorying and re-assigning functions currently performed by the central government. Under this conception of *bunken,* the law's outcome would simply be a uniform national list of what must, or must not, be done by the central and local governments. There is no recognition or authorization of a creative use of governing power to either generate or terminate activities and services for the public as needs arise or disappear. One horrifying implication is already evident: the Bunken Committee may end up with uniform roles and jobs for all the prefectures, cities, towns, and villages, and give the Ministry of Local Autonomy the power to regulate these local governments' performances and evaluate them using uniform standards. This would be a perfect antithesis of *bunken.*

Okinawa will be drawn into this kind of "reform," and the outcome may not be favorable to Okinawa. In fact, Okinawa may emerge from it with *less* power to govern itself. The "principles of local self-government" (*chihou jichi no hon-shi)*, referred to in the constitution and paid lip service to in the Bunken Law, should empower local governments by dis-empowering the central government, where power is excessively concentrated today. At present, the Japanese state's regulations reach down to the most minute aspects of every-day life. Many can be more expeditiously attended to by the nearest town hall. The example popularized by former reformist Prime Minister Morihiro Hosokawa is that a town remote from Tokyo, say in Kumamoto where he was governor before he moved into national politics, has to apply for and secure the approval of the Ministry of Transportation before it can move a bus stop even one yard from its previously approved spot. Does the power to decide where bus stops should be located belong to the state or to towns? Thousands of questions like this are being debated by the Bunken Committee. At this rate, the Bunken promotion movement will never reach the true *bunken* (division of sovereignty) between Japan and Okinawa.

ONE COUNTRY, TWO SYSTEMS

So far the impression within Japan is that all doors that might lead toward Okinawan independence are shut tight. This is disappointing, but one consolation is that there are doors, which if presently closed, might be opened in the future. In the last few years, Okinawans have discovered still another door. This is their enthusiastic cooperation with the Japanese state on one of its pet projects—namely, internationalization. In the hope of contributing to that national goal, the government of Okinawa Prefecture has adopted a cosmopolitan-city formation plan and a prefecture-wide free trade zone (FTZ) proposal. By turning the whole prefecture into a free trade zone and combining that with a comprehensive land-use plan, Okinawa hopes to become another Hong Kong or Singapore in the sense of a territory wide open to international trade and investment with few impediments. Since Japan is still highly protectionist, the free-trade prefecture of Okinawa would institutionally have to remove the protectionist and regulatory barriers erected around Japan and forge its own rules for economic and other transactions based on the principles and practices of free trade. Japan will then consist of two economic areas with different systems: Okinawa with a free trade regime and the rest of Japan behind its conventional protectionist and regulatory barriers. Thus "free" trade would not only free trade, but most importantly, would free Okinawa from Japan.

The vision of a prefecture-wide FTZ has captured the attention of economists in and outside of Okinawa, and a number of fairly sophisticated books and articles have appeared on the subject within a short period. Reams of policy proposals and counter proposals have been produced. Since its receipt of Okinawa's FTZ proposal, the Japanese government has also kept Tokyo think-tanks busy. Obviously, the FTZ idea as debated in Okinawa implies something quite serious for the Japanese government.

The conventional rationale for an FTZ is that it promotes exports and generates export-led economic development. But Okinawa's resources are meager and have no comparative advantage in large-scale manufacturing industries. As far as manufacturing is concerned, the dearth of investment by Japanese manufacturers in Okinawa despite a quarter century of economic integration with Japan testifies to Okinawa's comparative disadvantage. Okinawa's FTZ idea is entirely different from the conventional one. Okinawa wants the FTZ to promote imports.

The logic of the import-promoting FTZ for Okinawa runs as follows: From the standpoint of Okinawa, there are two kinds of imports and exports: (1) imports from the world at large and (2) imports from the Japanese mainland (in short, Japan). Similarly, there are (1) exports to the world at large and (2) exports to Japan. The Okinawan FTZ would "import" goods and materials duty-free from the world at large and after appropriate processing and packaging, "export" the final-use products to Japan. From the protectionist Japanese standpoint, this is outrageous because "imports" into Japan via the Okinawa FTZ are expected to have price advantages that are damaging to import-competing Japanese producers. At the same time, Okinawan producers operating in the FTZ, which would be the entire prefecture, would make profits and expand their activities, employing more Okinawan workers and contributing to Okinawa's economic growth. In other words, Okinawa's import-promoting FTZ has a "diversion effect" in that it would shift production and employment from higher-cost producers in Japan to lower-cost producers in Okinawa. But if the Okinawan economy grows as a consequence, Okinawans will also import more from Japan.

This diversion effect would not be the only outcome of the Okinawan FTZ. Okinawans would also benefit from cheaper products and experience an increase in real income. In the aggregate, this benefit would probably be larger than the other benefits mentioned above. Since domestic Japanese prices are generally higher than international prices, the Okinawan FTZ will bring Okinawa's prices down below those of Japan and toward international prices. The Japanese government has been spending trillions of yen to help Okinawa's economic development without ever paying attention to the most economical way to obtain the same results. The cost of the FTZ to the Japanese government is merely to free Okinawa from Japanese import duties and trade barriers. But, of course, dismantling a regulatory regime is the hardest thing for bureaucrats to do.

Aside from the standard FTZ benefits mentioned above, Okinawa is also welcoming to foreign investors. Okinawa has sunshine, unspoiled beaches, a distinct cultural tradition, a potentially convenient geographical location, an easy-going non-xenophobic people, educated human resources, and many other factors that are not counted as advantages in conventional approaches to economic development. If Okinawa were made freely accessible to other countries, foreign business people would discover hitherto unnoticed economic opportunities. Okinawa is already a major tourist center with further potential. The Japanese government's technical assistance programs that are sited in Okinawa are popular among Asian trainees. Okinawa's universities are receptive to foreign students and many of their faculty are foreign-trained. With its semi-tropical climate, Okinawa is also well-suited to become a retirement destination for Japan's aging population, much as Florida and Arizona are in the U.S.

With further investment in infrastructure, Okinawa can be an international hub for trans-shipment, telecommunications, travel, conventions, finance, medical care, recreation, and many other kinds of services. The list goes on. After a complete opening to world commerce, Okinawa might become a cosmopolitan country through which *hito, mono, kane, waza* (people, goods, money, and arts) flowed freely. Okinawa would be economically self-sustaining within the international market.

This is, of course, a dream scenario. Everything depends on the first step: the complete opening of Okinawa to the world. And this is where the first hurdle lies. When the prefecture-wide FTZ idea was communicated to the Japanese government, one member of the Diet instinctively rejected it, saying "No way!" The reason was the same old unitary state of Japan, which would not allow two systems in one country. Okinawans argued that since it was also the policy of the Japanese government to open Japan as completely as envisaged in the Okinawan plan, giving a go-ahead signal to Okinawa was consistent with the national policy. The "two systems" would converge in the future, depending upon how fast Japan deregulates. The government did not agree: at no time would Japan have two systems. The FTZ proposal was then scaled back to a few acres along the coastline with some tariff concessions and incentives for incoming investment. Okinawa hopes gradually to enlarge the limited FTZ, eventually encompassing the whole prefecture.

The enormous volumes of research and design that went into the FTZ project produced many valuable findings about the existing obstacles to free trade stemming from cumbersome regulations and arbitrary bureaucratic discretion. These findings, kindly put, would make valuable inputs into the government's ongoing efforts at regulatory reform. They can also be described, less kindly, as a diagnosis of cancer in the Japanese body politic. Ironically, Okinawa is in a position to play doctor for Japan.

It is well known that economic globalization renders national sovereignty more and more meaningless. In Europe, for example, the European Union has already swallowed up much of the sovereignty of the constituent states. Globalization is also encroaching on Japanese sovereignty, although far more slowly than in Europe. By taking advantage of this trend, Okinawa may at least provide the initiative for more internationalization and globalization, leading the less willing Japanese government to do what it nonetheless says it intends to do. There might be some psychic reward for Okinawa in being able to lead, if only in ideas.

THE SPIRIT OF INDEPENDENCE

Being asked to choose between independence and subordination as a description of current Okinawan-Japanese relations, one cannot help but choose subordination at the moment. But as I have tried to show, it is subordination under protest. The Japanese government, aware of the rumbling resentment in the prefecture, tries to appease Okinawans with money. Okinawans increasingly realize that in the 1960s they made a mistake in wanting to "return" to Japan. As Ouyama Choujo puts it, Japan was not the fatherland of Okinawans.

The spirit of independence has strengthened over the years. In May 1997, a month after the "special" legislation to revise the Military Land Law, there was a two-day forum in Naha to consider the possibilities of Okinawan independence. The forum was organized by an ad hoc coalition of concerned citizens, and participants came from Japan, Korea, Taiwan, the U.S., and, of course, Okinawa. Among them was a well-known advocate of Okinawan independence, Arakawa Akira. In the midst of Okinawa's reversion craze in the late 1960s and early 1970s, he vigorously opposed reversion and argued for independence. His remarks at the end of the May 1997 independence forum were touching. He said that he almost cried seeing the large crowd passionately debating Okinawan independence, since his had been a very lonely voice for many years.

Thirty years ago, Okinawans subordinated themselves to the Japanese state believing, erroneously, that it actually adhered to the "peace constitution" of 1947. Now they are in protest against subordination to Japan. What next? In the absence of better data, one may join Arakawa in extrapolating the growth of pro-independence sentiments over time and imagining real independence at the far end of this trend.

BIBLIOGRAPHY OF JAPANESE AND OKINAWAN PUBLICATIONS ON OKINAWAN INDEPENDENCE

Hirano Takuya. 1998. *Okinawa zenken* FTZ *no chousen* (The Challenge of Okinawa's Prefecture-wide Free Trade Zone). Tokyo: Doubun Shoin International.

Kurima Yasuo. 1996. *Okinawa keizai no gensou to genjitsu* (The Illusion and Reality of the Okinawan Economy). Tokyo: Nihon Keizai Hyouronsha.

Makino Hirotaka. 1996. *Saikou Okinawa keizai* (Okinawan Economy Reconsidered). Naha: Okinawa Taimusu Sha.

Miyagi Hiroiwa. 1998. *Okinawa jiyuu bouekiron* (Free Trade for Okinawa). Naha: Ryukyu Shuppansha.

Okinawa Dokuritsu no Kanousei wo Meguru Gekironkai Jikkou Iinkai (Steering Committee for the Forum on Possibilities of Okinawan Independence), ed. 1997. *Gekiron: Okinawa dokuritsu no kanousei* (Radical Debate: Possibilities of Okinawan Independence). Naha: Shisuikai.

Ouyama Choujo. 1997. *Okinawa dokuritsu sengen* (A Declaration of Okinawan Independence). Tokyo: Gendai Shorin.

Taira Asao. 1998. *Nihon no ikkoku niseido* (One Country, Two Systems in Japan). Tokyo: Hon no Izumi Sha.

Takara Tetsumi. 1997. *Okinawa kara mita heiwa kenpou* (The Peace Constitution As Seen From Okinawa). Tokyo: Miraisha.

Yoshida Kouichi. 1998. *Okinawa dokuritsu no susume* (A Push for Okinawan Independence). Tokyo: Bungeisha.

IV.

OKINAWA: THE PROTEST MOVEMENT

WOMEN AND MILITARY VIOLENCE

Carolyn Bowen Francis

Okinawans have tended to use key events in their history to serve as watersheds marking changes in their lives. One such date was recently added to the list of 20th century watershed events, which includes the Battle of Okinawa (April-June 1945) and the reversion of Okinawa to Japan (May 15, 1972). The new date, September 4, 1995, is burned indelibly into the memories of every woman, man, and child in Okinawa, it being the day on which three U.S. military personnel abducted a 12-year-old Okinawan school girl off the street in a northern Okinawa community, shoved her into their rented car, drove her to a deserted beach, where they covered her mouth and bound her hands and feet with duct tape, and took turns raping her.

Occurring during the year commemorating the 50th anniversary of the Battle of Okinawa and the end of World War II, the girl's courageous act in refusing to remain silent and instead reporting the rape to local authorities, set in motion a chain reaction of shocked outrage throughout Okinawa. Parents, teachers, and students, many of whom had up until now remained silent on the troubling issue of the mammoth U.S. military presence, rose up as one, raising their voices to declare, "No More!" in the largest, most broad based and longest lasting citizen protest in postwar Okinawan history. Their response sent unexpected tremors reverberating not only throughout Japan, but also throughout the U.S., ultimately shaking the very foundations of the U.S.-Japan defense relationship spelled out in the U.S.-Japan Security Treaty and the more detailed U.S.-Japan Status of Forces Agreement.

OKINAWAN WOMEN RESPOND TO RAPE

This explosion produced the activist Okinawan women's movement, which first began to raise the issue of U.S. military violence against women in Okinawa ten years earlier at the Third U.N. World Conference on Women in Nairobi.

The 1995 rape actually occurred during the Fourth U.N. World Conference on Women then being held in Beijing. Seventy-one Okinawan women had spent over a year preparing workshops on issues of concern to Okinawan women to present to that conference. Their major themes were 1) peace; 2) the environment; 3) traditional customs that discriminate against women; 4) labor issues; 5) the aging society; and 6) an Okinawa women's network. Under the theme of peace, four separate workshops were organized on "structural military violence against women in Okinawa," "Japanese military sexual slavery and the Battle of Okinawa," "the anti-nuclear weapons movement in Okinawa," and a "women and peace photographic exhibit."

All of the Okinawan participants attending the Beijing conference felt buoyed up by the support and solidarity of women from throughout the world, as they realized how many others faced problems similar to theirs. The five members of the last Okinawan workshop group to make their presentation, on the issue of "structural military violence against women in Okinawa," returned home to Okinawa on September 10, elated by the outpouring of support their workshop had received. The Beijing Conference had also reaffirmed in its *Platform for Action* the statement made in the 1993 Vienna Declaration at the World Conference on Human Rights that "Rape in the conduct of armed conflict constitutes a war crime against women." Their elation was short-lived, however, for they were met at the airport in Okinawa by colleagues who informed them of the rape, the news of which had only been made public two days earlier.

The women who had been in Beijing went into action immediately, calling a press conference for the following day, September 11, to issue a statement. In their statement they 1) strongly protested the rape; 2) called for an apology and compensation to the victim and her family; 3) demanded that the U.S. military commander in Okinawa establish a prevention program to address crimes against women, sexually transmitted diseases, and AIDS; 4) called for the three rape suspects to be turned over to Japanese authorities for prosecution; 5) called for the removal of the U.S. military presence from Okinawa; and 6) demanded an immediate response to their statement. This statement was also delivered to the U.S. Consul in Okinawa.

The same group organized a "Rally of Okinawa women,

children, and islanders against military violence," held 12 days later on September 23. This rally provided an opportunity for ordinary Okinawans to express their thoughts and feelings concerning the rape, since the program included a "One-minute Speech" open-microphone hour. Long lines of women waited their turn at floor mikes to pour out their anger, sorrow, and sense of helplessness. After sitting together and talking in small groups several women broke their silence to declare that they, too, had been raped by U.S. military personnel in years past, but had borne their secret in silence and shame until now.

Many other citizens' groups protested the rape, culminating in the October 21 rally organized by the Okinawa Prefectural Assembly that drew 85,000 participants. During that rally, Governor Masahide Ota apologized for having been unable to protect the 12-year-old girl, and a Futenma High School student implored, "Please return our peaceful and quiet Okinawa to us!"

As both Japanese and overseas mass media flocked to Okinawa to cover the rape incident, some reporters sought to identify and communicate with the victim, her family and persons in her community, while others treated the story in a sensational way. In response to this, on September 27, Suzuyo Takazato, the chairperson of the group that had gone to Beijing, issued an appeal to the mass media to exercise restraint in covering the rape case, in order to avoid further violating the human rights of the victim.

Many Okinawan women had long dreamed of opening a rape counseling center. They realized this was a crucial time to demonstrate their seriousness, and so on October 25, 1995, the Rape Emergency Intervention Counseling Center—Okinawa (REICO) was established. It provides a telephone hotline service and face-to-face counseling for victims of sexual violence. When requested, REICO staff members also accompany victims of sexual violence to report their rape or to seek medical care. REICO has also conducted training sessions for police officers in how to conduct investigations of rape and other sexual violence in a manner supportive of the victims.

A NEW OKINAWAN WOMEN'S MOVEMENT

Realizing that their activities could not continue indefinitely under the structure of the "Beijing '95—Okinawa Committee," on November 8, 1995, these women established a new organization called Okinawa Women Act Against Military Violence (OWAAMV). At their first general meeting on November 29, over 100 women, including teachers, full-time homemakers, part-time workers, young mothers, retired women, university students, elected officials, and women in prefectural and municipal government joined the organization. Two co-chairpersons and a steering committee were elected for a six-month period, until the time of the next general meeting. Keiko Itokazu, a prefectural assembly member, and Suzuyo Takazato, a Naha City assembly member, were elected co-chairpersons, and they have continued to serve in that capacity since then.

The goals approved for the first 6-month period were: 1) To organize study meetings throughout Okinawa on the U.S.-Japan Security Treaty and the U.S.-Japan Status of Forces Agreement, in terms of the concerns of women as outlined in the Beijing Conference's *Platform for Action*; 2) To provide information on Okinawa to persons elsewhere in Japan and overseas, particularly in the U.S., using some of the new networks established at Beijing; 3) To attend all military rape trials in Okinawa; and 4) To travel to the U.S. to inform American women about the problem of military violence against women in Okinawa (including Okinawan women, Filipinas working in bars and clubs around the bases, women from mainland Japan in Okinawa who become victims, and women in the U.S. military and dependents of American military forces who are victimized).

During November 9-21, 1995, a 12-day women's sit-in protest and signature campaign was held in front of the Okinawa Prefectural Office building to raise Okinawan citizens' awareness about military violence against women. On November 17, a 25-member delegation traveled to Tokyo to appeal to the Japanese Prime Minister, the Foreign Ministry, and the U.S. Embassy, and to hand over 55,000 signatures protesting the rape and U.S. military presence in Okinawa.

On February 1, 1996, a document entitled *Postwar U.S. Military Crimes against Women in Okinawa* was published in both Japanese and English in preparation for the group's first trip to the U.S. This First Okinawa Women's America Peace Caravan included thirteen women who, from February 3 to 17, visited San Francisco, Washington, D.C., New York, and

Honolulu. They met with women's, peace and environmental groups, university students and faculty, and churches; and they called on elected representatives and U.S. government officials to address the issue of the U.S. military presence in Okinawa and the problems it creates for women. Caravan members also asked the U.S. government: 1) To investigate all past U.S. military crimes that constitute human rights violations against women and girls; 2) To establish a concrete plan for the reduction and ultimate removal of all U.S. military forces from Okinawa, especially the Marines; 3) To strengthen the U.S. military's personnel orientation and continuing education program, especially for military personnel sent overseas, so that they will respect the human rights of citizens in the local host community, especially women and children; 4) To implement the Beijing *Platform for Action* and to revise the U.S.-Japan Security Treaty and the related Status of Forces Agreement to ensure that these documents conform with the Platform; and 5) To send international experts on women's rights and the environment to Okinawa to investigate and evaluate the situation there.

The Peace Caravan also visited the New York office of the U.N. Commission on Human Rights. In response to advice received there, the women prepared a written request to the Commission to send a Special Rapporteur to Okinawa to conduct an on-site investigation of the violations of women's human rights by U.S. military forces.

Invitations to speak on five U.S. university campuses convinced Peace Caravan members of the importance of also taking their concerns before university students in Okinawa. During the two months following their return to Okinawa, caravan members responded to invitations to speak a number of times at 5 of the 6 universities in Okinawa.

When the rape trial verdict was handed down on March 7, 1996, many mass media reporters asked members of Okinawa Women Act Against Military Violence whether they considered the 7-year and 6-1/2 year prison terms too light or too heavy. Refusing to be trapped into answering such a simplistic question, the group responded instead by issuing "An Appeal for the Recognition of Women's Human Rights." They called for revisions in the 100-year-old Japanese legal code to recognize the rights of women and their right to sexual self-determination. And they called for the creation of a social climate in Japan that would provide women greater freedom and equality in Japanese legal, administrative, health care, and educational systems.

After the first Peace Caravan to the U.S., members were besieged with speaking requests from groups throughout Japan. During the next six months, various members spoke about 100 times, and such invitations have continued to pour in. Since 1997, in response to requests for information on its activities and the situation in Okinawa, Okinawa Women Act Against Military Violence has published a Japanese-language newsletter.

To commemorate the first anniversary of the rape of the Okinawan schoolgirl, a "Seven Days to Eliminate Violence against Women" program was held. This centered around the visit to Okinawa of Betty Reardon, the Peace Education Department Director from Columbia University's Teachers' College. She conducted teach-ins and workshops for adults, university and high school students at various locations throughout Okinawa. On September 8, 1996, there was a prefecture-wide referendum on the U.S. bases, in which almost 90% of those voting rejected the U.S. military presence in Okinawa.

On November 29, 1996, the women's group appealed to Governor Ota, urging him to declare his opposition to the new proposal of the U.S. and Japanese governments to construct an offshore helicopter base to replace the U.S. Marine Corps Air Station at Futenma. On the following day, they held a women's rally and marched to the U.S. military forces headquarters. Since that time, they have joined with other peace and women's groups in opposing the construction of the new offshore helicopter base, viewing it not only as ecologically dangerous but also as constituting a U.S. military buildup rather than a reduction of the military presence in Okinawa.

In 1997, when debate on the revision of the Special Measures Law for Land Required by the U.S. Military Bases was taking place, a 25-member women's delegation was organized to go to Tokyo. On April 3, they presented a protest statement to National Diet members, held a press conference and attended Diet deliberations. Members also joined a sit-in demonstration in Okinawa, and then returned to Tokyo to participate in a Tokyo citizens' rally and watch the Diet vote, which approved the revision on April 17.

Okinawa Women Act Against Military Violence served as

co-organizer and host for the International Women's Network Meeting, held in Okinawa May 1-4, 1997. This conference included participants from the Philippines, Korea, mainland Japan, and the U.S. to consider and strategize on issues related to militarism and women. The group has also supported a citizens' lawsuit against the Japanese government for its heavy financial subsidy of the U.S. military presence in Japan, declaring it unconstitutional, and one of its members is among the several hundred plaintiffs. And the Okinawan women supported the full-page ad that ran in the *New York Times*, calling for the removal of U.S. military forces, especially Marines, from Okinawa.

On November 24, 1997, as ambassadors from 24 countries were planning to attend the Japanese government's ceremony to commemorate the 25th anniversary of Okinawa's reversion to Japan, the Okinawa women waged a FAX campaign, informing them of the actual situation in Okinawa, before they attended the ceremony.

During 1998, two of the group's representatives attended a non-governmental organizations' (NGO) consultation held in New York prior to the 42nd session of the U.N. Commission on the Status of Women. There they reported on the Okinawa situation in group sessions on "Violence against Women," "Violence against Women in Situations of Armed Conflict," and "The Girl Child." On May 8-9, twenty-five members participated in the Tokyo Action Program's protest of the proposed offshore helicopter base in northern Okinawa. On May 15-16, the Okinawan women organized "Two Days of Silent Protest" outside Gate 2 of Kadena Air Force Base. Participants proceeded in silence to the base gate every two hours throughout the day, carrying white flags on which were written the experiences of sexual violence victims. The following day, the women joined a more general Okinawan citizens' protest in which a human chain was formed around the U.S. Marine Corps Air Station at Futenma. Once again the groups called for the unconditional return of the base.

Between October 3 and 15, 1998, thirteen members of Okinawa Women Act Against Military Violence travelled to the U.S. for the Second Okinawa Women's America Peace Caravan and the Second International Women's Network Meeting. Their first stop was a 5-day visit to Los Angeles and San Diego, where they participated in a forum on military base toxic contamination together with citizen groups concerned about toxic contamination in the Philippines, Korea, Panama, Puerto Rico, the U.S. and Okinawa. An open citizens' forum on Okinawa, and two meetings for university students held on the UCLA campus also provided opportunities to exchange information.

In Washington, D.C., Peace Caravan members participated in the Second International Women's Network Meeting, which focused on the theme "What Constitutes Security for Women and Children?" In addition to conference sessions, participants from the Philippines, Korea, Okinawa, mainland Japan, and the U.S. met with local groups to discuss such issues as violence against women, defense spending, bilateral security treaties, and the effects of military bases on the local community. A Congressional staff briefing was also organized on "Violence against Women and the U.S. Military: Voices from Asia and the United States."

When they arrived at the airport in Washington, D.C., Peace Caravan members heard the news of a hit-and-run traffic accident that occurred on October 7 in central Okinawa. A U.S. Marine who was driving his private vehicle while under the influence of alcohol hit an Okinawan high school girl on a motorbike. The girl died one week later without ever regaining consciousness. The Peace Caravan members drafted a protest statement, which was signed by all 60 participants at the International Women's Network Meeting and directed to the U.S. President, the Japanese Prime Minister, the U.S. Ambassador to Japan, and the Commander of the U.S. forces on Okinawa.

THE MESSAGE AND THE MESSENGERS

Perhaps the name of the three-year old organization—Okinawa Women Act Against Military Violence—embodies both its style and its message. In both languages, the word "act" distinguishes it from many other women's and peace groups with longer traditions. Coming into existence during the year commemorating the 50th anniversary of the Battle of Okinawa and the end of World War II, stimulated by the Fourth U.N. World Conference on Women in Beijing, and shocked by the September 1995 abduction and rape of a 12-year-old Okinawan schoolgirl, the group has focused on action aimed at effecting change in Okinawa.

The core members and organizers are women who have long been concerned about and involved in women's issues, particularly issues related to violence against women, and the impact of war and the U.S. military base presence on the Okinawan community.

Three members of the core group, Suzuyo Takazato, Chieko Aguni, and Carolyn Francis, believed that most of the 50th anniversary ceremonies in Okinawa were focused too exclusively on the military battlefield. They therefore composed and read a *Requiem for Women* on the occasion of the 1995 international peace meeting, held each year on June 23, the day designated as Okinawa Memorial Day. The *Requiem* recalls not only the experiences of Okinawan women during the battle, but also the suffering of hundreds of young Korean women brought to Okinawa by the Japanese military and forced to serve as sexual slaves of the Japanese soldiers. Many were killed or left to fend for themselves when the battle ended. The *Requiem* also describes the new battle against women's and children's bodies that began once the guns were silenced, a battle that continues to this day. It ends by issuing a call to all people to join hands for global peace.

The seven members of the Beijing workshop on "Military Structural Violence and Women" were also among the core organizers of Okinawa Women Act Against Military Violence. They had compiled statistics and put together documents for distribution in Beijing, including a *Military Violence and Women Chronology*, which begins in 1609, when the Satsuma Clan (subsequently the southern part of Japan) invaded the unarmed independent Southeast Asian trading and crossroads nation, the Kingdom of the Ryukyus. The chronology documents the rape of an Okinawan woman by a sailor accompanying U.S. Commodore Matthew Perry when he landed on Okinawa in 1853, en route to Japan to establish U.S.-Japanese trading and diplomatic ties. The chronology also describes the prewar and wartime sexual violence committed against women and girls by Japanese soldiers, and the postwar U.S. military sexual violence.

Other founding members of the group included women labor union members who had participated in the Third U.N. World Conference on Women, held in Nairobi in 1985. There, they had presented a workshop and distributed a booklet *Okinawan Women: Our Struggle in Overcoming Discrimina-*

tion against Women, and the Labor Movement and Women's Liberation in Japan. They had returned from Nairobi and organized the annual Naha City Unai (Sisterhood) Festival.

From the beginning, the driving force behind Okinawa Women Act Against Military Violence has been Suzuyo Takazato, a longtime advocate for women, former Tokyo Metropolitan Women's Center telephone hotline counselor and Naha City women's counselor, and currently in her third term as Naha City Assembly member. Speaking of her experience as a women's counselor in Okinawa, she says:

> I have listened to the personal stories of women who continue to live with the physical and emotional trauma resulting from military sexual violence they suffered during Okinawa's postwar upheaval, when many women had no choice as the family breadwinner but to work in the GI clubs and bars that sprang up around the U.S. military bases. I personally witnessed soldiers returning from the Vietnam frontlines to take out their pent-up rage and terror on innocent Okinawan women and girls. Analysis shows that the effect of the military's training of young recruits in killing and violence turns them into war machines. The learned violence spills over into their off-duty time, robbing community women and girls of their security and human rights.

> We began to compile a list of documented cases of U.S. military sexual violence against Okinawan women and girls from the postwar period until the present time to take to the U.S. on the First Okinawa Women's American Peace Caravan in February 1996. At that time, we documented 64 cases by reading through police records and newspapers, and interviewing survivors and witnesses. We continued our investigation when we returned to Okinawa, and during the next two years, we added many new cases to the list. By the time we left for the U.S. on the Second Peace Caravan in October 1998, the list had grown to 236 cases, with the youngest victim being a 9-month old baby girl and the oldest being a 65-year-old woman. But we realize that this number really represents only the tip of the iceberg, because Okinawan society makes it difficult for women to

come forward and report sexual violence. There is both the shame it is thought to bring on women and their families, and the effect it may have on girls' chances for marriage.

We know that when military personnel return home to the U.S., their training in violence returns with them; thus, the targets of violence now become their American wives and girlfriends. For these reasons, I believe we must work together to achieve not only an Okinawa free of military bases and military forces. We must also transcend national barriers and create a peaceful global society that is free of military violence.

A member of the group's steering committee, Sumiko Toguchi, is also Secretary General of the Federation of Okinawa Prefecture Women's Organizations and an Environmental Counselor appointed by the Japanese Government. She looks at the U.S. military base presence in Okinawa from the perspective of the environment. As a child growing up in northern Okinawa, she recalls what happened to her family's land and the land of the villagers in her small community as a result of the Battle of Okinawa:

My village was a prosperous agricultural community on the northwest coast of Okinawa Island. All of the villagers took shelter in the wooded mountain area during the battle. Afterwards, we were rounded up into detention camps, where we were investigated by U.S. military officials. We lived in tents in the camps until we were finally allowed to return to our home areas. We walked back to our community with the other families, eager to return home and begin our lives anew. We arrived back home late at night after a long day's trek. When we looked down on our village from the top of a nearby hill, all we could see in the darkness was a broad white expanse where our village had once stood. When it became daylight, we took another look and, to our amazement, we saw what appeared to be sparkling snow covering the ground. We hurried down the hill and, approaching our village area, we found that the entire village had been covered with crushed white coral three meters deep in order to turn it into a U.S. military landing-strip. So of course, all of the families in our community had to relocate to other areas to begin their postwar lives. Years later, after Okinawa's reversion to Japan in 1972, the village land was officially returned to each landowner, but the crushed coral remained, and we all knew that even if we had the resources to remove the coral from our land, the soil would no longer be arable.

This personal experience has led to my strong concern for environmental contamination and destruction resulting from the U.S. military presence in Okinawa. I have traveled to the U.S. to examine the toxic contamination and cleanup process within domestic military bases. It is most unfortunate for Okinawa that Article 4 of the U.S.-Japan Status of Forces Agreement states: "The United States is not obliged, when it returns facilities and areas to Japan, on the expiration of this Agreement or at an earlier date, to restore the facilities and areas to the condition in which they were at the time they became available to the United States Armed Forces, or to compensate Japan in lieu of each investigation." Furthermore, the reality is that no Okinawan is allowed to enter a U.S. military base to investigate the amount and type of toxic contamination, but we know that large amounts of PCB, lead, cadmium and other toxic wastes exist.

Harumi Miyagi, a Naha City employee and editor of a 10-year women's history project, also bears a deep concern for women as a result of her personal experience. She participated in the Second American Peace Caravan. Born on Zamami Island, one of the small islands in the offshore Kerama Island Group on which the U.S. military forces first landed on March 26, 1945, prior to the massive invasion of Okinawa Island on April 1, she described for Americans the wartime experience of her island:

Soon after the Japanese military arrived, everyone realized they had not come to protect Zamami islanders from the approaching U.S. invasion. Soldiers raped island women and distributed hand grenades to heads of families with instructions for their use. When the signal was given, each family was to form a circle around the grenade and pull the pin, as mass suicide was seen to be more honorable than capture by the American demons. While many islanders died, survivors were surprised to find the American military invaders treated them kindly at first, dispelling the myths of Japanese wartime propaganda. But Zamami people were shocked when the Americans, who had come to save them from the Japanese soldiers, also began to carry off our island women to deserted areas to rape them.

Listening to my mother's stories of wartime and postwar Okinawa, and witnessing the effects of the military presence on my island left a lasting impression on me. I have devoted much of my career to analyzing militarism, irrespective of the country. This, in turn, led me to begin collecting statistics and documents, and to interviewing survivors and witnesses regarding their experience of military violence against women in Okinawa.

Fujiko Nakasone is a retired junior high school math teacher from Okinawa City, and also a member of the Second American Peace Caravan. She shared with Americans her experiences as a teacher in a U.S. military base town:

Students in schools around the U.S. Air Force Base at Kadena, the largest U.S. base in Asia, lose an average of two years during their twelve years of education, due to class interruptions resulting from the constant high level of noise caused by military aircraft flying overhead. The physical problems they suffer include nervousness and an inability to concentrate, hearing loss, headaches and stomachaches.

Furthermore, a recent 3-year study conducted by the Okinawa Prefecture Public Health Association revealed that infants born to mothers living in Kadena Town, the community adjacent to Kadena Air Base, have the lowest average birth weights of any community in Japan. Kadena Air Base occupies 83% of Kadena Town land, and the 14,000 Kadena Town citizens crowd into the remaining 17% of the town.

My students used to say, "If you compare Kadena Town to a steak, the U.S. military is the meat and we are the fat around the edge."

Yuka Iha was a founding member of DOVE (Deactivating Our Violent Establishments), a young Okinawans' group founded in 1997. In 1998, she was an exchange student at a community college in Massachusetts and the youngest member of the Second Peace Caravan. She talked about what it is like to grow up close to the military bases in Okinawa:

> I've always lived close to a military base. Even elementary and junior high school students are afraid of all the accidents and violence. We used to say that if there were ever a war, Okinawa would be the first to be bombed because of all its bases. Some high school and college students like to become friends with GI's to speak English and learn about American culture. I have had many girlfriends who had GI boyfriends and I have heard many terrible things from them. I became interested in trying to understand what the U.S. military really is.
>
> I want the U.S. military to leave Okinawa, but I know it is difficult. Sometimes I feel more anger toward Japan than toward the U.S. military. Japan has betrayed Okinawa. It doesn't care about Okinawan people, only about its relationship with the U.S. and the U.S.-Japan Security Treaty. Some American military people say, "Okinawa belongs to America." They don't understand the feelings of Okinawan people.
>
> Sometimes students in my college here in America say, "Why are you always talking about Okinawa?" Even the Japanese students say that. But I love Okinawan culture and people. I'm proud of being Okinawan!

THE ROLE OF OKINAWA WOMEN ACT AGAINST MILITARY VIOLENCE

Some of the group's critics say that it focuses only on women and on individuals, not on the broader issues, and that it is too emotional in its approach. On the other hand, some supporters in other parts of Japan and overseas say that the group offers them hope, and although they realize that members must become weary with their frantic pace of activities, they urge the group to continue its unique task.

It is true that Okinawa Women Act Against Military Violence originated as a response to one small Okinawan girl who raised her voice to say "No!" to military violence. But its members have discovered that the surest way to gain the attention of American and Japanese audiences who do not really want to hear the U.S.-Japanese security relationship criticized is to share their personal experiences. These can then be enlarged upon to discuss the broader issue of the long-term U.S. military presence in Okinawa and its effects on society.

The Okinawan women do not deny that their movement focuses on people more than on land or on abstract issues of military policy. Their concern is also for individual American youths who are lured into the military system, and the devastating effect their training has both on the youths and on the society to which they ultimately return. This destructive military system also brings violence and destruction to the people, culture and environment of the host community, Okinawa. Thus the women's organization has become committed to the task of reducing and eventually eliminating the ongoing suffering of the people of Okinawa, and to restoring true peace and security to the islands.

GOVERNOR OTA AT THE SUPREME COURT OF JAPAN

Masahide Ota

Governor Ota was elected in 1990 for his pledge to end the American military occupation of parts of Okinawa. Okinawa's land on which the military bases are built is subject to lease renewals every five years. The lessee is the Government of Japan, which then turns over the leased land free of charge to the stationed American military forces under the terms of the U.S.-Japan Mutual Security Treaty. In September 1995, Governor Ota refused to cooperate with the Japanese Government in the procedure required by the Land Acquisition Law.

Invoking the relationship between the Japanese state and its subordinate prefectures stipulated in the Local Autonomy Law, the prime minister of Japan sued Governor Ota at the Fukuoka High Court, Naha Branch, seeking a court order for the governor to execute the duties delegated to him. Governor Ota argued against the connection between delegated duties under the Local Autonomy Law and cooperation with the forcible acquisition of Okinawa's land for use by the American military. In February 1996, the court supported the prime minister. Dissatisfied with the ruling, Governor Ota appealed to the Supreme Court of Japan.

On July 10, 1996, Governor Ota testified before the grand bench of the Supreme Court. The media and newspapers reported that the justices appeared to be favorably impressed with the governor's presentation. However, on August 28, 1996, the Supreme Court announced a very unfavorable verdict on the governor's appeal. It even appeared to treat this case with profound disdain. The court was open for about one minute and closed as soon as the chief justice finished reading the two-line verdict: "[We] reject and dismiss *(kikyakusuru)* the appeal. The court expenses shall be borne by the appellant."

Governor Ota's testimony before the Supreme Court was based on the text published in the *Ryukyu Shimpo*, July 11, 1996. This translation was first published in *The*

Ryukyuanist, No. 35 (Winter 1996-97).

THE TEXT OF OTA'S TESTIMONY

I am Ota Masahide, Governor of Okinawa Prefecture. I heartily thank you for giving me the opportunity to make a statement of opinion *(iken chinjutsu)* before this court.

To begin, I would like to explain the background of my appeal to the Supreme Court following my refusal to sign the documents in lieu *(dairi shomei)* of the landowners concerning the forcible acquisition of their land for the stationed [U.S.] armed forces *(churyugun)*.

What I would like to say before anything else is that among my people, the longing for peace is very strong. The reason is: not only did we sacrifice almost one third of our population in the Battle of Okinawa toward the end of the Pacific War, but our cultural heritages from our ancestors— valuable national treasures—were totally destroyed. Our rich, verdant land was literally transformed into scorched earth. Not only that. Okinawa was a small kingdom called Ryukyu until it was annexed by Japan by the process known as *Ryukyu shobun* (punishment of Ryukyu) during the period from 1872 to the 1880s. For ages, the Ryukyu Kingdom had been widely known, even abroad, as an unarmed land of courtesy *(shurei no kuni)*.

This was because King Shoshin, who was on the throne in the late 15th and early 16th centuries, forbade people to carry weapons. The fundamental state policy he established was to maintain the little kingdom in peace by friendly trade with foreign countries. In addition, after its invasion of Ryukyu *(ryukyu shinryaku)* in 1609, Satsuma strictly prohibited people from bearing arms in order to forestall Ryukyuans' possible rebellions. This also [ironically] helped the islanders enjoy the reputation as a peace-loving people *(heiwa aiko no tami)*.

On the basis of the above historical background, the [late] Professor William Lebra of the University of Hawaii, in his *Okinawan Religion: Belief, Ritual and Social Structure* (1966), concluded that the cultures of Japan and Okinawa are fundamentally different. That is, in contrast to Japan's "warrior culture," Okinawa's is notable for an "absence of militarism." Other scholars define Okinawan culture as a "feminine culture" *(josei bunka)* or a "culture of moderation" (*yasashisa no bunka*).

[The late] Mr. Nakahara Zenchu, a well-known scholar of Okinawan studies, researching the *Omoro soshi*, which is a collection of 1554 old folk and religious songs ranging in age from the 12th to the 17th centuries, was impressed with a total absence of words connoting ruthless killing *(satsuriku)* in these songs. Nakahara inferred that Okinawans at that time had none of it [killing] on their consciousness *(sono ishiki ga nakatta)*.

[THE IMPACT OF THE U.S. MILITARY BASES]

In this way, my prefecture is dedicated to a way of life that shuns and abhors armed conflict. Many people in Okinawa are greatly troubled by the fact that contrary to their wishes, they have become participants in the killing and maiming of other people by allowing military bases in Okinawa, from which the American forces have been deployed for military operations in other lands, as in the Korean War earlier, and then the Vietnam and the Gulf wars.

It may also be pointed out that the military bases in Okinawa are extremely dense, a situation well described by a certain American journalist as Okinawa being in the bases, rather than the bases being in Okinawa. In area, Okinawa is only 0.6 percent of Japan, but about 75 percent of facilities exclusively used by the American armed forces stationed in Japan are concentrated in this small prefecture.

The American military bases occupy about 11 percent of the total area of the prefecture and about 20 percent of Okinawa Island. Moreover, the bases are concentrated in the middle and southern parts of the island which, with a population density amounting to 2,198 persons per square kilometer, are among the most densely populated areas of Japan. In addition, by virtue of the Status of Forces Agreement based on the U.S.-Japan Security Treaty, 29 areas in the sea and 15 air spaces are also controlled by the American forces. As a result, my people are not free to use [much of] their land, sea and air. We wonder whether the nation-state [we belong to, that is, Japan] can really be called a sovereign state *(shuken kokka)*.

Under these circumstances, planned urban development *(machizukuri)* is impossible, let alone the growth of industry. Since the reversion [of Okinawa to Japan], the [Japanese]

Government has implemented three ten-year economic encouragement and development plans (*shinko kaihatsu keikaku*), investing 4 trillion yen in the construction and maintenance of infrastructure.

As a result, roads and harbors have considerably improved, but regrettably, achievements are unsatisfactory in matters like the elimination of economic differentials [vis-à-vis Japan as a whole] (*kakusa zesei*) or the laying of foundations for suitable development *(jiritsuteki hatten no kiso joken no seibi)*. These are the basic objectives of the economic encouragement and development plans. In particular, industries that may generate sustainable development have not been nurtured. The prefecture's per capita income per annum still remains 74 percent of the national average, or less than half of Tokyo's. Besides, the unemployment rate is about 6 percent, twice as high as the national average. Moreover, the unemployment rate of youth in their teens and twenties reaches a serious 12 percent.

This condition reflects not only the wrinkles created in our economy *(shiwayose)* by the excessive burden of the bases, but also the difficulties that hinder the rise of unique local industries *(jiba sangyo).* The urbanization process itself has been distorted. In my prefecture, "cities"—like Naha, the capital, especially, and others like Urasoe, Ginowan, and Okinawa—have come into being as erratic sprawls around the bases, without the benefit of zoning. These cities are not solid enough to withstand natural disasters. For purposes of safeguarding the lives and livelihoods of the people of my prefecture, an urban redevelopment that [by widening streets] permits operations of fire trucks and ambulances is indispensable.

For example, in Kadena Town, where Kadena Air Force Base is located occupying about 83 percent of the town, more than 14,000 people crowd into the remaining 17 percent. Under these circumstances, it is almost impossible to live as [decently as] humans should.

As may be seen from these realities, it is not an exaggeration to say that the military bases forcing a special land use pattern on us have been the greatest problem of postwar Okinawa.

[ORIGINS OF FORCED ACQUISITION OF LAND]

The forced acquisition of land for military use occurred [in Okinawa] both before and during the war. Prior to the abolition of the [Ryukyu] domain and the establishment of the [Okinawa] prefecture *(haihan chiken)* in 1879, the Meiji government directed the Ryukyu Kingdom to undertake several reforms toward Japanization *(nihonka),* such as the abolition of the traditional embassies to China and of the investiture [of the king by the emperor of China] *(sakuho),* as well as the adoption of the Japanese era name [Meiji]. The reforms also included permanent stationing in Okinawa of an army unit from the Sixth Division of Kumamoto.

The Ryukyu Kingdom agreed to all the reforms but one, the permanent stationing of Japanese troops *(Nihongun no jochu),* which it resolutely rejected. The Ryukyuan government argued: "no matter how much one might strengthen military preparedness in these little islands, a success would be impossible to attain in defense against enemy attacks;" "arming the little island-state might cause suspicions on the part of other countries and invite an invasion;" and "as in the old saying that 'softness tames toughness well' *(ju yoku go wo seisu),* it is wiser to maintain the state in peace by courteous and friendly relations with the people of the neighboring countries."

But the Meiji government insisted: "Since the government has the duty to protect the safety and stability *(annei)* of the territory and population, where to station the armed forces is a matter for the government to decide; no one has the right to oppose [the government]." The government then arbitrarily and forcibly dispatched an army unit to Okinawa. On the pretext that land was needed for barracks, drilling grounds, shooting ranges, hospitals, and so on, the Meiji government selected an area amounting to 61,600 square meters at Kohagura between Shuri and Naha and speedily proceeded to a forcible purchase of the land in the area. Since this was an area of fertile and superior farmland, the Ryukyu government requested the Meiji government to reconsider and offered an alternative site for free. The Meiji government rejected the request and, as planned, decided on basing the dispatched troops at Kohagura.

In this way, Okinawa, formerly a peaceful nation-state *(heiwa kokka)*, had no choice but to go along with a military state *(gunkoku),* Japan. This, one may say, was the beginning of Okinawa's fortification *(Okinawa no kichika).*

As this example illustrates, the tendency of central government policy to override everything else, including the local will, has continued unabated in Okinawa. During the [Pacific] War, farmland was semi-forcibly taken and used for air fields in the name of Japanese defense.

[LAND ACQUISITION BY THE AMERICAN MILITARY]

After the war, nothing changed. The expropriation of land continued by ordinances and decrees of the American military as if the war had never ended. Since documents like family registers and land ledgers were lost in the ravages of war, the confirmation of titles to privately-owned land was extremely difficult. One cannot deny that this situation made the arbitrary acquisition of land by the military easier. Moreover, the acquisition was forced, the troops brandishing "bayonets and bulldozers," as my people well remember.

Over the period from 1953 to 1956 or 57, there were "island-wide struggles for [the defense of] land" (*shima gurumi no tochi toso*) in Okinawa. A group of Okinawa's high-level administrative leaders visited America twice in search of a solution to the land problem. In a sense, today's forcible land-use problem is a replay of that of the 1950s.

A distinctive characteristic of the land problem observed throughout this history from the prewar period to the present is that much of the land that has become the object of forcible acquisition is farmland belonging to farmers. Until recently, the key industry of Okinawa was agriculture. The farming folk who lost their lands were compelled to emigrate to [faraway] countries like Bolivia looking for places for permanent resettlement, or to work [in odd jobs] on the bases giving up traditional farming. As numerous records indicate, in Okinawa where the proclivities for ancestor worship are strong, land is not a mere plot of soil in which to grow crops. It is not a commodity, something that can be considered an object for buying and selling. If I may paraphrase further, land is an irreplaceable heritage graciously bequeathed to us by our ancestors or a spiritual string that ties us to them. My people's attachment to their land is firmly rooted, and their resistance against the forcible taking of their land is similarly strong. What must be pointed out in this connection is that the military bases on the mainland of Japan sit on land that is 87 percent state-owned, while more than 30 percent of the land used by the bases in Okinawa is privately owned. Especially in the central area of Okinawa Island, where the bases are concentrated, 75 percent of the land used by the bases is privately owned. Moreover, there are differences [in government policy] between mainland Japanese and Oki-nawan bases, as may be seen in the delays in reaching agreement on noise prevention or [permissible] kinds of mil-itary maneuvers. My people consider these differences as amounting to discriminatory treatment [of them by Japan and America] and are increasingly dissatisfied with it.

In addition, incidents and accidents originating in the American bases never cease. Atrocious cases like last year's rape of a little girl are repeatedly taking place.

[THE GOVERNMENT'S PROMISES AND PEOPLE'S EXPECTATIONS]

At the time of Okinawa's reversion to Japan, the Diet adopted a resolution about realignment and reduction (*seiri shukosho*) of the bases in Okinawa. [But] its implementation has largely been neglected.

With the collapse of the Cold War structure *(reisen kozo)*, my people expected the realignment and reduction of the bases in Okinawa to make progress, if belatedly. But, according to the U.S. Department of Defense report, *United States Security Strategy for the East Asia-Pacific Region*, published in February of last year [1995], the American forces in the East Asia-Pacific region would be maintained at a troop strength of 100,000 *(jumannin taisei)*. And at the U.S.-Japan summit scheduled for November of last year it was suggested that the two countries might redefine the Mutual Security Treaty and readjust the use of the American bases in Japan to more globalized perspectives. From all of this, my people feared that the functions of the bases in Oki-nawa might be reinforced *(kyoka)* and perpetuated *(koteika)* through the 21st Century.

Under these circumstances, anyone responsible for the administration of my prefecture would find it difficult to accept a further reinforcement and perpetuation of the bases. Therefore, I could not favorably respond to [the task of] witnessing and signing *(tachiai/shomei)* [the documents] concerning the forcible use of land by the stationed forces. I believe that my decision was the only choice available to me as a governor responsible for a prefectural administration that should protect the lives and livelihoods of the people of the prefecture.

I do not have to tell you, since it is obvious, that I do not think that the base issue can be resolved in one day *(itcho isseki)* by a refusal to witness and sign [the land documents]. For 50 years since the end of the war, my people have been forced to live side by side with military bases and to suffer their enormous impact *(sono juatsu)*. This means, without exaggeration, that we have fully cooperated with the Mutual Security Treaty.

The 1972 reversion was a return to the rule of the pacifist Constitution *(heiwa kenpo)* and should have been a great turning point for Okinawa. What my people sincerely wished for at the time of the reversion was a reduction of bases at a rate at least comparable to that experienced on the mainland *(hondonami)*, together with the restoration of human rights *(jinken)* and the establishment of home rule *(jichi)*.

[NOTHING HAS CHANGED]

However, today, a quarter of a century after the reversion, the condition of Okinawa has hardly changed. Today, just as before, the extensive bases packed with military functions remain. Incidents, accidents, and pollution on account of the bases keep appearing. This is a far cry from the meaning of reversion my people desired. The Status of Forces Agreement, Article 2, permits military bases to be built in any area of Japan under the authority of the Mutual Security Treaty—the so-called "bases anywhere formula" *(zendo kichi hoshiki)*. If so, then why should Okinawa alone shoulder the excessive burden? One would be hard put to understand it.

Many people in Okinawa do not wish to transfer their sufferings to others. However, if the Mutual Security Treaty is important for Japan, they believe that responsibility and burdens under the treaty should be assumed by all Japanese citizens. If not, many of my people point out that the outcome is discriminatory and goes counter to [the principle of] equality under the law.

In Okinawa, there are about 1.27 million Japanese nationals. Although this lawsuit [formally] concerns the prime minister's order to a prefectural governor to carry out certain duties *(shokumu shikko meirei sosho)*, I believe that it implies issues of basic human rights such as constitutionally guaranteed property rights, people's rights to a life in peace, and [the prefectures'] right to home rule. Because of these constitutional issues, all Japanese nationals everywhere should be actively concerned with Okinawa's base issue as one that impinges on their own basic human rights. In that sense, Okinawa's base issue is not peculiar to one local area—Okinawa—but is eminently general as Japan's problem with implications for Japan's sovereignty and democracy. Is that not so?

[I DEMAND, REQUEST, WISH . . .]

In searching for the solution to the base problem, beginning with as many as five trips to the United States, I have seized every opportunity to ask the governments of Japan and the United States for a realignment and reduction of bases as well as the prevention of damages due to them. My efforts have produced results: for example, according to an interim report of the Special Action Committee on Okinawa (SACO) announced last April, it was decided that [the land used by] the Futenma Air Station was to be returned completely. In this manner, there has been some progress in the realignment and reduction of bases in Okinawa. Yet, in almost all cases of base return, a prerequisite is the transfer of the bases to other areas or facilities in Okinawa. This reinforcement of bases is strongly opposed by the municipalities and residents affected by it. The situation is extremely serious.

I strongly demand that those who make decisions about base transfers actually come and see the areas affected and carefully examine the impact of the bases on people's lives, the natural environment, and the ecosystem.

Up until now, Okinawa's history has been determined by others. Now, of its own free will, Okinawa Prefecture has generated an "Action Program for the Return of Bases" demanding a planned and phased return of [the land used by] the American military bases by the year 2015. The prefecture is also engaged in the formulation of a "Grand Design of an International City, Okinawa," which sets Okinawa's course of development in the 21st Century. All this aims at building a base-free, peaceful, and green Okinawa that can withstand natural disasters and that can literally be an "international" city that facilitates exchanges of people, goods, and information *(hito, mono, joho)* with Japan and Asian countries in fields like technology, economics, and culture.

I wish to transform the military bases into production sites to serve peace and human happiness and to reactivate the potential of my prefecture's geographical uniqueness and its long history of friendly relations with Asia-Pacific nations. I wish to entrust the future of Okinawa to its transformation into an international city, a hub of peace that pulls Japan, Asia and the rest of the world together.

In conclusion, I would like to note that my people expect the Supreme Court, as the guardian of the Constitution, to render a positive *(sekkyokuteki)* judgment concerning the military base issue in Okinawa. I sincerely request the Supreme Court to examine the past and present of my people who, denied the benefits of the Constitutional principles, have been living under the oppression of military bases, and to grant a judgment that may open up a future filled with broad possibilities for Okinawa, a future that may generate dreams and hopes for its youth. That is all I have wanted to say for my "statement of opinion."

THE HELIPORT, NAGO, AND THE END OF THE OTA ERA

Chalmers Johnson

On November 30, 1997, the *Yomiuri* published the results of an opinion poll it had commissioned from the Gallup organization concerning Japanese and American attitudes toward the U.S.-Japan Security Treaty. In Japan, 1,952 people were interviewed; in the U.S., 982 responded. In an accompanying article, Joseph Nye, one of the Pentagon's principal architects of the policy of keeping 100,000 American troops in Japan and South Korea in peacetime, tried to put a positive spin on the poll's results. While he acknowledged "some perception gaps between the two countries on military cooperation, mainly over details for implementing new defense cooperation guidelines," he professed to believe that the poll reveals "Japan and the United States share common interests in the Asia-Pacific region."

My reading of the same statistics was far less sanguine. When respondents were asked which nations or regions they believed might pose a military threat to their own country, 69 percent of the Japanese named the Korean Peninsula, whereas 58 percent of U.S. respondents gave the Middle East top billing. Only 26 percent of the U.S. respondents believed that the Korean Peninsula posed a military threat. So much for some of those shared common interests.

However, if a military conflict did break out in Korea and the U.S. took military action there, almost 30 percent of those polled in the U.S. believed that Japan should join the U.S. in military action and another 42 percent believed Japan should provide the U.S. with logistical support, including supplies and the refueling of U.S. warships and aircraft. By contrast, only 11 percent of the Japanese believed they should refuel U.S. ships and aircraft, and even smaller percentages would support providing maintenance and repairs, or arms and ammunition.

Half of the Americans polled believed Japan should offer the use of its civil airports and ports, but only 20 percent of the Japanese agreed. Only 4 percent of the Japanese respondents thought that Japan should join the U.S. in military action if a conflict broke out on the Korean Peninsula, and 23 percent believed Japan should actively not cooperate with the U.S.—this in an area that 69 percent of them regard as a potential military threat.

When it comes to conflicts in other areas neighboring Japan, the gaps in attitudes grow even wider. Almost 53 percent of the Japanese believed that their military should stay exclusively within their own territory, including territorial waters and airspace, and 41.5 percent believed any military cooperation by Japan should be limited by the current interpretation of its constitution. In the U.S. the percentages of respondents agreeing with these propositions were only 20 percent and 14.8 percent respectively. Some 38.8 percent of the American respondents believed Japan should participate in front-line operations in the event of a neighboring conflict that threatens Japan, whereas only 2.3 percent of the Japanese supported such an activity.

In addition to these glaring disparities in what each country expects of the other, there are similar differences in their knowledge about the new security guidelines. These are the the plans for mutual cooperation in time of war that Japan and the United States signed in New York in September 1997. They include the memorable example of Orwellian double-talk that "The concept, 'situations in areas surrounding Japan,' is not geographical but situational." Even though their language is bureaucratic and intended to cover up as much as it exposed, the intent of the Guidelines is to make Japanese bases available to the United States whenever the U.S. declares an "emergency," that is, to return Japan and Okinawa to the occupied status they had during the Korean and Vietnamese wars. During early 1999, the Japanese Diet passed legislation giving the Guidelines legal force.

In the *Yomiuri* poll, two-thirds of the Japanese, as opposed to only one-third of the Americans, claimed any familiarity with the guidelines. Thus in the event of an actual conflict, Americans not only risk being disappointed by Japan's response: they are quite likely to be shocked and unpleasantly surprised. A mutual security treaty in which there is a 30-point gap in popular understandings of what the treaty entails, and further 30-point disagreements over who should do what in times of troubles, does not seem like a treaty in which anyone should place much confidence.

There is a further statistic that should give both sides pause. While approximately half of both Japanese and U.S. respondents thought that the U.S. military presence in Asia should be maintained—which Joseph Nye cited as evidence of "the broad public support in both countries for the reaffirmation of the Japan-U.S. Security relationship"—40.9 percent of the Japanese and 20.4 percent of the Americans wanted the U.S. military presence reduced. These are sizeable percentages, and the fact that the "hosts," the Japanese, outvoted their "guests" by two to one in calling for a reduction of troops must tell us something. Most likely, it should tell us that we have become an unwelcome army of occupation rather than of liberation, and that if security is the air we breathe (to use Professor Nye's tired analogy), the air surrounding Japan's American bases is decidedly unhealthy.

SPECIAL ACTION COMMITTEE ON OKINAWA

This unhealthy air became even more fetid around the northern Okinawan town of Nago as a result of the Japanese and American governments' reaction to the 1995 rape incident. The rape led to a protest by 85,000 Okinawans and a prefecture-wide plebiscite, Japan's first such vote, in which a majority of the voters called for the reduction and ultimate removal of foreign troops from Japanese soil.

In order to try to contain and deflect this movement while pretending to be responsive to it, the American and Japanese governments undertook several initiatives. These included postponing the scheduled visit of the American president to East Asia from the autumn of 1995 to the spring of 1996, so he would not have to take immediate responsibility for what American troops and their officers had done. When President Clinton finally did meet Governor Masahide Ota of Okinawa at the April 1996 summit meeting in Tokyo, he contrived not to respond or to say anything to him at all.

Meanwhile, amid profuse apologies from lesser American officials, the U.S. and Japanese governments set up a Special Action Committee on Okinawa (SACO) to recommend ways "to reduce the impact of U.S. military operations and training on the people of Okinawa." In its final report of December 2, 1996, SACO recommended, among other things, that Futenma Marine Corps Air Station, located in central Okinawa and entirely surrounded by the city of Ginowan, be closed. It is an acknowledged urban disaster area in which accidents from low-flying aircraft and environmental pollution are unavoidable. SACO suggested that Futenma be replaced by either a floating or an anchored, sea-borne airfield located slightly off-shore in northern Okinawa island.

This proposal became known as "the floating heliport," and the chosen site was the small impoverished town of Nago—or, more exactly, its seacoast suburb of Henoko. Henoko is the site of the Camp Schwab Marine base (and three other smaller U.S. military facilities), and so its citizens were presumed to be amenable to the expansion of the numbers of American troops. During the Vietnam War, Schwab supported some two-to-three-hundred brothels and bars and was notorious for its noise, accidents, and environmental damage. There are still some 3,000 U.S. Marines and attendant personnel stationed at Camp Schwab today, and the new heliport would double that number.

The proposal to build a floating airport at Nago does not, of course, meet the publicly proclaimed terms of the April 1996 Clinton-Hashimoto agreement to reduce the presence of U.S. forces on Okinawa. Nago is still in Okinawa. The two leaders allowed the public to believe that they planned to relocate facilities to other Japanese islands or back to the U.S., but in the fine print to their summit agreements they decided that Futenma had to be relocated elsewhere within Okinawa since no other Japanese prefecture would take it. As usual they paid no attention at all to the attitudes of the people on whom they were about to inflict an untested, experimental airport.

The people of Nago objected. Offshore from their town a large coral reef is home to the dugong, a manatee-like marine mammal said to have been mistaken by 18th century European seamen for a mermaid and now protected under international law. The seashore is also where endangered turtles come to lay their eggs. The residents of Nago well remember the 1960s and 1970s, when the nearby Marine base produced noise, pollution, military accidents, and sexual assaults, and they did not want a rerun. On August 13, 1997, a newly formed anti-base group in Nago submitted a petition containing 19,734 signatures, more than half of all of Nago's eligible voters, calling for a local referendum on the heliport. The city authorities submitted the bill to the City Council. After intense and divisive debate, with Tokyo openly lobbying against letting the people vote, the Nago Government on December 11, 1997, officially scheduled the referendum for December 21. It also began accepting absentee ballots. Of Nago's 38,176 eligible voters, absentee voters constituted just under 19 percent, making them of great significance in the final count. It was later revealed that construction companies had tried to falsify absentee votes in favor of building the heliport.

Of course, not everyone was opposed. Nago has a depressed rural economy and Prime Minister Hashimoto's government promised lucrative construction contracts and other economic benefits if a majority of the voters would support the proposed heliport. Hashimoto also threatened that *if* the Nago voters failed to approve of the heliport, "nothing will change," meaning that Futenma would then not be returned to Okinawa for peaceful development. In this way, he managed to pit Okinawans against each other and forced Governor Ota to take a publicly neutral stance.

THE NAGO REFERENDUM

In the weeks preceding the referendum, members of Japan's Self-Defense Forces who were stationed or born in Okinawa were ordered to go from house to house in Nago, urging residents to support the heliport. And the weekend before the vote Fumio Kyuma, the director general of the Defense Agency, himself visited Nago to harangue voters. An attempt was also made to rig the voting by offering four choices instead of the usual two. The choices were:

•I agree with the construction plan.

•I oppose construction.

•I agree because promised anti-pollution and economic measures can benefit the community.

•I oppose construction because such benefits are unlikely.

The third option, "I agree because . . ." was doubtless invented to draw more yes votes than if the choice had been starkly "yes" or "no." But had only this choice been included, the ballot would have been grossly unfair because "yes" voters would have had two options, which could have been added together, whereas the "no" voters would have had only one choice.

In the event, this strategy backfired. The final result of the December 21, 1997, plebiscite in Nago, with 80 percent of the eligible voters casting their votes, was as follows:

I agree with the construction	2,562)
I agree because . . .	11,705) 14,267 or 46.2 percent

- -

I oppose construction	16,254)
I oppose because . . .	385) 16,639 or 53.8 percent

In other words, those who were opposed were simply opposed, no matter what economic inducements were offered, whereas those who decided to vote *for* the heliport took advantage of the softer wording; very few were willing to support the heliport outright.

Since the plebiscite was non-binding, Prime Minister Hashimoto and the LDP took the position that they could ignore it and go ahead and build the floating heliport anyway. But combined with the referendum of August 4, 1996, when the citizens of the city of Maki in Niigata Prefecture voted down construction of a nuclear power plant, and the September 8, 1996, prefecture-wide referendum in Okinawa, when 53 percent of the voters demanded a reduced U.S. military presence on the island as a whole, it had become harder for Tokyo to ignore the will of local voters. People in local areas have become irritated by the central government's attempts to foist projects on them that it would not think of building in the localities of powerful LDP politicians. Before the Nago vote, the people of Okinawa Prefecture as a whole had already spoken to say that they wanted to lighten the burden of hosting U.S. military installations. The local plebiscite, almost never used in Japan until the late 1990s, has become by far the most important institution in the country through which ordinary citizens can democratically express their will.

Following the referendum, the mayor of Nago, Tetsuya Higa, who had supported the heliport, said that he still favored the heliport but then abruptly resigned his office. In the subsequent mayoral election, Tateo Kishimoto, backed by the LDP, the Defense Agency, and the Pentagon, emerged victorious. However, unsuspected by the pro-base forces, Kishimoto was also an Okinawan patriot. It was revealed that he had long been a one-tsubo landlord—that is, one of the several thousand Okinawans who hold handkerchief-sized plots of land under the American bases as a way of protesting Japanese-American expropriations. On taking office, he declared that he would leave policy on the heliport to the prefectural government—that is, to Governor Masahide Ota—and take no part in helping Tokyo build it.

THE LDP TAKES OVER IN OKINAWA

Ota, who faced reelection in the fall of 1998, had been a thorn in Tokyo's side ever since he refused to override the property rights of dissident Okinawan landlords who did not want to continue leasing their land for the use of American bases. Despite Ota's very considerable reputation as a scholar, which elevates his national and international standing over any of his LDP critics, the Japanese central government and its press appendages, particularly the *Yomiuri,* attacked and ridiculed him in every possible way. Pentagon officials, usually half Ota's age, learned to copy the behavior of their counterparts in the Japanese Defense Agency. Two days prior to the Nago mayoral election, Ota declared that the people had already spoken in the referendum. As a matter of elementary democracy, he therefore abandoned his position of neutrality. He said he opposed moving Futenma anywhere else in Okinawa and that it should be moved to mainland Japan or to the territory of the United States.

This position so infuriated the leaders of the LDP in Tokyo they decided to freeze out Ota and cut off all statutory subsidies from the central government to Okinawa prefecture. The party and the *Yomiuri* also launched a campaign of defamation against Ota, complaining that he had not shown proper appreciation for all that Prime Minister Hashimoto had tried to do for Okinawa since the rape incident. The result was to saddle Japan's poorest prefecture with an unemployment rate of over 9 percent, twice the national average. In the gubernatorial election of November 15, 1998, Governor Ota lost his bid for a third term as governor of Okinawa. His challenger, the Liberal Democratic Party-supported candidate, Keiichi Inamine (former chairman of Ryukyu Petroleum), took 52.1 percent of the vote compared to Ota's 46.9 percent. Voter turnout was 76.5 percent, fourteen percent higher than four years earlier.

The LDP orchestrated the outcome from Tokyo, and Inamine ran a clever campaign. He adopted positions as close to those of Ota as possible—for example, Inamine too came out against the floating heliport—but he promised that he could reopen the money pipeline from Tokyo. Five days before the election, the LDP announced that it was abandoning the heliport idea and would negotiate with Inamine over where to move Futenma Marine Corps Air Station. Two Marine hit-and-run cases occurred just prior to the election (one resulting in death), but this time U.S. Ambassador Thomas Foley literally ran to the Foreign Ministry to apologize and offer financial compensation. The people of Okinawa, already worn down by the relentless pressure of the Pentagon, seem to have settled for money instead of the ideal of self-government.

But the forced retirement of the most effective prefectural governor in postwar Japan does not mean that the Okinawan problem is solved. The U.S. expects to keep its forces in Okinawa indefinitely and have Japan continue to pay for them through the "sympathy budget." Governor Inamine has no solution to the problems of too many bases in too crowded a space, and Okinawa is just waiting for the next rape, or accident, or revelation of environmental pollution that will again bring Japanese and global attention to the festering problems.

THE HAMILTON REPORT

Tokyo can think of no alternative to the Nago heliport, least of all moving Marine Corps Air Station Futenma to a location on the Japanese mainland. It knows that opposition in mainland Japan would be as fierce as that in Okinawa but more effective, since it would involve mainstream Japanese rather than the exploited ethnic minority the people of Okinawa have become. Throughout this complex, contentious process, officials of the Pentagon maintained an almost complete silence on the policy issues involved. However, Robert Hamilton, a former U.S. Marine Corps artillery battery commander who was stationed on Okinawa from 1986-88, visited Okinawa and the proposed site for the so-called new "heliport" in late 1996 and offered the following sober analysis (from *JPRI Working Paper* No. 28, January 1997):

A general description of a facility like MCAS Futenma is instructive. In addition to the obvious landing areas required, hangar space for all helicopters is needed for maintenance and protection from the harsh salt water environment. Next, a lot of space is needed to store the large variety of parts and tools required to keep these highly complex machines in operation. And do not forget about storage space for aviation fuel, and also a guarded area for ammunition, since this is a military operation. Furthermore, every military air facility needs a fully stocked and manned medical facility on the premises, since accidents do occur, requiring immediate lifesaving services. Also required is a mission-capable fire and rescue operation, which requires considerable space. I could go on, but the picture should be clear.

The Pentagon proposes replacing Futenma's 1,188 acres (640 acres equal 1 square mile) in the densely populated city of Ginowan with a steel platform less than a mile long. Any offshore facility adhering to U.S. Department of Defense safety, environmental and security standards and meeting military mission requirements will probably end up looking more like the giant Kansai Airport in Osaka than what is currently being described as a modest and down-sized facility.

As for the idea of building a floating facility in the open sea off the coast of Okinawa, there is quite a trade-off in placing the facility far enough offshore to solve the noise pollution problem. Anyone who has ever experienced a major typhoon on Okinawa will realize that such a typhoon would turn Okinawa's first floating air facility into Okinawa's first underwater air facility, with the greatest sinking of U.S. military assets into the Pacific Ocean since Pearl Harbor. To stand any chance at all of surviving the island's long typhoon season, the floating facility would have to be heavily anchored to the sea floor and surrounded by giant seawalls, and this construction would cause great damage to the beautiful coral reefs of Okinawa.

However, even if the engineering and environmental problems could be solved, a more basic policy problem remains. Currently on Okinawa, serious and committed young American men and women who have volunteered to serve in their nation's armed forces are increasingly being viewed as mercenaries to be isolated and caged away from the local populace in peacetime, and only to be set loose in times of military emergency. The proposed move of the Futenma air station to an isolated off-shore area only accentuates this.

As for the proposed relocation of MCAS Futenma to another site, the Okinawan people have spoken, and their concerns must be addressed. Instead of behaving like indigent travelers looking for a place to stay, I wish the American base negotiators would begin discussions on a move to either Hawaii or the West Coast of the United States. The training for the Marines would certainly be much better at these American locations, and such a proposal might also prompt the beginning of a sorely needed domestic debate in Japan on the implications of a genuine security alliance with the United States.

THE GAO REPORT

Meanwhile, Congressman Duncan Hunter, a right-wing Republican representing California's 52nd Congressional District located east of San Diego in El Cajon, California, and chairman of the House Military Procurement Committee, asked the U.S. General Accounting Office (GAO) to look into the matter. Hunter was not concerned about the Okinawans, but he did want to know what impact the implementation of the SACO recommendations would have "on the readiness and training of U.S. forces stationed on Okinawa." Coming from San Diego, the largest concentration of military force anywhere on earth, Hunter's request reflected local concerns. His constituents are interested in whether the Marines are comfortable on Okinawa and are being well taken care of by the Japanese and American governments. The report he received is surely not the one he was looking for.

The GAO report, entitled *Overseas Presence: Issues Involved in Reducing the Impact of the U.S. Military Presence on Okinawa: Report to the Honorable Duncan Hunter, House of Representatives* and dated March, 1998, constitutes the only publicly available document from the American government on its activities in Okinawa in the late 1990s. Since this report received no known coverage in the American press or other news media and even its existence has only been reported in Okinawa and Japan, I am hereby offering some excerpts.

The GAO report is important because it reveals that the proposed heliport relies on technology that has never been tested and that, for one configuration, does not even exist. It reveals that, as Hamilton also argues, the heliport cannot perform the functions currently assigned to the base at Futenma. It reveals that the heliport would be vastly more expensive than Futenma and that the Japanese and American governments cannot agree on who should pay for it. It also reveals that the heliport, if ever built, would inflict serious environmental damage on northern Okinawa island and that officers of the Department of Defense knew all these things and chose to remain silent.

The GAO conducted its research, including an on-site visit, from June 1997 to March 1998. It interviewed many Department of Defense and Department of State officials in Washington, Tampa (the U.S. Special Operations Command, which is responsible for the contingent of Special Forces based on Okinawa), Honolulu, Tokyo, and Okinawa. It talked with two ocean engineering professors at the University of Hawaii. It talked with no Okinawans.

Copies of the GAO Report were sent to the Chairmen and ranking minority members of the House Committee on National Security, the Senate Committee on Armed Services, and the House and Senate Committees on Appropriations; and to the Secretaries of State, Defense, Army, Navy, Air Force, and the Commandant of the Marine Corps. The U.S. government cannot claim that it is unaware of the conditions it has created on Okinawa. Excerpts below from the GAO Report have been grouped topically. They are direct quotations from the GAO Report, except for italics, inserted for emphasis.

WHY AMERICAN FORCES ARE IN OKINAWA

Discontent among the people of Okinawa regarding the U.S. military presence and its impacts has been rising for years. The chief complaint is that the Okinawa prefecture hosts over half of the U.S. forces in Japan and that about 75 percent of the land U.S. forces occupy in Japan is on Okinawa. They also believe the U.S. presence has hampered economic development. (p. 2)

To demonstrate a commitment to peace and security in the Asia-Pacific region, the United States has about 47,000 servicemembers, about half of all U.S. forces deployed in the Pacific region, stationed in Japan. Of the 47,000 U.S. servicemembers in Japan, over half are based on Okinawa, a subtropical island about 67 miles long and from 2 to 18 miles wide, with coral reefs in many offshore locations. In fiscal year 1997, U.S. forces on Okinawa occupied 58,072 acres of the land in the Okinawa prefecture. (p. 14)

The Status of Forces Agreement, signed on the same day as the treaty [the Treaty of Mutual Cooperation and Security, signed in January 1960 by the United States and Japan], permits the United States to bring servicemembers and their dependents into Japan. . . . The agreement also (1) required the United States to return land to Japan when the land is no longer needed, (2) specifies that the United States will perform maintenance on bases it occupies in Japan, and (3) relieves the United States of the obligation to restore bases in Japan to the condition they were in when they became available to the United States. U.S. *Forces-Japan* (USFJ) *has interpreted this latter provision to mean that the United States is not required to conduct environmental cleanup on bases it closes in Japan.* (p. 15)

To determine DOD's views on the benefit or necessity of having U. S. forces stationed on Okinawa, we interviewed officials and obtained relevant documents, including the Quadrennial Defense Review report. . . . *Because it was outside the scope of our work, we did not evaluate any alternatives to forward deployment. However, in a June 1997 report, we concluded that DOD had not adequately considered alternatives to forward presence to accomplish its stated security objectives.* (p. 19)

The III Marine Expeditionary Force, the primary Marine Corps component on Okinawa, consists of the (1) 3rd Marine Division, the ground combat component; (2) 1st Marine Air Wing, the air combat component; (3) 3rd Force Service Support Group, the logistics support component; and (4) command element. (p. 24)

Warehouses hold war reserve supplies on Okinawa that would support U.S. operations, including 14,400 tons of ammunition, 5,000 pieces of unit and individual equipment, and 50 million gallons of fuel. (p. 25)

MCAS Futenma's primary mission is to maintain and operate facilities and provide services and materials to support Marine aircraft operations. MCAS Futenma covers 1,188 acres of land and is completely surrounded by the urbanized growth of Ginowan City. (p. 27)

The land at MCAS Futenma is leased from about 2,000 private landowners by the government of Japan. . . . MCAS Futenma has a runway and parallel taxiway that are about 9,000 feet long as well as an aircraft washrack, maintenance facilities, vehicle maintenance facilities, fuel storage facilities, a hazardous waste storage and transfer facility, a control tower, an armory, and other facilities needed to operate a Marine Corps air station. (p. 29)

THE HELIPORT

The U.S. and Japanese government established a working group to examine three options for replacing MCAS Futenma. The options were relocation of the air station onto (1) Kadena Air Base, (2) Camp Schwab, or (3) a sea-based facility to be located in the ocean offshore from Okinawa Island. . . . The government of Japan has decided to locate the sea-based facility offshore from Camp Schwab. However, at the time of our review some residents living near the propose site had opposed having the sea-based facility near their community, but U. S. officials are proceeding on the basis that the facility will be built. (p. 29)

The United States has established a runway length requirement of about 4,200 feet for the sea-based facility. Arresting gear would be located about 1,200 feet from either end of the runway to permit carrier aircraft to land. (p. 31)

During regular operations, about 66 helicopters and MV-22 aircraft (when fielded) would be stationed aboard the sea-based facility. The MV-22 can operate in either vertical takeoff and landing mode, like a helicopter, or short takeoff and landing mode, like an airplane. . . . The Pacific Command has established a 4,200-foot runway for all MV-22 operations based on aircraft performance and meteorological data. The Marine Corps study indicates that a 4,200-foot runway is sufficient for most training and mission requirements. However, the study also stated that for missions requiring an MV-22 gross weight near the maximum of 59,305 pounds, the aircraft would have to operate in its short takeoff mode and would require a runway of 5,112 feet under certain weather conditions. (p.30)

The United States planned to locate the headquarters, logistics, and most operational facilities aboard the sea-based facility and most quality-of-life activities, including housing, food service, and medical and dental services, ashore at Camp Schwab. . . . Due to a lack of DOD dependent schools in the Camp Schwab area, only unmarried servicemembers will be housed at Camp Schwab. (p. 31)

A pontoon-type sea-based facility would essentially be a large platform that would float in the water on pontoons. The structure would be located about 3,000 feet from shore in about 100 feet of water. Part of the platform would be below the water line. To keep the sea relatively calm around the platform, a breakwater would be installed to absorb the wave action. *The breakwater would be constructed in about 60 feet of water atop a coral ridge. . . . According to documents that we obtained, no floating structure of the size required has ever been built*. In addition, Naval Facilities Engineering Command officials told us that construction of a breakwater in about 60 feet of water would be "at the edge of technical feasibility." (pp. 32-34)

A pile-supported sea-based facility essentially would be a large platform supported by columns, or piles, driven into the sea floor. The structure would be located in about 16 feet to 82 feet of water and relatively closer to shore than the proposed pontoon-type sea-based facility. *According to Naval Engineers, about 7,000 piles would be needed to sup-*

port a structure of the size proposed. (p. 34)

The semisubmersible sea-based facility relies on technology that does not yet exist, according to documents provided by DOD. . . . Semisubmersible sea-based facilities are limited by current technology to about 1,000 feet in length. (pp. 36-7)

Technological challenges may arise because no sea-based facility of the type and scale envisioned has ever been built to serve as an air base. . . . *The sea-based facility would have to survive natural events such as typhoons, which strike within 180 nautical miles of Okinawa Island an average of four times a year.* During a typhoon, personnel would evacuate the sea-base facility, but the aircraft would remain aboard the facility in hangers to ride out the storm, according to 1st Marine Air Wing officials. (p. 38)

If Kadena Air Base is not available for MV-22 operations, the Marines would have no alternative U.S. military runway of sufficient length on Okinawa to support MV-22 missions at its maximum weight and maintain safety margins in certain weather conditions. . . . Naha International Airport would be available as an emergency landing strip for U.S. military aircraft. (p. 39)

COSTS

Japan pays part of the costs of the U.S. forces stationed in its country with annual burden-sharing payments that totaled about $4.9 billion in fiscal year 1997. [¥544 billion at US$1=¥111, the rate used by USFJ.] The annual payments fall into four categories. First, Japan paid about $712 million for leased land on which U.S. bases sit. Second, Japan provided about $1.7 billion in accordance with the Special Measures Agreement, under which Japan pays the costs of (1) local national labor employed by U.S. forces in Japan, (2) public utilities on U.S. bases, and (3) the transfer of U.S. forces' training from U.S. bases to other facilities when Japan requests such transfers. Third, USFJ estimated that Japan provided about $876 million in indirect costs, such as rents foregone at fair market value and tax concessions.

Last, although not covered by any agreements, Japan provided about $1.7 billion from its facilities budget for facilities and new construction. (p. 16)

The Congressional Research Service believes that the Department of Defense (DOD) overstates the true value of burden-sharing payments from Japan because such costs as base lease payments and rents foregone are costs unique to operating in Japan. DOD would not pay these costs if troops based in Japan were relocated to bases in the continental United States. (p. 16, n. 3)

The sea-based facility is estimated to cost Japan between $2.4 billion and $4.9 billion to design and build. . . Based on a $4-billion sea-based facility design and construction cost, U.S. engineers have initially estimated maintenance costs to be about $8 billion over the 40-year life span of the facility. *Thus, annual maintenance would cost about $200 million, compared with about $2.8 million spent at* MCAS *Futenma.* At the time of this report, the United States and Japan were discussing having Japan pay for maintenance on the sea-based facility. *If Japan does not pay maintenance costs, then the U.S. costs related to the* SACO *recommendations could be much higher.* (p. 37)

ENVIRONMENTAL DAMAGE

If environmental contamination is found on bases to be closed under the SACO process, cleanup could be expensive. . . . USFJ and Marine Corps Bases, Japan, officials believe that the United States is not obligated to do environmental cleanup at bases to be closed. Nevertheless, a 1995 DOD policy calls for the removal of known imminent and substantial dangers to health and safety due to environmental contamination caused by DOD operations on installations or facilities designated for return to the host nation overseas. . . . In fact, Marine Corps Bases, Japan, and other Okinawa-based U.S. forces were informed by a letter dated August 25, 1997, from the Government of Japan's Naha Defense Facilities Administration Bureau that the toxic substances mercury and polychlorinated biphenyls were found on the Onna communications site. The United States had closed the base and returned the land to Japan in November 1995 (a land return unrelated to the SACO process). The letter indicated that the presence of these substances has prevented the land from being returned to its owners and thus being available for reuse. The letter concludes by requesting that the United States conduct a survey, identify any contamination that may exist, and clean up bases scheduled for closure in the future. (p. 47)

The United States and Japan, along with a substantial number of other countries, support an international coral reef initiative aimed at conservation and management of coral reefs and related ecosystems. Coral reefs are in the area in which the sea-based facility is tentatively to be located. . . . Two sea-based facility options currently under consideration have the potential to harm the coral reefs. The pontoon-type facility requires the installation of a large breakwater and several mooring stations onto the seafloor. The pile-supported facility requires several thousand support pilings that would need to be driven into the coral reef or seafloor and reinforced to withstand storm conditions. *Both of these option require at least one, and possible two, causeways connecting them to shore facilities. Numerous scientific studies show that large construction projects can cause damage to coral reefs and the nearby coastal areas.* (p. 48)

OKINAWA SUFFERS ON

As of early 1999, nothing had changed. The heliport at Nago remains on the table as an option, but no one in Okinawa, including Governor Inamine, supports it. In November 1998, the U.S. Defense Department issued a new East Asian Strategy Report (the DOD deliberately held it up until after the gubernatorial election in Okinawa in order not to inflame the voters into supporting Governor Ota). It reaffirms the Nye Report and states that the United States intends to maintain an imperial presence in northeast Asia even after the two Koreas reunite and as far into the future as the DOD can imagine. The Marines remain at Futenma, daily threatening the lives, hearing, and property of the people of Ginowan, who have been offered no alternatives other than enduring the presence of the uninvited Americans in the center of their city.

On April 29, 1999, Japanese Prime Minister Keizo Obuchi

tossed a potential bombshell into this situation. He announced that Japan would hold the July 2000 summit meeting of the heads of the Group of Eight Nations in, of all places, the small Okinawan town of Nago, population 55,171. It is Japan's turn to host the summit meeting and in choosing to do so in Nago, Obuchi overruled the Ministry of Foreign Affairs, which ranked Okinawa last among eight possible regional sites in Japan for such a gathering. Even though it will be the beginning of the typhoon season, the Japanese government anticipates that some 8,500 officials and journalists from around the world will attend. If Bill Clinton comes, as is expected, he will be the first president to visit Okinawa since Dwight Eisenhower in 1960. (President Eisenhower stopped briefly on his way to a summit meeting in Tokyo to celebrate renewal of the U.S.-Japan Security Treaty, which was suddenly cancelled because of rioting against the treaty. The first sitting American president to visit mainland Japan was Gerald Ford.)

It has already been announced that Clinton will use Kadena Air Force Base, presumably because he does not want to cause a riot at either Naha International Airport or Futenma. The president has said to the press that he hopes the issue of relocating Futenma will be settled before he arrives in Nago, conveniently forgetting that he could solve the problem by simply ordering the Marines back to the United States. Opinion in Japan is divided on whether Obuchi may have intended to force this option on Clinton or whether he instead has thrown the Nago residents a carrot prior to compelling them to accept the new airport.

In any case, neither the Japanese nor the American government has shown the slightest interest in justice for Okinawa, only in dividing and deceiving its people in order to make their protests ineffective. This situation has existed for well over half a century.

V.

OKINAWA: A FUTURE WITHOUT

AMERICAN BASES?

THE JAPANESE-AMERICAN SECURITY TREATY WITHOUT A U.S. MILITARY PRESENCE

Shunji Taoka

(A Dialogue, March 1997)

(1) JPRI: What do you think of the idea advanced by former Prime Minister Hosokawa and the Japanese Democratic Party of an "alliance without U.S. bases?" Is it a realistic conception?

Taoka: I do not think it is an unrealistic dream. It is one of the long-term goals advocated by the leader of the Democratic Party of Japan, Yukio Hatoyama, and also by Morihiro Hosokawa, who was a very popular prime minister from 1993 to 1994. They want to maintain the Security Treaty but without a U.S. military presence during peacetime. In other words, they call for an alliance with the United States but without American military bases in Japan. The aim of this policy is to maintain friendly relations with the United States in the post-Cold War era. Hatoyama hopes that this goal can be achieved by the year 2010.

(2) JPRI: To separate the alliance and a U.S. military presence seems like a novel idea for Japan. Is it possible?

Taoka: Basically, an alliance and a military presence are two separate matters. The United States has nearly fifty allies—some nominal and some de facto. But only in five are there more than 10,000 U.S. service personnel stationed. They are Germany, Japan, Korea, Italy, and the United Kingdom. Historically speaking, equal allies in peacetime rarely stationed troops in each other's territory. In the early part of this century, Japan was allied with Britain and then with Germany. But neither Britain nor Germany had military bases in Japan. Long before the creation of the Japanese Democratic Party, I argued that Japan should shift from a *teishoku* dinner mentality (a full fixed-course meal) to ordering à la carte from a menu of four different items—(1) friendly relations with the United States, (2) an alliance, (3) a U.S. military presence in Japan, and (4) financial support of U.S. forces.

A full-course mentality reflected Cold War conditions but is much less appropriate to the international relations of the coming century. The military aspect of the U.S.-Japan alliance is of declining importance because of the collapse of the Soviet Union and the rapid hollowing out of Russian forces in East Asia. The main purpose of the U.S.-Japan alliance was to contain Soviet expansionism in East Asia. Now that American and Russian leaders have declared that their two nations are virtual allies, Japan's security environment has fundamentally changed.

(3) JPRI: You do not think North Korea is a threat to Japan?

Taoka: Russia opened diplomatic relations with South Korea in 1990. China followed suit in 1992. North Korea is virtually isolated and on the verge of economic collapse. In the early part of this century, Korea was called "a dagger pointed at the heart of Japan" because it seemed likely that Russia would occupy it. Today there is no possibility that Russia will take up the dagger. By 2010 the situation on the Korean peninsula is likely to have been resolved. Even today, the GNP of South Korea is almost twenty times larger than that of the North and its population is twice as large. The gap between their national potentials is of the same order as that between the United States and Mexico. North Korea's GNP is about half that of Okinawa's, Japan's poorest prefecture.

(4) JPRI: How about China? Isn't it building up its modern military power?

Taoka: Contrary to widespread perceptions in the United States, Chinese conventional military power is declining. The numbers of China's combat aircraft, submarines, surface ships, and army personnel have all decreased in recent years, and the obsolescence of its equipment is obvious. China has attempted some modernization of its forces, but the pace has been slower than that of Taiwan, South Korea, or Japan. For example, since the early 1990s it has imported only 48 Su-27 fighter aircraft from Russia, but it must soon retire some 4,500 old fighters, mostly MiG17s, MiG19s, and MiG21s. It has purchased two "Kilo class" submarines from Russia, but they will not be able fully to replace some 60 obsolete submarines.

Since 1986, Beijing has experienced increasing fiscal deficits in spite of its economic growth, largely because local officials try to keep tax revenues in their provinces. China lacks a national taxation system, and its central government relies upon remittances from the provinces. The introduction of a national taxation system would lead to tremendous problems and could cause the break-up of the country. During the mid-1990s, there has been almost zero real term growth in Beijing's revenues. Chinese leaders acknowledge that pursuit of selfish interests and corruption, which has been a traditional Chinese problem, have contributed to the country's increasingly critical financial situation. Military officers, too, are actively engaged in making money as part of the new "market economy." They have shown surprising mercantile talents. Generals often refuse to be transferred from lucrative districts. In this sense, China is not a modern nation even compared with India and Pakistan.

(5) JPRI: If such prominent leaders as Hatoyama and Hosokawa believe that the military threat to Japan has diminished, why do they still call for the maintenance of the alliance with the United States?

Taoka: The traditional foundation of international alliances has been the perception of a "common threat" or the belief that "thy enemy's enemy is thy friend." Contrary to these contentions, many Japanese believe that the U.S.-Japan alliance should be maintained because of its political significance and the common interests and values shared by the two nations. Continuation of the alliance is beneficial for Japan and, it is hoped, also for the United States.

(6) JPRI: If such Japanese leaders believe in a continued alliance with the United States, why then do they advocate an end to the U.S. military presence?

Taoka: In order to preserve the alliance into the 21st century, the two nations must continuously work to adjust its terms to the changes in the international environment. Today, the two governments must ensure that the dramatic changes that have taken place since 1989 are reflected in the alliance.

The Japanese public tends to perceive the U.S. bases in Japan as relics left over from the post-World War II occupation era. They have persisted for more than fifty years only because of the Cold War. The American public, on the other hand, tends to feel that the United States is doing Japan a favor by stationing troops there and protecting Japan. Since both Japanese and American perceptions have some truth to them, the gap between them could undermine the alliance. In order to ensure that the alliance retains the approval of the Japanese and American people, it is necessary to reduce the burdens on both sides and to avoid friction as much as possible.

(7) JPRI: Does the Japanese public view the Security Treaty this way?

Taoka: Public opinion surveys indicate that about two-thirds of the Japanese people want to maintain the alliance but also want the U.S. military presence reduced (see, e.g., the *Asahi Shimbun* poll published on May 15, 1996, in which 70 percent favored the alliance with the U.S. but 67 percent wanted the bases reduced). We conjecture that Americans would answer the same questions in similar ways.

(8) JPRI: Are American service personnel unpopular in Japan?

Taoka: No. Generally speaking, they are well accepted as friendly people. But it is human nature to welcome a friend who visits one's home occasionally but to be much less receptive to a friend who stays in one's house for weeks. The Japanese government does not like taking the awkward position of telling its friends that it is time for them to leave. I believe that a reduced U.S. military presence in Japan would improve friendly relations and guarantee the treaty's survival into the next century. The Japanese would welcome occasional visits of the U.S. fleet and other military units for joint training and rapid deployment exercises. I hope that joint naval patrols of the Western Pacific will become possible.

(9) JPRI: What do you think is the best way for the U.S. to maintain cooperative security relations with Japan while giving up its military bases there?

Taoka: Administrative control of the U.S. bases in Japan could easily be transferred to the Japan Self-Defense Forces with guarantees of access to American units. The only three bases for the exclusive use of the U.S. Navy outside the U.S. are Guantanamo Bay in Cuba and Yokosuka and Sasebo in Japan. In Europe, U.S. Navy vessels use the ports of friendly navies whereas at Yokosuka and Sasebo, ships of Japan's Maritime Self-Defense Forces are allowed to use only small parts of these extraterritorial facilities even though the Japanese Government bears almost 100 percent of the cost of maintaining them. This situation is one example of the prerogatives the U.S. forces claimed during the occupation era that have continued for more than fifty years into the present. Such abnormal situations should not be maintained into the next century. Even at Subic Bay before the American withdrawal, a Filipino admiral was in command of the base, albeit nominally, even though the Americans paid rent to use Subic's facilities.

(10) JPRI: People at the Pentagon say that the U.S. bases in Japan are indispensable for the security of Japan, the United States, and the Asia-Pacific region. Some Japanese say the same thing. But you do not think so?

Taoka: Whether bases under the exclusive control of the United States are really necessary for the security of the U.S., Japan, or the Asia-Pacific region must be reexamined. As long as Japan and the United States are friends and allies, U.S. ships and aircraft can use Japanese Self-Defense Forces facilities. If friendly relations between Japan and the U.S. should diminish, exclusively American bases could no longer be maintained in any event because the geographical and financial situation of the American bases in Japan is very different from that of the bases at Gibraltar and Guantanamo Bay.

(11) JPRI: So, do you mean that U.S. forces should be allowed to use Japanese military facilities in the next century?

Taoka: Yes. In order that U.S. forces have guarantees of access to Self-Defense forces facilities in the 21st century, some new arrangements will be necessary. These include, for example, priorities for the use of some piers at Yokosuka and Sasebo and the stationing of the necessary U.S. personnel to staff offices and storehouses at Japanese bases. Japan must also guarantee the use of ship-repair facilities for U.S. Navy vessels. Japan should also allow for exclusive use by U.S. forces of a few communications facilities on Japanese territory but on the condition that they will not be used to eavesdrop on or conduct intelligence collecting activities against the host nation, as they do now.

(12) JPRI: Such arrangements seem to contradict somewhat the goal of "alliance without a U.S. military presence in Japan."

Taoka: Giving these privileges to U.S. forces in Japan might appear to contradict the goal of an "alliance without an American military presence." But this is only a necessary and realistic compromise in order to maintain a *pax Americana,* supported by American naval and air power, which is in Japan's national interest. Realistically, the goal should be an alliance with a minimal foreign presence. The goal for the foreseeable future should be "almost zero" exclusively American facilities in Japan.

(13) JPRI: Won't major reductions of U.S. forces in Japan lead to Japan's military build up?

Taoka: I know that some Americans and Japanese express concern that if the U.S. military presence is reduced, Japan will have to expand its own defense forces. This view ignores the fact that there are no U.S. military units in Japan that are directly committed to the defense of Japan itself. For example, there is no combat unit of the American army in Japan except for a special forces battalion of approximately 400 men. One Marine division, actually one infantry regiment and one artillery battalion, is stationed in Okinawa, the southernmost islands of Japan, for dispatch to the Middle East or Korea in an emergency. There are two U.S. Air Force fighter wings made up of 54 F-15s and 36 F-16s based in Japan, but they are intended for the defense of South Korea. Since 1959 the air defense of Japan has been the responsibility of the Japanese Air Self-Defense Force with about 300 fighter aircraft. There is no doubt that the U.S. Navy contributed to the security of Japan in the Cold War days by maintaining a favorable naval balance with the Soviet fleet. But the U.S. Navy's role has been global, just as the role of the British Navy in the 19th century contributed indirectly to the security and prosperity of the United States. The major difference is that the United States did not permit the British Navy to maintain bases in the United States and did not provide "host nation support."

Since there will be no "gap" in Japan's defenses if the U.S. military presence is reduced, there will be no need to expand the Self-Defense forces. The situation in Japan is thus very different from that in Germany before 1989 and in Korea today.

(14) JPRI: Some American military officers assert that the U.S. military presence in Japan is necessary to prevent a resurgence of Japanese military expansion. What is your response?

Taoka: Some Americans try to defend their post-World War II prerogatives in Japan by claiming that an American military presence in Japan is required in order to prevent a "resurgence of Japanese militarism." Because many Americans seem to have formulated their image of Japan from World War II movies and from Japan's current industrial capabilities, this so-called cap-in-the-bottle view has gained some influence in the United States, in my observation. I believe that it is ridiculous, based on two points.

First, about 75 percent of the cost of maintaining U.S. forces in Japan—about $6 billion per annum, or more than $120,000 for each of the 42,000 American military personnel in Japan—is provided by Japan. If the American troops are there primarily to watch Japan, this amounts to a case of the prisoners paying large salaries to their own prison guards.

Second, fears of Japanese militarism are paranoid. Japan has nothing to gain from the use of military action to overturn the present world order. Perhaps more than any other nation, Japan benefits from international trade, as signified by its annual trade surplus of over $100 billion. Japan is the world's number one status quo power, enjoying more than $1 trillion in personal savings (over 50 percent of the global total of savings) and some $700 billion in overseas assets.

The age of colonialism is over, and the former colonial territories that gained their independence after World War II can now trade with Japan without any restrictions being placed on them by their colonial overlords. Such nations in the Asia-Pacific region have become very good trading partners of Japan's. Both sides enjoy co-prosperity as a result of these commercial ties established after World War II. Japan neither needs nor has the incentive to attempt to alter this ideal situation through the use of military force. No Japanese politician or military officer advocates a policy of military expansion, which is obviously contrary to both Japan's national interest and public opinion. There is no more likelihood of resurgent militarism in Japan than there is of the reintroduction of slavery in the United States. Both are simply outmoded.

(15) JPRI: What do you think of the possibility of Japan's acquiring nuclear weapons?

Taoka: Although the conventional military threat to Japan has diminished, Japan is still open to the threat of nuclear pressure or blackmail from its neighbors who are armed with nuclear weapons. Because Japan is a signatory to the Nuclear Non-Proliferation Treaty, which in 1995 became a permanent treaty, it has foreclosed the option of acquiring a nuclear deterrent capability. Since an anti-ballistic missile defense can never be a perfect guarantee against a nuclear attack, the only logical solution for Japan is to maintain the alliance with the United States and hope its "nuclear umbrella" can deter any possible attempt at nuclear blackmail. This should be acceptable to the United States because it, too, does not want Japan to build its own independent nuclear deterrent or to ally itself with other nuclear armed nations.

(16) JPRI: One of the reasons the Pentagon gives for keeping U.S. forces in Japan is that because of Japan's generous host-nation support, it is less expensive to base them there than calling them back to the U.S. Will Japan continue its financial support in the next century despite the end of the Cold War?

Taoka: Finance is a more realistic issue than questions of nuclear blackmail. A fiscal crisis is now gripping the Japanese government. As of the end of fiscal year 1996 (March 31, 1997), Japanese government debt will amount to ¥221 trillion (circa US$2 trillion). In addition, local Japanese governments' debts amount to about ¥220 trillion. Japan's total public debt of about $4 trillion is close to 90 percent of Japan's gross national product. This financial crisis is directly affecting the Japanese government's ability to finance its support of the U.S. forces in Japan. In fiscal year 1996 this support amounted to ¥486 billion (approximately $4.2 billion), excluding such indirect expenses as foregone revenues from government-owned land used by the U.S. forces.

(17) JPRI: Then how long can Japan continue to provide financial support for the U.S. forces? Is it going to be suspended soon?

Taoka: The Japanese Government will abide by its existing five-year special agreement to provide financial support for the U.S. forces. But with the expiration of the agreement at the end of fiscal year 2001 (March 2002), Japan will have no choice but to reduce these expenditures. Rising public discontent with tax increases and cuts in public services in order to cope with the fiscal crisis will make continued large subsidies to foreign troops quite difficult.

This kind of criticism is already strong in Okinawa. Its people pay taxes to the Japanese Government, which then uses these tax revenues to keep U.S. bases on their islands. Even though Okinawa prefecture receives large subsidies from the central government as compensation for the heavy concentration of U.S. military bases, the Okinawan people feel that only a small group profits from these payments. They tend to think that those who benefit from the American bases are only land owners (to whom the Japanese Government pays rent for land used by the American bases), construction companies, and civilian employees of the Americans, who also receive their contracts or salaries directly from the Japanese Government.

Rather than waiting for an abrupt cut in financial support for the U.S. forces in 2001, the two governments should today start preparing to adapt to the post-Cold War situation and the financial constraints on Japan. One way to begin to adapt to these conditions would be to reduce significantly the U.S. Marine units on Okinawa, which constitute 63 percent of the American military personnel in the islands and occupy 75 percent of the base areas in the islands.

(18) JPRI: Although the U.S. Marines in Okinawa may not contribute directly to the defense of Japan itself, they may contribute to regional stability, which is also important to Japan.

Taoka: I agree, so I have said that a realistic compromise would be to retain only the 31st MEU (Marine Expeditionary Unit) of approximately 2,000 personnel on Okinawa and move the other Marine units to Hawaii or Guam. The four U.S. amphibious vessels homeported at Sasebo can transport only the 31st MEU, which is therefore a realistic force level. The 31st MEU could be used for various missions, including non-combatant evacuation operations from crisis areas and relief from natural disasters. The United States Navy does not have in-theater sea-lift capacity to move other Marine units from Okinawa to "real forward areas," such as South Korea or the Middle East. The U.S. Navy's amphibious transport capability is 2.5 brigades, which is slightly less than a division even though the United States has three Marine divisions. If other U.S. Marine or Army units were using the limited amphibious and airlift capacity for an emergency in Korea or the Middle East, most of the Marines in Okinawa today would be temporarily stranded there as troops in exile. Americans should realize that Okinawa is not a real forward area because strategic transportation is required to send troops from there to possible war zones.

(19) JPRI: How about North Korea? Many American officials have said that withdrawals of U.S. forces from Japan could trigger a North Korean attack on the south. Do you agree?

Taoka: No. As you have said, one reason given by the Pentagon for continuing to station the 3rd Marine Division in Okinawa is that reducing its presence in any way would send a "wrong signal" to North Korea. But the U.S. Army's 2nd Division is already deployed along the DMZ, and the combined air superiority of the U.S. and ROK air forces is overwhelming. If North Korean leaders should become so irrational or desperate as to launch an attack in the face of the U.S. Army and U.S. Air Force presence in South Korea, one must ask how one Marine division, actually one regimental combat team, located 1,300 km from the DMZ—the distance from Berlin to Sardinia—would help deter them? More to the point, a war in Korea implies the clash of million-man armies on each side. The effect of one lightly equipped Marine regiment airlifted from Okinawa would be negligible in such a context.

(20) JPRI: Why do you and some Japanese politicians say that the U.S. Marines on Okinawa should be moved to Hawaii or Guam but not to California or Australia?

Taoka: The Governor of Hawaii and the Congressman from Guam have both expressed their desire to have the Marines based in their territories. One regiment of the 3rd Marine Division is already stationed in Hawaii, even though its divisional headquarters are in Okinawa. Moving the headquarters, the one infantry regiment, and the one artillery battalion from Okinawa to Hawaii would improve the overall command and control structure of the division. The Governor of Okinawa has said that such a redeployment would please the people of Hawaii, Guam, and Okinawa and that he would be glad to help finance it. There is no question but that there would be strong public support in Japan for its government to help finance the cost of the troop movements and construction of necessary facilities in Hawaii or Guam.

(21) JPRI: As a military historian and analyst, do you think that the U.S.-Japan alliance can be maintained into the 21st century?

Taoka: Yes, I think so. Certainly the end of the Cold War weakened the foundation of the U.S.-Japan alliance. It now resembles a building located on soft, shifting earth. With their statements of determination to maintain present force levels and to cooperate more fully in an emergency, the two governments are trying to save the building by reinforcing it. But making a house heavier when it is already located on soft ground only increases the problem. American and Japanese leaders should instead think of ways to make the structure lighter, which I believe is the best way to ensure that the alliance and friendly relations will persist in the coming century.

SUSTAINABLE DEVELOPMENT IN OKINAWA FOR THE 21ST CENTURY

Masayuki Sasaki

In the Okinawan gubernatorial elections of November 15, 1998, Masahide Ota, the progressive incumbent, was defeated in his bid for a third term by Keiichi Inamine, a candidate backed by local business groups and the prefectural wing of the Liberal Democratic Party. While Ota stuck to his commitment to get rid of the American bases, which for him also represented a major step toward the autonomous development of the prefecture, Inamine blamed Ota's administration for the recession. Inamine promised to secure economic development funds from Tokyo by agreeing to build somewhere in the north of Okinawa Island a joint civil-military airport (one combining American military and Japanese civilian functions) with a time limit of fifteen years attached to the U.S. military component.

During the final stages of the campaign, when the issue had been narrowed to one of "base removal versus economic promotion," the government in Tokyo gave strong backing to the Inamine camp by suddenly announcing, with exquisite timing, that it had abandoned the idea of an offshore base, thus seeking to nullify Ota's promise to get rid of the bases. After Inamine's victory, the government in Tokyo reopened the Okinawa Policy Conference (Okinawa Seisaku Kyogikai), thereby ending a ten-month freeze imposed since Ota's announcement in February 1998 that he would not support construction of an offshore base. Tokyo also promised that it would include an item for Okinawan development in the budget for the coming year.

There is no doubt that Inamine's policies, linking base construction with economic promotion, succeeded in winning the support of the Okinawan public, which was looking for some way out of economic stagnation. Some 375,000 Okinawans voted for Inamine. However, some 340,000 anti-base voters supported Ota, and a public opinion survey conducted during the campaign found 65 percent still in favor of removing the bases from Okinawa. Moves by Inamine to construct a new base within the prefecture will not be easy to implement. Furthermore, Okinawa prefecture's pursuit of large-scale public works as the center-piece of its economic stimulus policies is bound to hinder further the autonomy of the economy. On the eve of the 21st century, Okinawa seems to have chosen the most difficult of paths.

MOVING BEYOND A BASE-DEPENDENT ECONOMY

After two years research and investigation, the Study Group for a Sustainable Society in Okinawa (headed by Professor Ken'ichi Miyamoto of Ritsumeikan University in Kyoto and of which I am a member) takes the view that the way forward into the 21st century is not through the old pattern of dependence on U.S. bases and public works. We emphasize instead endogenous development that mobilizes the energies of the anti-base struggle in order to realize a sustainable society within Okinawa's environmental and resource endowments. In considering Okinawa's prospects for the 21st century, we stress the continuing importance of the *Principles for Okinawan Economic Development* initially put forward by Miyamoto together with Masahiko Kuba (formerly of Ryukyu University) at the time of reversion in 1972 and reformulated several times since then. These are:

(a) To work to transform the base-dependent economy into a normal economy.

(b) To secure the immediate and unconditional return of the main means of production and livelihood, including land, water, transport, and energy, to be used for Okinawan economic development. Their actual use should be decided by a Ryukyuan government (for example, by the Okinawan prefectural government under the present structure) on the basis of popular participation.

(c) To pursue an autonomous mode of development within a framework of preserving the environment and the culture rather than following the mainland development pattern of putting narrow economic interests ahead of all others.

Okinawa has sought to pursue the ideal of peace and cultural exchange within the rapidly developing East Asian region. Because it is suited to being a model of a sustainable society in which humanity lives in symbiotic balance with nature in a fertile, sub-tropical environment, we now wish to add to these three principles the proposal that Okinawa also follow the path of "sustainable development" and that it should seek to become a sustainable society.

Since reversion to Japan in 1972, the Special Measures Law for Promoting Okinawan Development of December 1972 established the goals of "eliminating the gap with the mainland" and "providing the basic conditions for autonomous development." This legislation has been twice extended. In the current Third Okinawan Promotion and Development Plan, which covers the decade from 1992 to 2001, the goal of making the most of Okinawa's regional distinctiveness and turning it into "a center for exchanges with the south" was added to the other two goals.

During the quarter century since 1972, the Japanese government has spent some five trillion yen of public funds in Okinawa, mostly on public works. The goal of "eliminating the gap" with the rest of Japan has been achieved in the sense of providing roads and other forms of infrastructure that are on a par with the rest of Japan. The goal of autonomous development has not been achieved in any sense. Instead, the workings of a system in which local administration is fiscally dependent on subsidies from Tokyo has cut off all sprouts of autonomous development and deepened dependence on the central government. Combining the old base-dependent economy with the subsidy-dependent economy created after reversion has tended to crush all distinctive elements within Okinawa and deprived it of the energies that come from self-government. To proceed with a development process that maintains Okinawa's distinctive natural environment, self-government, including control over the whole range of fiscal administration, must be recovered. Okinawa must replace the standardized construction projects carried out under subsidies from the central government with projects that it itself develops.

THE INTERNATIONAL CITY PLAN

The Ota prefectural government's planning for the future emphasized two aspects—first a Base Return Action Program, which sought to eliminate the bases completely by the year 2015, and second, an International City Plan. Under the three keywords of "peace" *(heiwa)*, "symbiosis" *(kyosei)*, and "autonomy" *(jiritsu)* the International City Plan aimed at converting Okinawa from an Asia-Pacific military bastion into "a center of international exchanges contributing to sustainable development." It aimed at securing the national government's recognition of the principle of "one state, two systems," which would provide the basis for the rapid growth of the Okinawan economy. Once Tokyo agreed to "one state, two systems," Okinawa would then create a Singapore-type international city on the sites left by the closure of U.S. military bases, most of which are concentrated on prime territory in the center and south of the main island of Okinawa. Reductions in the corporate tax rate and suspension of visa requirements in the Free Trade Zone were part of the plan. The Ota prefectural government conceived of its International City as the culmination of the Third Development Plan period, due to end in 2001. Many people welcomed the International City idea as offering Okinawans a 21st century vision, but numerous economists took the view that attracting businesses from the outside and relying on specific "big ticket" projects would still do little to advance Okinawa's economic autonomy.

In April 1997, when the "one state, two systems" demand ran up against strong opposition from central government ministries, the Okinawan government set up a "committee for deliberation on industrial promotion and deregulation," under the chairmanship of the prominent economic writer and commentator Naoki Tanaka. Keiichi Inamine, then representing the world of finance, was a member of that committee, and it was he who presented its report to Governor Ota. The draft, published on September 1, 1997, called for the creation of a prefecture-wide Free Trade Zone in Okinawa. In concrete terms, this meant that foreign goods imported into the prefecture (with the exception of some primary products) would be exempt from tariffs and other charges. It also meant that Japan would have to adopt a special tariff system with reduced tariffs on goods processed within Okinawa using imported materials, liberalize imports through elimination of the import quota framework, speed up and simplify import procedures, cut the corporate income tax, exempt investors from local taxes, and deregulate the transport and basic services sectors. The idea was to implement an All-Okinawa Free Trade Zone by the year 2001.

However, various critical views were expressed by agricultural and industrial groups fearing sudden exposure to international competition. It was agreed that the system should be confined to certain sectors and its implementation delayed till 2010, the target date for abolition of tariffs by the advanced countries agreed to by APEC (the Asia-Pacific Economic Cooperation forum). However, as Yasuo Kurima, a professor at Okinawa International University, has pointed out, there are real problems with implementing a free trade zone in Okinawa since the prefecture's agriculture is protected by tariffs and the import quota system of the Japanese government. These will not be easily given up.

On November 4, 1997, the Okinawan prefectural government, taking note of dissent and opposition within the Prefectural Assembly and from industrial groups, drew up a final draft, entitled, "A New Industrial Promotion Policy for the International City," and presented it to the Tokyo government's Okinawan Policy Conference. Changes in this draft included limiting the Free Trade Zone to specific designated factories and duty free shops within the prefecture and delaying its introduction until 2005 with only gradual expansion thereafter. Opposition by industries within the prefecture, which had been feeling a sharp sense of crisis over the intensification of competition that would follow deregulation and abolition of tariffs, caused this retreat. In the polarization of views within the prefecture, agricultural organizations and some business groups distanced themselves from the Ota government.

In April 1998, based on a revision of the Special Measures Law for Promoting Okinawan Development, a scaled-down Okinawan Special Free Trade Zone was set up. In concrete terms it provided for a 35 percent reduction of corporate income taxes for enterprises located in the zone, reduced taxes on investments, created a special incentive system, and eliminated duties on materials and producers' goods. For a start, the Nakagusuku New Port was designated as part of the Zone. However, at this point it remains unclear what industries the prefecture will be able to attract, and so far the only item recognized under the tariff removal system is processed beef for fast foods such as instant noodles.

It would seem difficult to expect autonomous development to proceed from an International City plan based solely on deregulation and the attraction of foreign businesses into a Free Trade Zone. Instead, endogenous development needs to be at the center of planning. The Okinawan Prefecture Industrial Creativity Action Program, launched by the prefecture's Department of Commerce and Labor in June 1997, deserves consideration in designing an industrial policy that will convert Okinawa into a sustainable society. The chief problems are how to mobilize the energies of the Okinawan towns and villages for economic development and the need to cultivate industries that contribute to autonomy and flexibility. The experience of Yomitan Village constitutes a relevant case study in endogenous local development.

ENDOGENOUS DEVELOPMENT GROWING OUT OF THE ANTI-BASE MOVEMENT: THE CASE OF YOMITAN VILLAGE

Yomitan village has already begun the process of endogenous village revival and development. It is striving to become a "humanistic village sensitive to the environment and culture" by combining the creation of new industries with the promotion of traditional crafts. Situated in the middle of the main island of Okinawa, Yomitan village has a population of 35,000. It is pursuing the sort of regional development in which local people themselves engage in autonomous, self-directed, creative activities. It describes itself in lofty terms as a "village that dreams of earning a Nobel Peace Prize."

In any consideration of Yomitan's history of regional development, the influence of the bases is crucial. This village was the site of the U.S. Army's first landings on Okinawa, and it suffered the loss of around 3,000 people during the subsequent Battle of Okinawa. After the war, the U.S. military appropriated village land, and at the time of reversion in 1972 bases still occupied 73 percent of the village. Following a fierce and concerted struggle by the village executive office, the local assembly, and the people, some of the land was returned in 1978, but even now bases account for 48 percent of the village. Because of their experience of battle and the history of postwar Okinawa, the people of Yomitan are profoundly pacifist. They have held fast to the principles of village-centeredness, local solidarity, and harmony with local surroundings, under the banner of "peace, culture, and creativity," in opposition to "bases, war, and destruction." The same village energies that were first concentrated on base removal have been turned to the promotion of traditional and market industries and a distinctive kind of resort development. In May 1997, they completed the construction of a new city hall, built on former U.S. base land.

Yomitan cultivates its distinctive traditional arts and crafts and has risen to prominence because of its pottery *(yachimun)* and weaving *(yuntanza hazaui).* Its pottery has developed steadily since 1972, when the so-called Living National Treasure, Jiro Kinjo, accepted the village's invitation to set up a kiln. In 1978, when the former Kadena Ammunition Storage Area was returned, it was reborn as Yachimun village. Currently, it is the largest pottery center in Okinawa, with 36 kilns in operation. Sales through the village-run cooperative store are steady and local potters also conduct classes for village people. From the point of view of the promotion of culture and industry, this is a good example of how former base lands may be put to use.

Weaving has been in decline since the war but was revived by the village under the slogan of "creating beauty through the hands and hearts of women." They now produce kimono fabric, table cloths, kimono sashes, and neckties, and output is steadily increasing. Every year fifteen new weavers are trained, and in 1989, 235 people were employed as weavers. The number declined in 1994 to 184, but Yomitan village continues to promote its weaving, seeing it as both an industry based on tradition and an art based on everyday life.

THE YUNTANZA VILLAGE DEVELOPMENT COMPANY AND ITS NETWORKING SYSTEM

In 1992, Yomitan set up the Yuntanza Village Development Company to promote new industries and a relationship of exchange and cooperation among different industries. It started with a capital of fifteen million yen, of which one million each came from the eleven members of the Chamber of Commerce and ¥50,000 each came from 80 local people, including public employees of the village office. Its stated principles are "to enhance the economic worth of Yomitan by creating organic linkages among the natural, historical, cultural, and human assets, tangible and intangible, held in common by the people of the village" and "to create new businesses that combine the economic functions of a resort location with the existing local economic conditions." The company has played a key role in regional development and the promotion of new industries, from processing *beni-imo*, a red sweet potato that is a specialty of Yomitan village, to the sales of pottery and neckties and other products of Yomitan weavers and the launching of new industries in conjunction with resort entrepreneurs from outside.

This small village development company has had a large and multi-faceted impact upon the local economy. Its accomplishments include:

(a) By fostering cooperation among local cultivators of *beni-imo*, it has created a semiprocessing industry, producing *beni-imo* paste for use in various kinds of cakes, breads, ice cream, and so on.

(b) It has provided incentives for all the farming families of the village to profit from the sale of their *beni-imo*. Since the task of peeling the sweet potatoes is done by local people, including the elderly and the handicapped, *beni-imo* cultivation and processing has contributed to a participatory economy in which all residents can share.

(c) The company has opened up markets in Tokyo, Nagoya, Osaka, and other cities, as well as in the village itself and elsewhere in Okinawa. By linking processing and manufacturing on the one hand and marketing on the other, it has enhanced the profits of the entire region. Both the acreage devoted to *beni-imo* in the village and the size of the harvest have increased rapidly. At a time when the output of other agricultural products such as sugar cane is declining, the development of *beni-imo* and other local speciality products has played an important role in helping to stabilize agricultural income.

(d) At a site within the village adjacent to a resort hotel, the Yuntanza company set up a satellite company called the Zampa Golf Club. It uses biotechnology rather than agricultural chemicals for course maintenance. Zampa advertises that "We protect the natural environment from the harm of agricultural chemicals, and we protect the health of golfers and workers." After demonstrating the effectiveness of their biological agents in this way, they then set up an affiliated company, Bio-Yomitan, to develop and seek business outlets for its environmental-protection technologies.

Industry linkages around the development of the *beni-imo* as a local specialty product have flowed from agriculture to manufacturing and also to the commercial sector of retail outlets and then to the advanced industry sector of biotechnology. Yuntanza Company is at the center of the network, and it serves as the base for industrial development. At present it is a stock company, but in fact it bears many of the marks of a nonprofit organization. This can be seen from its management philosophy, under which even though the company is now producing profits it pays no salaries to its managers. In other words, it strives to contribute to the industrial development of the village through strengthening the networks of local culture and industry, and it is expected to continue playing a central role as a nonprofit organization in future industrial development. Furthermore, as an organization that connects local culture and industry, backed by the residents, it revives in a contemporary form the traditional mutual help association of Okinawa's indigenous society.

ENVIRONMENTALLY SENSITIVE RESORT DEVELOPMENT

One of the basic principles of Yomitan village, utilizing its naturally beautiful seaside locale, is to include resort development as part of village building. Yomitan strives to combine balanced development in which the resort and the village are mutually dependent and beneficial for the livelihood and local culture of the village. It wants resort development to enhance local commercial services and use local products in order to enlarge the village's overall commercial base. In contrast to the common model of resort development that relies on outside capital, Yomitan has set forth the following principles:

(a) Partnerships with outside capital. Yomitan Village's resort development began with large-scale resort hotel construction by private capital on former base lands along the coast. The village and the incoming businesses drew up a development protocol, and the plan of the resorts went ahead based on local history and culture combined with the building of hotels. Disagreements between the outside businesses and village policy could lead to revisions following discussion, but the village's final decision always prevailed and it retained its sovereignty. Elsewhere in Okinawa, by contrast, in districts such as neighboring Onna village, the common pattern has been for outside developers to buy land for hotel sites and develop them as they saw fit. In Yomitan hotel sites can only be leased, with the ownership and rental rights remaining in the hands of the local landowners.

(b) Environmental protection framework. Yomitan has blocked excessive damage to the natural environment through by-laws that require golf course developers to introduce biotechnologies and forbid the use of agricultural chemicals. Waste water from resort hotels must be put through a three-stage purification process so that it can be used locally for irrigation. The hotels meet the costs of this processing. Businesses that do not agree with the village's position on protecting the environment are not allowed to undertake development.

(c) Private beaches are banned. Although private beaches are forbidden in Okinawa prefecture under the regulations on coastal usage, in practice a number of resorts, including the famous Onna Village, have enclosed beachfront land in such a way as to prevent free public access to the beach. Yomitan has not only forbidden private beaches but has developed a municipal beach, using funds that the two large-scale resort hotels operating within the village have donated to the village.

(d) Linkages with local industries. By agreement with the hotel management, the Yomitan resorts use local agricultural produce in their restaurants, in contrast to the practice of resorts developed by outside capital, where there is virtually no contact between the resort chain and local farmers. Yomitan intends to use resort development to strengthen such local linkages. One unusual example of this is the practice of setting up a "Yomitan morning market" within the grounds of the hotels. Village people and the Yuntanza Company set up stalls where hotel guests and local residents can buy locally produced fresh vegetables and fruits.

(e) Generation of local employment. Under an agreement with the hotels to give employment preference to local people, each hotel management hires from a local employment agency a maximum of 250 people for its staffs of about 450 people. Contracts for services such as cleaning are given to other local businesses that give preference to handicapped people.

It should be clear that resort development in Yomitan is markedly different from the sort of development by outside businesses that has caused so many problems elsewhere in Okinawa and Japan. Because local capital is too scarce for Okinawa to undertake resort development on its own and because a lot of businesses have already come in from the outside, there is a limit to how fast Okinawa can shift to endogenous resort development. Furthermore, taxes paid by existing hotels are a major revenue source for Yomitan village, making up 11 percent of its property tax revenues and 6.7 percent of total village tax revenues. Under these circumstances, the important thing for future Okinawan resort development is for local government authorities to enter into partnership agreements with outside capital under which they retain ultimate control.

The endogenous local development of Yomitan village is based on the clear understanding of the village authorities and residents, mostly farmers and small and middle-sized businessmen, that the basic industry of the village is agriculture. Other villages may differ somewhat, but Yomitan-style local development has the following broad characteristics.

First is the cultivation of local industrial linkages using networks among the residents. It is necessary to construct a system based on the sort of cooperation and solidarity that characterized the communities of old Okinawa, the village corporatism called *yuimaru*. The best approach for now is to rely on a kind of contemporary nonprofit organization for the promotion and revitalization of local districts in which the local people can be collectively engaged in planning and implementation.

Second is the principle of control over and partnership with outside capital. Since the 1970s, Okinawa has permitted large-scale resort development by mainland businesses, and such development continues today. But Yomitan village has demonstrated through its village development company, Yuntanza, that Okinawans can retain some control over outside capital.

Third is the way in which endogenous local development draws upon base removal energies. Since there are still many large-scale U.S. bases in Okinawa and in most cases the bases incorporate the lands most suitable for industry, they represent a serious opportunity cost to Okinawa. The return and efficient use of the bases is an urgent task for Okinawan industrial promotion in addition to being the fervent desire of the Okinawan people on other grounds. The efficient use of base lands has been discussed in various documents, including the "Base Return Action Program" and the "Plan for the Establishment of an International City," but mostly these schemes have been conventional proposals for large-scale, outside-capital projects not at all based on Okinawa's distinctiveness. It would be highly desirable to convert these plans into grass roots, resident-participatory, endogenous regional development proposals, bringing to bear the energies generated in the base return movement.

Yomitan village's experience is a model, but it is not the only example in Okinawa. Ogimison village in Yanbaru in the extreme north of Okinawa Island is pursuing its regional promotion and revitalization through a revival of traditional crafts such as the manufacture of *bashoufu* (banana hemp cloth) and the development of the distinctive *shikasa* juice from a local variety of citrus fruit. The city of Nago, also in the north and close to the U.S. Marine base at Camp Schwab, is drawing up comprehensive plans based on the assumption that its distinctive location and conditions are not disadvantages, as they might seem when seen from Tokyo or Naha, but positive advantages to be fostered. The residents of Ishigaki Island have taken a stand for their own version of "island promotion" in opposition to letting outside resort developers buy local land. Yet it seems that insufficient attention is still being paid by the prefecture as a whole to assessing these experiences and comprehensively carrying them forward.

CONCLUSION

Governor-elect Inamine has been quoted as saying that it will be necessary to draw up completely new plans for the 21st century, since "the international city plan is like a rice cake that just exists on paper and has no substance in reality." It is true that this plan started out from vague notions of an "international city" built around a "free port" and a "free trade zone" and was not derived from the realities of the Okinawan economy. Moreover, it took too roseate a view of the realities of the global economy in which international investment capital flows abundantly. However, it did incorporate the lofty goals and ideas of transforming Okinawa from an Asia-Pacific military encampment into an international citadel for peace, internationalism, eco-tourism, reliance on natural energy resources, and exchanges within the world of sub-tropical cultures. Since global investment capital has brought the Asian economy to crisis, I take the view that it is necessary to draw up a "21st Century Plan for Okinawa" containing the following points.

(a) A "21st Century Okinawa Plan" must take into account the whole prefecture, including towns, villages, and outlying islands. Its key words should be peace, environmental preservation, cultural distinctions, welfare, and creativity. Its chief aim should be the conversion of Okinawa into a sustainable society.

(b) Priority should be given to constructing systems that foster indigenous cultural and industrial creativity rather than large-scale projects such as airports and harbors and the bringing in of foreign or mainland businesses as major players. Locally generated development should be supported by technical development and training. In concrete terms, this could mean establishing (or reinforcing) advanced research and educational facilities in bio-engineering and the policy and information sciences to help design environmentally friendly industries and an environmentally friendly society. It could also mean the establishment of a facility for training actors for a future national dance theatre.

(c) The prefecture should set up a central foundation for the support of endogenous development which would draw upon the experiences and wisdom of local government authorities, villages, and traditional cooperatives. It would give financial, technical, and administrative support to small, cooperative or non-profit organizations striving to set up enterprises in the fields of environmental preservation, contributions to peace, new technologies (including multi-media technology), the arts and crafts, welfare, and eco-tourism, especially to women entrepreneurs in these fields. It would also seek ways comprehensively to expand the network-style industrial structure.

(d) The system of public works practiced up until now by the Okinawa Development Agency should be reformed and self-government in Okinawa (including fiscal authority) should be greatly expanded in order to foster creative businesses that are sensitive to the natural environment of the prefecture.

The peoples of the Asia-Pacific region have become objects of speculation by international investment capital. These invasions by foreign capital are destroying the Asian peoples' economic foundations. Adoption by them of endogenous development strategies as outlined here could constitute a beacon of hope. Okinawa might thus become an international model for peace and sustainable development.

[Note: A version of this article first appeared in Japanese in *Sekai,* January 1999, pp. 104-112.]

OKINAWAN DILEMMAS: CORAL ISLANDS OR CONCRETE ISLANDS

Gavan McCormack

In the late 1990s, the words "Okinawa" and "problem" are almost synonymous. The "problem," as most commonly understood, is that these lush, semi-tropical Japanese southern islands host a huge U.S. military base structure, which their people clearly do not want. But there are other reasons for seeing Okinawa as problem-bound. I believe that Okinawa is a microcosm through which the unsustainability of the Japanese system as a whole becomes visible. The poverty of a simply "cut the bases; expand development" formula for the future of Okinawa is demonstrated by the fact that the Japanese government now insists that the only way forward is to combine both, bases and development, and promises to do just that. Certainly, the bases should be removed, but just as certainly, I believe, development must be re-thought.

The achievement of "parity with the mainland" *(hondo-nami)* has been the driving force of Okinawan politics for the past generation, but it has been a Sisyphean quest: irrespective of the effort devoted to it the goal seems ever to recede. The bounty of nature, the beauty of the environment, and the sophistication of its culture, were Okinawa's distinctive "affluence," but they are being sacrificed in the quest for this chimerical mainland-style affluence that depends on the constant creation of new and artificial needs rather than the satisfaction of real ones.

The relationship to the Japanese state and economy also has obvious implications for Okinawan identity. So long as the gospel of the 1960s and 1970s was mainland parity, Okinawa's problems would be resolved by elevation and absorption within the higher mainland state; its distinctiveness was almost equivalent to its backwardness. The superiority of Japanese political and economic organization was believed with unquestioning fervor, and the aspiration to share its vitality and dynamism was universal. But are the Okinawans just sub-tropical Japanese, or are they/do they wish to be a different people? And if the answer is the latter, is the Japanese state of today capable of reconceptualizing and restructuring itself as a multicultural, diverse, politically and economically decentralized polity? Could a "one-state, two-systems" formula be discovered that might accommodate the different aspirations of areas such as Okinawa?

BACKGROUND

The chain of islands—around sixty of them inhabited and many more not—that make up Okinawa stretch for 1,100 kilometers (683 miles) along the Western Pacific between Japan's Kagoshima prefecture and Taiwan. The two most northerly islands of Tanegashima and Yakushima, which lie between 30 and 31 degrees north, were cut off from the Ryukyu kingdom during the 16th century and so they are excluded from consideration here. Slightly further south, however, between 28 and 29 degrees, the island of Amami, also administratively now a part of Kagoshima prefecture, is sufficiently close in cultural identity and political history to be thought of as part of the Ryukyu group.

The main island of Okinawa is situated between 26 and 27 degrees north, but further south, between 24 and 25 degrees, lie the Miyako and Yaeyama Islands (or the Sakishima Group), much closer to Taiwan than to anywhere else in Japan. With Okinawa island, they constitute part of Okinawa prefecture. Administratively, the degree of control from mainland Japan, in fact from the southern Kyushu administrative center of Kagoshima, weakened with distance, and a distinctive Ryukyuan (for most purposes identical with Okinawan) cultural identity developed in various of the islands, Okinawa itself being most notable.

Geologically the islands, linked to the Asian continental landmass until a million or so years ago, are now separated from it by a gulf sufficiently deep and dangerous to have allowed the emergence in relative isolation of a rich and distinctive botanical and zoological environment. One measure of this is that each ten square kilometers of Okinawan territory is biologically more than twenty times richer in life-forms than its equivalent elsewhere in Japan. In purely botanical terms, the differential is probably greater, as much as 45 to 1 according to one source. Such are its riches that

Okinawa is sometimes referred to as "Asia's Galapagos." The climate is humid and sub-tropical, with an average year-round temperature in Naha, the Okinawan capital, of 22.4°C (72°F). It is 16°C (60°F) even in the winter month of January, which is also the month when the cherry blossom is celebrated. The average rainfall is 2,000 millimeters (about 79 inches) a year, somewhat higher than the average for the rest of Japan, and half of it falls in the summer typhoon season between May and September. Much of the rain tends to flow quickly to the sea via the very short Okinawan rivers (the longest of which, the Urauchi on Iriomote Island, is a mere 19.4 kilometers, or 12 miles).

In pre-modern times, the combination of mild sub-tropical climate and good rainfall with a rich marine reef environment made life relatively comfortable. From the 15th century a flourishing autonomous state, the Ryukyuan Kingdom, emerged, developed its distinctive cultural and artistic style, and engaged in trading and cultural relations throughout the East and Southeast Asian region. Although it later became virtually obliterated from conventional historical memory, pre-modern Okinawa was an open, non-militarized, economic, cultural and political system, flourishing on the frontiers of the early modern Asia-Pacific. It constituted a vital and distinctive realm, from which the emerging 21st century Asian-Pacific order might learn much.

Nineteenth century visitors referred with pleasure to the lush and relaxed atmosphere of Okinawa (then known to the outside world as the Ryukyus, or the Loochoos), and when the U.S. Navy's Commodore Perry sailed in on his Black Ships, en route to open Japan in 1853, his scientific advisers reported on a fertile, friendly, and prosperous state, a "most rich and highly cultivated rural landscape," with an agriculture more akin to horticulture, in a "system which could scarcely be improved," and its villages "quite romantic, and more beautiful than any of like pretensions I have ever seen." The French missionary, Furé, who spent the years 1858-61 in Naha, described the villages as "resembling the beautiful gardens of England." It was by then diminished from its flourishing 16th century peak and maintaining a precarious autonomy through judicious expressions of respect towards its two powerful and sensitive neighbors: the kingdom of Satsuma (one of the domains, centering on Kagoshima, making up the loosely linked Japanese state

263

structure) to the north, and the Ch'ing court in Beijing to the West. Having no armed forces, the Okinawan kings relied on their relative remoteness and their diplomatic skills to preserve their autonomy. As the new world order of expansive, rapacious, and militarized modern states spread in the era that followed Perry, that soon changed.

Once Imperial Japan constituted itself as a modern state (1868), it moved quickly to consolidate its frontiers. To the south that meant extinguishing the independence of the Ryukyus and incorporating them as Okinawa prefecture (1879), thereby opening the way to the process of assimilation as a discriminated frontier province, and impoverishment. By the time of the Osaka Industrial Exposition of 1903, Okinawan "natives" were on display, along with Ainu and Taiwanese aboriginal people, as primitives. Ultimately Okinawa was sacrificed by imperial Japan in the catastrophic conflagration of March-to-June 1945, when one-quarter of the population died. Thereafter the Japanese backwater, Okinawa, became the American "hub of the Pacific." It remained an American military outpost for the next twenty-seven years, a kind of East Asian Panama. In Japan proper, the U.S. occupation ended in 1952; in Amami, the most northerly of the Ryukyu islands, in December of the following year; but in Okinawa itself and its adjacent islands it lasted until 1972.

Despite political reversion, the U.S. military presence on the island of Okinawa was maintained virtually intact. The best agricultural lands, and much of the seas and skies, remained subject to U.S. military control. Two decades later, the Cold War ended and the enemy against whom the base structure had been directed collapsed, but the base complex (75 percent of U.S. military facilities in Japan, and 20 percent of the land area of Okinawa's main island) was still preserved with only minor modification. Some redefinition was negotiated following major protests in the late 1990s, but as the terms of the new U.S.-Japan Defense Guidelines became known during 1997 and 1998 it became clear that the Okinawan demands would not be met. The subordination of the islands to military purposes would be not one jot diminished.

REVERSION AND DEVELOPMENT

Okinawa was undoubtedly neglected, both during the

prewar and wartime decades, as the most backward Japanese prefecture (ultimately devastated by war), but also during the 1945-72 U.S. period. Its industrial and social infrastructure of communications, education, health and welfare was inadequate; the economy during these two and a half decades heavily depended on revenue from the bases; and there was no plan for Okinawan development as such. Twenty-five years after reversion, however, discontent still remains strong. The richest lands and most important locations remain outside Okinawan control, which makes it impossible to draw up any integrated plan for the development of Okinawa as a whole. Okinawan people feel that they are third-class citizens in their own land, with key decisions affecting them being taken by overlords in Washington and Tokyo. Furthermore, the bureaucratic and corporate power of Tokyo is so much greater than that of local Okinawa, and Tokyo priorities are rooted in the interests of Japan as a state or in the global economy, that a distinctively Okinawan identity has been difficult to conceive or implement. The sense of grievance and victimhood is strong. The Okinawan problem is how to convert these essentially passive and negative sentiments into a positive sense of subjectivity and shared Okinawan identity, and to generate an Okinawa-first scenario for the future.

During the Ota administration of the 1990s, the debate was reopened on strategies to take Okinawa in the direction of a promised land of demilitarization and prosperity. Despite the militarization of the 1945-72 period, at reversion Okinawa enjoyed certain large assets: its forests, coral reefs, rivers and fields were more or less unspoiled, its lagoon fisheries abundant, its climate mild, and its agriculture rich and sustainable. Essentially, in the 25 years that followed, in the name of "development," the patterns of mainland Japan's political economy were superimposed on Okinawa. The economy of post-reversion Okinawa has been described in terms of "three K's:" *kichi* (bases), *kokyo jigyo* (public works) and *kanko* (tourism)—a triple external dependence, partly on Washington but largely on Tokyo. Locally generated *(naihatsu-teki)* elements gradually shrank, sustainability diminished, and Okinawa became in many respects just like anywhere else in Japan. The bounty of nature was squandered or depreciated, and the once base-dependent economy bequeathed by the U.S. gradually evolved into a public-works-dependent economy.

After 1972, the agriculture and fisheries sector slowly diminished in importance, and manufacturing remained at a low level. Bases slowly declined in economic significance from 19.4 percent of revenue to 5 percent. This was far from insignificant: at ¥160 billion per year, the income from the bases was more than that from primary and secondary industry combined, and it was nearly half as much as the income from tourism. The most distinctive feature of the economy of post-reversion Okinawa (and Amami), however, has been the centrality of public works. Okinawa ranks Number One among Japanese prefectures in terms of the dependence of its economy on public works. In the 27 years from reversion in 1972, just under ¥5 trillion was poured into Okinawa, 90 percent of which went into public works or infrastructure development.

The subsidies from Tokyo were funneled via the major Tokyo ministries, especially Construction (roads and dams), Agriculture and Fisheries (land "improvement" and forest roads), and Transport (harbors). The system worked to extend to Okinawa the characteristic patterns of Japanese-style development, and the unmistakable stamp of these bureaucratic fiefdoms is more sharply etched for the fact of having been concentrated in a relatively short time. The early years of reversion, from 1972, were also the years of the ascendancy of "Kakuei" politics, when Prime Minister Kakuei Tanaka was pursuing his agenda of "reconstructing the Japanese archipelago."

The two central fruits of this period in Okinawa were the Kin Bay project and the Okinawa Marine Expo of 1975. Upon reversion, the islands were divided into various development zones, in accordance with Tokyo designs for decentralized growth. Mainland business was to be induced to invest and thereby bring the islands up to the industrialization levels of the rest of Japan. The Kin Bay project (on the east side of Okinawa's main island) amounted to a plan for a huge industrial base, to be built on a 33,000 hectare (81,543 acre) site of reclaimed land, which would comprise crude oil storage facilities, a refinery, a petrochemical plant, steel works, shipyards, a nuclear power plant, and an aluminum refining plant. By the time of the first "oil shock" of 1973, the oil storage and refinery were already operating, and a road had been built across the Bay irrevocably altering its ecology. But the rest of the grand scheme was never fulfilled, nor were the other designated zones developed. The Marine Expo of 1975 was planned and implemented. It was not only an event, but the central element in a program of road, harbor and airport construction, water and sewage works, and regulation *(seibi)* of rivers and coast. The Marine Expo of 1975 gradually shaded into a profound long-term transformation out of which the tourist industry also evolved.

YANBARU: ITS PAST AND FUTURE

Okinawa's political economy has three primary poles—military bases, public works, and tourism. Yanbaru, the large, 27,000 hectares (66,717 acres) sub-tropical forest in the northern part of Okinawa Island, illustrates all three. About one third of it is under U.S. military control (the Northern and Aha Training Areas), and has thus been preserved more-or-less intact, set aside by the U.S. for jungle training. Under the joint U.S.-Japan agreement of 1996, half of this U.S.-controlled area is slated for return, provided various conditions are met, by the year 2002.

The forest is largely made up of low (300 to 400 meters) hills covered with evergreen oak *(itajii* and *urajirogashi)*, various subtropical trees, wild orchids, azaleas, wild cherry, ferns, mistletoe and other distinctive shrubs and flowers. It is also home to many kinds of rare and distinctive native fauna, including the flightless bird known as the Okinawa rail *(Yanbaru kuina)*, the Pryer's woodpecker *(noguchigera)*, pygmy woodpecker *(kogera)*, Ryukyu scops owl *(konohazuku)*, Ryukyu robin *(akahige)*, and many unique or extremely rare species of turtle, rat, frog, snake, butterfly, moth, newt, fish, beetle, and other insects. However, the best current estimate is that only about 10,000 hectares is today really pristine, broadleaf forest, and most of that (ca. 6,000 hectares) because it falls within the U.S. base jurisdiction. In the 25 years of reversion, half of the area returned has been subject to various forms of development, ranging from clear-cutting to "undergrowth removal," in the process of "cultivated natural forest regulation works" *(ikusei tennen-rin seibi jigyo)*.

The Japanese model of development attributes a peculiar significance to what is known as *seibi*. *Seibi* is a characteristic modern Japanese word, common in general combinations such as *infra-seibi* (provision of infrastructure), or with words for roads, city water supply and sewage, rivers, coastline, ports and harbors. It means "regulating," "straightening out," or perhaps most simply the "fixing" of land, river, and sea—the conquest of the environment. As Okinawa came to the modern Japanese system late and in a poor, semi-destitute condition, it was in no position to query the wisdom or appropriateness of imposing over the delicate coral and sub-tropical forest environment the same public works practices and the same collusive structures of mainland Japan's "construction state." During the quarter-century that followed reversion, these patterns and practices were firmly established, and the land, rivers, coast and coral were indeed subjected to *seibi.*

The fate of the Yanbaru rivers after reversion is instructive. Between 1974 and 1997, six dams were built, three more are under construction, and at least one more is planned. On the eastern side of the Yanbaru, the chain of dams form a cascade of mountain water channeled south, tumbling from Benoki, via Fungawa, Aha, Shinkawa, and Fukuji Dams, and a set of pipes and tunnels, to the more densely populated central and southern parts of the island. On the western side, the waters are channeled via a chain of nine pumping stations which sit astride the mostly small rivers, siphoning off their water into the same southward-directed complex of pipes and pumping stations to the central and southern parts of the island. The water, which constitutes the life-blood of the Yanbaru, is now appropriated almost exclusively for the center and south of the island, for town water, resort water, and agricultural and industrial water. The link between mountain and sea is broken, the flow of nutrient to the coral and marine life cut off, and mouths of the enfeebled rivers gradually become blocked. Although the upper reaches and watershed areas of the dams still remain within the U.S. military zone, the hand of the Japanese construction state has already reached across this frontier sufficiently to prefigure its eventual intent.

SEIBI: FIXING THE LAND

The decades of Okinawa's return to Tokyo were decades of rapid degeneration in the quality of Japan's forests as a whole, and that tendency has been reproduced in Okinawa.

The same policy and market forces operated to give priority to economic exploitation over environmental conservation or ecological preservation. Although the short-term economics of the market dictated the clearing of old forest and the planting of fast-growing varieties of pine, the sub-tropical forest, once cleared, tends quickly to lose its thin layer of nutrient top-soil, which washes into river and sea. Five-thousand hectares (12,355 acres) of Yanbaru forest was converted to plantation, and the income of Kunigami Village now derives almost wholly from its heavily subsidized forest works and chip plant. The village has reportedly already earmarked for logging the Northern Training Area forest due to revert to it in the new century.

From the narrow, economic viewpoint, the continuing process of "development" made a certain sense, if only because the employment effect of such projects was considerable. By the late 1990s, there were some thirty public works contractors in Kunigami (population 6,000), all of whom therefore had a vested interest in the forest's continuing development-cum-depletion. Yet the economic value of plantation forest is likely to be short-lived and far outweighed by the long-term costs of coping with the complex damage caused. The mountains, especially those subject to clear-cutting and re-forestation *(zorin),* lose their capacity to retain water and soil drains off, clogging river and coast, species are lost, and rivers and sea degenerate.

Between 1977 and 1994, the Okuni Forest Road was constructed for 35.5 kilometers (22 miles) through the heart of the Yanbaru. Costing over ¥4.5 billion (80 percent from national and 20 percent from prefectural funds), this five-meter-wide, concrete-based, bitumen road opened the forest to development. The new road also opened the forest to hitherto unknown feral animals—dogs, cats and mongoose—as well as to 4-wheel-drive vehicles which brought poachers, thieves, tourists, and even (according to some reports) groups of karaoke addicts who set up all-night stalls in the darkness of the forest. Thanks to this "development," pollution and garbage proliferate, and the prospects for survival of the forest's wild inhabitants are diminished.

"Land improvement" *(tochi kairyo)* is another policy with wide environmental implications. It means clearing, straightening, draining, and engineering of lands, usually for agricultural purposes. In Okinawa's case such improvement

269

was supposed to help farmers plunged into crisis by the shocks accompanying reversion and opening to the mainland's agricultural market. However, during the 1970s and 1980s, Tokyo was simultaneously paying farmers elsewhere in the country to take their fields out of production and opening sector after sector to the global market. If Japanese farmers elsewhere found that difficult, those in Okinawa found it doubly so. The rationale of Okinawan land improvement was not so much designed seriously to promote Okinawa's agriculture (let alone its agricultural competitiveness) but to incorporate Okinawa into the national *doken kokka* system of public-works-based, collusive and corrupt political economy. Undoubtedly some Okinawans welcomed it as part of what they believed to be the attainment of "parity with the mainland," particularly when at least the initial costs were met by Tokyo. But, as with so much else that was done, it was not spontaneously chosen and requested by Okinawa but imposed by Tokyo.

The effects of land improvement have been at best ambiguous. The major beneficiaries are the *dokenya,* often small-scale construction companies (as in Kunigami Village), which do the work and whose livelihood depends largely upon securing contract after contract. Some farmers also reap a benefit, but it is often short-lived and followed by costs likely to be much greater, in the sense that a major effect of the land improvement is soil runoff and discharge into rivers and sea. Every year, according to a 1993-94 study, some 320,000 tons of top-soil are washed from Okinawa's fields and forests into the rivers and sea, with land improvement being the major cause (57 percent), followed by agriculture (33 percent), and U.S. military activities (9 percent).

These various developments combined to bring to the Yanbaru something with which the rest of modern Japan is already familiar: the rule that levels of bio-diversity decline in almost inverse proportion as economic growth indices rise. Okinawa University's Jun Ui, the pioneer of modern environmental studies in Japan, estimates that since Okinawa's reversion 90 percent of the pristine nature of the island as a whole has been lost. By now, probably extinct species include the Okinawan giant bat, the Ryukyuan wood pigeon, the Daito long-beaked cuckoo, and the Daito wren, with many others threatened. Indeed, Yanbaru is home to no less than 88 of the 283 species listed as "endangered" for Japan as a whole.

So far as mammals are concerned, Yanbaru, with the rest of the Okinawan and Amami islands and also the South-eastern Ogasawara island group, constitute peculiarly precious places, home to nearly half (46 percent) of Japan's surviving mammals. Half of Japan's 174 land and sea mammal species are already either extinct or in grave danger of extinction, and the pattern for flora, other animals and insects, and bird life, is similar. In Amami, a staggering 247 varieties of birds have been recorded. Of Yanbaru birds, the Okinawa rail *(Yanbaru kuina)* is a particularly delicate species, vulnerable because it does not fly. Discovered in 1981, it went on the endangered list soon afterward. The Pryer's woodpecker *(noguchigera),* which burrows and nests only in the dead branches of old oak trees—and insists on building a fresh nest each year—is also very vulnerable. Policies that favor opening the forest to development and fast-growing and easily harvested varieties of timber for chipping, are inimical to birds such as these, and estimates of surviving *noguchigera* range from 80 to 200. The cause of such birds may be easy to promote because their delicate beauty is apparent even to the untrained eye, but the fate of all sorts of bats, bugs, beetles, butterflies, mice, rats, and so on, is no less crucial; the crisis affects the ecosystem as a whole.

Other, even quite remote, islands also suffered from the onslaught of agricultural "modernization." Hateruma is a tiny (15 kilometer circumference), more-or-less flat, island lying in the most southern latitude of any Japanese territory. With a population of merely 600, it has no river, relying upon careful cultivation of the waters that accumulate as the rains percolate into underground storage. With "improvement," however, much of its forest was cleared, including the wind-break stands, allowing storms to sweep unchecked across the island. The natural cycle of percolation and storage thus fails, and the underground water begins to dry up. The modernizers have offered a new solution—something that was never necessary before—a desalination plant. That means, of course, escalating water costs. Islanders have begun to fear that modernization and improvement may turn their little island into a desert.

However severe the problems of land development or improvement on Okinawa Island, as well as Hateruma and other outlying islands, the thinking at work in such cases is the same as that guiding assumptions about value and development throughout all Japan's regions: nature developed or improved is superior to raw nature, the former contributes to the GDP, while the latter has no economic significance. This is true even in the case of land at the center of the U.S.-Japan negotiations of 1996-97—the huge U.S. Marine Corps Futenma Air Station that sits astride Ginowan City just outside Naha and which the U.S. promised to return between 2001 and 2003. The post-return prospect for the patches of forest *(amekunomori)* that have survived or grown around the military facilities is for clearance and development of one kind or another, not for preservation. Developmentalism, in other words, is seen as the promise accompanying reversion, and not as a threat. In common with other regions that perceive themselves to be backward and are intent upon closing the gap with affluence, Okinawans tend to see their land and sea as a resource, rarely grasping the difference between what economists describe as resources on the one hand and nature as the ultimate ground and source of value on the other. The modern insistence on market rationalization, economies of scale, and maximization of growth, sits ill upon the complex harmonies of the sub-tropical natural order.

Since improvement of the land has been supposedly for the benefit of agriculture and fisheries, how has this sector fared since reversion? Okinawa's once self-sufficient rice economy was drastically shaken-up by the impact of imports first from the U.S., then from Japan proper. Having squared, rationalized, and often irrigated its fields, and having reorganized its agricultural sector to meet the requirements of bureaucratic Tokyo conceptions of it as an industry, Okinawan farmers are still hard-put to compete in the globally open agricultural commodity market. Cash crops—sugar, pineapples, pork, even flowers—are proving either marginal or exact so heavy a toll from the environment as to be unsustainable in the long term.

Sugar cane and pineapples were two crops thought to be specially suited to Okinawa. With liberalization of pineapple imports (1990), however, Okinawa's fruit was costing about two to three times the world market price. Its canneries shrank from 23 to 1 (1997), and only a heavy subsidy from Tokyo kept the industry going at all. A 1995-96 study found pineapple plantations, which accounted for only 3 percent of Okinawa's agriculture, responsible for over half of the soil run-off on the islands as a whole. Sugar cane was similarly problematic, with Okinawan sugar costing seven to eight times world market prices for raw sugar.

Some new agricultural sectors, such as the pork and (cut) flower industries, have been more successful. Both have a significant export orientation, but they too exact a different kind of price. In the case of flowers, the industry is increasingly conducted along mainland lines, in vinyl house structures with heavy reliance on energy and chemical inputs. Insecticides, at 3,661 kilograms (8,054 pounds) per year, are the most commonly used agricultural chemicals in Okinawa, and seven of the nine varieties employed are des-ignated as toxic. As for pork, Okinawa currently has 300,000 pigs, an inflated stock made possible by the adop-tion of extraordinarily lax effluent emission standards. With each pig producing effluent equivalent to between six and ten humans, wastes equivalent to those of between two and three million people are poured virtually untreated into the rivers and sea. As Ui notes, it is highly ironic that this should be the case, in the name of promoting an industry, even as vast sums are expended on the processing of human wastes.

SEIBI: FIXING THE WATER

Traditionally, the Okinawan population was concentrated in the center and south of the main island because this was where the richest sources of water were to be found, while the forested north of the island was left more-or-less untouched. A complex system of *ka,* springs or wells, was fed by rainwater as it percolated and circulated under-ground. This precious resource was carefully tended, high levels of purity were maintained and the gods of these springs were revered. When Perry's expedition observed Okinawa in the 1850s, they were especially impressed with Okinawa's "beautifully clear and pellucid streams" which seemed "universally distributed over almost every mile of its surface, and in the pure fresh springs, finding their way out from among the crevices of every hill side, and often near the summits." Immense care over water reticulation and the avoidance of erosion seemed to Perry to be the "central considerations in all their operations."

The Ministry of Construction has concentrated on the building of roads and water supply systems, and on the concreting of riverbeds and coastlines, determined to bring Okinawa up to mainland levels in these respects. In the decades since reversion, the traditional system of reliance on rivers and springs was replaced by a "modern," mainland system based on centralized, piped water and sewage systems. The cost of installation was prodigious, estimated at about ¥2 million per person, but cost was deemed an irrelevance because the money was all coming from Tokyo. As the populated sections of Okinawa were, from 1972 onward, transformed along the lines of mainland water practices, water consumption grew steadily, the traditional springs began to dry up, and the springs and rivers of central and southern Okinawa Island became polluted by a combination of agricultural chemicals and red-soil run-off from road and agricultural modernization works. Three of Okinawa's rivers now rank among the five most polluted rivers in Japan. Because the mainland practice of regulating rivers by concreting the bottom and sides (sanmenbari) has also been widely adopted, with disastrous effects on local stream ecology, much more water has to be extracted from the Yanbaru.

Whereas Okinawa's rivers were once renowned for their purity, today they are three-colored—red, white, or black, depending on the chemical composition of the different soils which, eroded and dislodged by public works, flow into them with the rains. Overall, and especially in the north of Okinawa Island, red (or red-yellow), the color of the highly acidic Paleozoic phyllite (agrillaceous schist), is the most common; after rain, the rivers and bays look as if nature itself were hemorrhaging. White is the color of the slightly alkaline Cenozoic Ryukyu limestone rock of the south of the island. Although less conspicuous it has the same causes and the same effect, especially in reducing sea transparency and stifling coral. Black is the color of the untreated wastes of the pig industry, especially in the center and south of the island. Perry's crew would be hard-put in the late 1990s to recognize in these red, black and white streams the "pellucid" waters that delighted and impressed them 140 years ago.

TOURISM

Tourism is a major Okinawan industry. The 1975 Marine Expo marked the beginning of mainland attention to the tourism potential of Okinawa's tropical climate and unspoiled beaches, presaging the wave of steel and concrete that was to sweep over the islands in subsequent decades. Growth in the industry was spectacular, from 800,000 visitors in 1974, just two years after reversion and the year before the Marine Expo, to 1.8 million in 1975 and 3 million by 1992, with a target of five million per year by the year 2002. Okinawa aims to join Hawaii and the Australian Gold Coast as a "super mega-resort" and part of the Golden Triangle of tourism.

Following the passage in 1987 of the Resort Law, the whole of Okinawa, including the outlying islands, became caught up in a frenzy of resort development schemes. On Okinawa Island itself, some thirty resort hotels and golf courses were built. Some involved the privatization of beaches and the creation of tourist enclosures, so that mainland visitors could enjoy a life-style of conspicuous consumption without the inconvenience of contact with local communities.

The Miyako Island group may be considered an example of the workings of "resortism." On Miyako Island itself, between 1987 and 1996, the village of Ueno (19 square kilometers; 1997 population: 3,186) constructed a remarkable resort, known as "German Culture Village." It featured a faithful reproduction of a medieval German castle (Marksburg), the "Fraternity Palace Resort Hotel," a golf course and other facilities, including a fine fishing port, although it has no fishing industry. The German connection amounts to the fortuitous rescue in 1873 of some German fishermen who were shipwrecked in waters off the village. There is no attempt to produce anything recognizably German, neither bread, nor beer, nor wine nor cheese, nor was there any significant German involvement in the planning and building of the village, although some advice was evidently rendered on medieval German thatching techniques. Built at the height of the bubble economy, 90 percent of the costs of the Culture Village were borne by Tokyo. It now sits, grandly if rather incongruously, in its remote rural surroundings, while local village authorities struggle to contain their operating losses and wait for the mass tourism that might one day make the Culture Village economically viable.

Setting aside the fiscal problems implicit in such grandiose projects, the availability of water alone also makes them dubious ventures. Miyako Island and its adjacent, smaller islands have no rivers. However, around 40 percent of Miyako's annual rainfall of 2,200 millimeters (86.6 inches) percolates through the porous limestone surface of the island and constitutes a well-nourished ground water supply. Since reversion, however, the forest cover on Miyako has been cut by half, to around 16 percent (against a national figure of 67 percent, or the Okinawan prefecture figure of 47 percent), and the natural water-retaining properties of the island have deteriorated. The island's first real water shortage occurred in 1994, while ammonium nitrate levels (mostly attributable to chemical fertilizer usage) have risen to worrisome levels. In short, the bureaucratic modern solution to the problems of Miyako has served to worsen its situation.

Tourism remains a key development strategy for 21st century Okinawa. The growth in the industry in the 1970s and 1980s was dramatic, but whether it can continue to grow and serve as a core industry in a future sustainable Okinawa must be open to some doubt. Tourism, as presently structured, calls for 1,000 liters (264 gallons) of water a day to satisfy the life-style requirements of each tourist (as against the average for the residents of the islands, even including the U.S. servicemen, of 370 liters, or 98 gallons a day). With the traditional *ka* now neglected and often unusable, and with the northern rivers already largely harnessed, and underground water reserves being rapidly drawn down and threatened by chemical pollution, the plan to double the current number of tourists seems questionable. The installation of desalination plants might offer one possible solution, but the trial plant which has begun to operate on Okinawa's main island, is small-scale, dependent on fossil fuel, and expensive.

COASTAL SEIBI AND CORAL

The damming and appropriation of river flow has fed a process of deterioration and erosion in coastal estuaries, for which the bureaucratic response has been: more *seibi*. Since reversion, the extent of the prefecture's coastline in a natural state has declined overall from 90 to 70 percent, but in the most populated island of Okinawa the figure is 49 percent (58 percent on its west coast). The wall of concrete continues to creep around all the islands, including even the shores of remote island marine parks. This process is known for budgetary purposes as "coastal preservation."

The fate of the coral reefs around Okinawa parallels that of the land environment. In global terms, the fate of the world's coral reefs has only relatively recently come to public attention. Whereas it took about 8,000 years for the world's forest-cover to be eroded by two-thirds, the global "marine forests" of coral were more-or-less intact until recent times. Coral reefs nourish a complex, bio-diverse ecology, comparable to rain-forests: they absorb around two percent of human emissions of CO_2 (500 million tons per year), as well as sustaining rich fisheries and helping to reduce global warming. But, like rain-forests, they are delicate and vulnerable before the rush of development. By now, 600,000 square kilometers, or about ten percent, of the world's coral is gone, and thirty percent more is expected to go in the next twenty years, even without taking possible global warming into consideration. Without forests and without coral reefs, mankind might survive, but it would be a fragile civilization, de-linked to a historically unprecedented degree from its natural surroundings.

Over 90 percent of Japan's coral is in Okinawa prefecture. The fertility of the coral reefs and the lagoons was a major source of prosperity and cultural distinctiveness in pre-modern Okinawa. Okinawan fishermen traditionally earned their living within the reef, taking an abundance of sea grasses, shellfish, crab, shrimp, octopus, and various kinds of fish. In many parts of Okinawa, people could simply walk out to the reef at low tide to fish. The island of Hatoma, for example, a mere square kilometer in area, until recently supported a population of 600 people by carefully harvesting an area six times as large within its reef-protected lagoon. Such was the bounty of the sea that Okinawan people rarely lacked protein.

The reef resource built over thousands of years has been drastically depleted in the decades since reversion. According to an official study published in 1996, the proportion of live coral around Okinawa Island is mostly less than five percent, and although healthy colonies are still to be found on other islands, they too are mostly shrinking. This means that it is still "coral," but in the same sense that a preserved Egyptian mummy is human: it is lifeless and inert, no longer the cradle of bio-diversity that coral is in its vital, healthy state. In the seas around Yanbaru, the tell-tale blood-red soil blocks river mouths, stems the flow of nutrient and river and marine life between land and sea, and stifles the coral. This can be done either directly, by asphyxiation, or by a process of chemical reaction whereby the acidity of water gradually rises under the load of aluminum ion, which is both highly toxic and highly soluble, reaching pH4.5 at the point of entry into the sea. This aluminum ion has recently been discovered to be a major component of the acid rain devastation in Northern European lakes. As it proliferates, the coral weakens and dies and native fish disappear.

Most native fish, including the Ryukyu *ayu,* or sweetfish, are now to be found only on the outlying islands, while imported fish predominate in the center and south of Okinawa itself. Degeneration of the reef environment has produced a steady decline in the traditional fishing industry, driving many to adopt the mainland-style, capital-intensive mode requiring powerful boats that venture far beyond the reef to specially constructed floating artificial reefs a number of hours' journey away. In this, as in other respects, Okinawa is becoming "mainland-ized." Unlike the rest of Japan, however, the coral-protected islands of Okinawa are directly threatened by global warming and the anticipated rise in the level of the oceans, since the former may well kill the coral, and the latter inundate it.

THE COLD WAR'S UNFINISHED BUSINESS

The "Okinawa problem" is inseparable from the role the islands were forced to play in the Cold War. Militarized, and turned into the key to the U.S. chain of East Asian garrisons, Okinawa now faces a choice between being incorporated in the nation-state-centered regional and global order as a hyper-peripheral, hyper-dependent backwater to be despoiled by the slash-and-burn of rampant development *(ran-kaihatsu)* or, alternatively, becoming a base for the creation of the 21st century's new, decentralized, sustainable and naturally balanced order. The latter could only be accomplished by a prodigious concerted effort, almost certainly of an international character.

Twenty-five years ago, at the height of the Cold War, Tokyo laid down, and Okinawa in general welcomed, a formula for reversion that combined retention of the U.S. bases with a set of policies to achieve parity with the mainland. Today, ten years after the end of the Cold War, the formula remains essentially unchanged. The bases may be more high-tech, more concentrated and rationalized geographically, but their strategic and military purposes, their sheer weight upon the landscape and society, have not been altered or reduced. The use of every instrument available to the Japanese state to foist a huge new offshore "floating heliport" onto Nago, in northern Okinawa Island, despite local opposition, was typical and likely to be repeated in the future.

As for parity with the mainland, the post-reversion era in Okinawa has been characterized by the imposition of metropolitan patterns, priorities, and engineering practices irrespective of climatic, geological, or socio/cultural differences. In place of the heavy and chemical industries of the 1960s and 1970s, we now see a series of fancy schemes woven around the ideas of internationalism, culture, environmentalism and leisure, with special projects—plans for a "cosmopolitan city," a "free trade zone," and a revitalized Northern District—plus a special tax status and perhaps visa-free status reminiscent of the "special industrial zone" promotion of 1972. Bureaucrats in Tokyo and Naha drew up the International City design out of left-over bits and pieces of the many desktop schemes developed during the 1980s bubble. The idea of Okinawa as some sort of go-between facilitating the Japan-Southeast Asia, or the Japan-China, relationships was also part of the reversion deal twenty-five years ago, but it came to nothing. The promise of a liberal transfusion of mainland money is the real bottom line.

These end-of-century scenarios are predicated on the assumption that the Okinawan people can be persuaded, cajoled, or pressured, rather than consulted or respected as an autonomous and subjective force. Whether it concerned the Nago base, or the various formulations of a "cosmopolitan" future, or the construction of new dams, Okinawan conceptions of modernity and value, let alone life, have rarely been considered. *Naihatsu,* or inner-directed or bottom-up orientation, is lacking. In crucial respects, the Okinawan people face the governments in Washington and Tokyo as late 20th century colonial subjects, recalcitrant "natives" to be brought to heel rather than citizens in a democratic polity.

And yet to say merely this is to miss an important point. To date, force has not been necessary to impose the Tokyo design because persuasion has worked, and it is far from clear that it will not continue to work into the next century. Why is it that the Okinawan people are so vulnerable to Tokyo's blandishments and manipulations? It seems likely that persuasion can work because they share the national religion of growthism and GDP-ism, and are as susceptible in the late 1990s to the slogans of development, progress, and industrialization as they were at the time of reversion in the early 1970s. Perhaps the sense of victimhood, strong in Okinawa because of the tragedies of the recent past, also predisposes people toward passive acceptance of externally-imposed solutions, for the victim is one "to whom things are done." Whatever the reasons, the fact is that the Okinawan problem is almost universally seen on the islands as one of bases, not development, and the problem of development is seen as one of how to maximize, not how to constrain, it.

I am not proposing that unspoiled, pristine and natural poverty is somehow preferable to developed prosperity. Development and growth are both positive and desirable, but the distinction has to be drawn between growth that is sustainable and that which is not. Since the Rio Conference of 1992, even the Japanese government, at least in theory, has recognized that growth may not be sustained for long at rates that outrun the regenerative and restorative capacities of nature. To the extent that they pay little heed to the fundamental requirements of long-term sustainability, Okinawan development strategies, based on the mainland model, offer only short-term prospects.

Furthermore, not only has the process of Okinawan development been unsustainable—as my discussion of the forests, coral, rivers, and agriculture should have made clear—but it has also been deeply flawed in purely economic terms. Dependency has deepened, nature (the crucial support of the economy) eroded, and sustainability shrunk, since reversion. The one great new industry successfully created has been public works, the archetypal problem sector of mainland Japan's economy. Without the transfusions of capital for bases, public works, and tourism, Okinawa as presently structured would collapse. The deepening fiscal crisis of the late 20th century Japanese state constitutes yet one more reason for doubting the long-term viability of the Okinawan economy.

This is not the place to develop an elaborate blue-print for a sustainable Okinawan economy, but some basic principles might be essayed. The resources Okinawa has are its people, seas, forests, rivers, and fields: their long-term health must be nurtured, and only within sustainable limits can the fish, farm, forest, marine, and tourism industries be maintained. In place of the tourist industry's preferred resorts, with their affectation of luxury, gourmet food, a profligate use of water, and the golf culture that epitomizes it, one might imagine more widely available *minshuku*-style accommodations for longer stay visitors, offering them a form of eco-tourism that explored the linkages between education, health, ecology, and culture. One might offer special tours for bird-watchers, butterfly-watchers, whale- and fish-watchers and stargazers, and facilities for poets, scholars, composers and artists to work for extended periods in close proximity to nature and in close contact with local specialist guides.

As for agriculture, it will have to return to the organic principles sacrificed in the pursuit of a share of the mainland market, since increasingly the market itself demands it, and since the costs for Okinawa of chemical agriculture are already too high. Likewise the application of ecological principles will involve a radical rethinking of traditional industries. The ecological philosophy of zero emissions, for example, should transform sugar cane from being merely cane for sugar into the raw material for a range of industries, including fuel, distillation, fermentation, and fibre (high quality paper and cellulose). The recovery of the reef and of the forest will be the prerequisite for establishing sustainable industries in those sectors, and both will depend upon high-level scientific expertise to understand and explore possible future applications for the largely unknown riches they offer.

The public works sector will require the most drastic restructuring, but its role as a major employer of local labor could be maintained even while its "works" role is reversed from laying concrete to removing it, from cutting to planting trees, from the plumbing of highly centralized, bureaucratically-dominated water systems to the task of recovering as much as possible the traditional, decentralized system. Many more highly skilled workers will have to be trained for these tasks, and as specialized marine and forest park rangers to maintain these resources. Far from countenancing further development in the conventional sense, the time has come to invest heavily in a long-term program to secure the forests and waters for coming generations.

Okinawa's human resources require careful cultivation as well. Along with mainland models of agriculture and industry that have proved either inappropriate or plainly damaging in Okinawa, mainland practices in education were also followed. Yet Okinawa is unlikely ever to pass through the stage of requiring its youth to be trained as salarymen for a mainland-style industrial wage-labor force, and mainland Japan itself is gradually awakening to the folly and wastage of its education system. The qualities of independent, imaginative thinking, and the cultivation of artistic sensitivity are likely to be the seedbed of a new entrepreneurialism for the 21st century. As even the economic value of non-homogenized culture grows, education for the 21st century will have to be revamped to meet such ends. During a visit to the Shiraho region of Ishigaki Island in 1989, it occurred to me that the demand within mainland Japan for the skills and arts of living, forgotten during the dour concentration on wage-labor and accumulation for high growth, were such that the dancers, singers, talkers and dreamers engendered by the traditional culture of Ishigaki (and other islands) might well play a 21st century role in Japan. Okinawa's social and cultural diversity may turn out to be as precious as the biodiversity of its nature.

The pursuit of such a local Okinawan development path will depend on the cultivation of Okinawan values and identity. No visitor to Okinawa can fail to be impressed by the difference between the values and priorities of life in Okinawan communities and elsewhere in Japan. Japanese manufacturing capitalism and its salaryman culture have made only the smallest inroads in Okinawa, and the pre-modern communitarian, celebratory, nature-rooted ways of thinking, sacrificed elsewhere in Japan, although eroded have not been lost here. The myths of a unique, superior Japanese identity, imperial or corporate, never had credibility here, and the Asia-Pacific, long a lived reality, was never an ideology.

INERTIA ON DISPLAY

Patrick Smith

The Japanese can neither love the Americans
nor endure being loved by them.
—Ambassador Sir Oliver Morland
to the British Foreign Office; Tokyo, 1963.[1]

The air station at Kadena is not merely the largest of the 39 American military bases in Okinawa; it is the largest the Pentagon maintains anywhere outside the United States. Including its munitions zone, it takes up nearly 12,000 acres, which is 83 percent of the territory of Kadena, a city of 30,000. They are among the local folk who will occasionally tell you, with some justification, "Okinawa doesn't just host American bases. Okinawa *is* an American base."

The entrance to Kadena is worth describing. Around it is a congested, tumbledown area of bars, crumbling shops, and badly built apartment blocks. Step inside the main gate, and the first thing you see is an 18-hole golf course lined with graceful pines. Then there is the gate itself. A guard waves cars through, saluting each. Next to him is a sign that reads, "10 DAYS SINCE THE LAST KADENA TEAM DWI UNIT." The count changes by way of numbered plaques. In civilian English, it was 10 days at the time of my visit since anyone had earned the base another hash mark by driving while drunk.

The city, the golf links, the gate between: This is a provocative arrangement, surely. It raises uncomfortable questions. While Americans seldom ask these questions, the Japanese more or less live with them. So let's pose them here, for they are not without import. How and why have Americans become so oblivious to the conditions they cause for others—in this case, as so often elsewhere, in the name of protecting them? Why do Americans so often claim privileges for themselves that they are unable to understand as such? Finally, why are we Americans so unaware of how we look and sound to others as we converse among ourselves?

Even for those lacking all distance, caught up in the business of the base or the city around it, these matters must sometimes creep into consciousness. Some may dismiss them as questions of morality, or of the liberal conscience, but that would be well wide of the mark. They are essentially questions of vision, which is something quite different. And when we talk about vision, we mean not just our ability to see others, but our ability to see ourselves—and finally ourselves among others.

There are many startling contrasts in Okinawa. Though its *per capita* income, at $25,000, is higher than Britain's or France's, it is nonetheless the poorest of Japan's 47 prefectures. Unemployment, at 9.2 percent, is more than twice the national average; in the cities it is 12 percent, and more than three-quarters of those without work are under 35. A great deal of Okinawa's income derives from subsidies, and Tokyo awards a sizable proportion of them to the cities and towns that live with American bases. The prefecture has a lively tourist industry, but its dependence on subsidies means that Okinawa is in many respects a ward of the national government. The No. 3 source of income is the bases—rents paid to local landlords, the salaries of base employees, money soldiers spend in the off-base bars and shops.

It makes for unexpected scenes, as at Kadena. Along the coast in the north, the town of Kin is 60 percent given over to Camp Hansen, which has shelled the surrounding hills into a moonscape that now erodes into a once-pristine sea. To the south, Futenma Air Station takes up a third of central Ginowan, a city of 84,000. It is a little as if one carved runways into, say, downtown Baltimore. Ginowan lives with noise levels that routinely disrupt sleep, classroom instruction, and ordinary conversation. Meet the mayor in any of these communities, and they can reel off a list of base-related calamities half a century long—everything from assault and battery to toxic spillage, aircraft accidents, and stray artillery shells. All around the prefecture you find suggestions of the wealth-and-poverty polarities ordinarily observed in developing countries—and more or less absent from respectable, egalitarian Japan. You see some of that tatty, contingent, not-quite-coherent living that tends to get done around military garrisons in foreign lands—which is a faded, emphatically bitter memory on the main islands.

One needn't go on. But to see Okinawa is to understand immediately why three-quarters of the U.S. facilities in Japan are crammed into the prefecture, taking up a fifth of its usable land. These facilities, contentious since they were established after World War II, are the reality of the U.S.-Japan relationship. So the question is simple: What does it mean that the reality of the relationship is best kept far from view?

Many strategic arguments are advanced to explain the U.S. presence in Okinawa. None holds up—not when examined in detail and not when considered more broadly. They all seem to suffer from either being part of a time warp—that is, they're outdated—or else they revolve around notions such as military "credibility," and "perception," as opposed to simple operational logic. Take one look at Okinawa, and you must certainly conclude that credibility and perception are at issue—but not in the way the Pentagon claims. The point here is to consider what the American presence costs Americans in a currency of far greater value than dollars. What does the scene at Kadena's gate cost the United States in terms of prestige? The question is never asked; there is little sign that Washington intends to ask it. But it needs to be asked on both sides of the Pacific if the price is not to rise precipitously.

I have thought for 10 years that the chief impediment to change in the U.S.-Japan relationship is an especially burdensome form of inertia. So much needs to be rethought and renewed between Washington and Tokyo—between Americans and Japanese—that no one knows where to begin. This inertia is on full display in Okinawa—as is its cost. A decade ago, the price paid for our trans-Pacific inertia was low. The post-Cold War world was new, and the Japanese were only dimly aware of what the new era would mean to them. Now, though, the price has begun to climb. What is the source of a nation's prestige abroad? In the post-Cold War world, this question is urgent.

Americans used to understand that prestige derived from principles, a way of acting among others that suggested a national character worthy of respect. But the Cold War changed Americans. Now we no longer show much interest in the matter of prestige—not on the ground, in any case.

The emphasis has shifted toward a concern with power alone. And in this America has pointed itself 180 degrees in the wrong direction. In the long term, at least, power alone will fall short in the post-Cold War world. It will not be enough to allow any nation to claim global leadership. Power alone can purchase only its own continuation—and it will not purchase even that indefinitely.

In early October 1998, when I was last in Okinawa, an 18-year-old girl died in a coma after a hit-and-run collision with an allegedly drunk U.S. Marine corporal. That incident threatened to bring the Okinawan question to the fore much as the rape of a 12-year-old by three American servicemen did three years earlier. The rape, as is well known, sparked widespread protests throughout Japan and prompted Okinawa's impassioned governor, Masahide Ota, to launch a rigorous campaign for the removal of all U.S. facilities by the year 2015.

Not long after this latest fatality, however, Ota was voted out of office. He had long enjoyed broad support for his stand against the U.S. presence. But after eight years of recession in Japan, Okinawans had become nervous about their economy. Ota's principles had begun to threaten those much-needed funds from Tokyo. The new governor, a local business executive named Keiichi Inamine, also professes to oppose the bases—no candidate who favored them could possibly win an election in Okinawa—but to him the bases are not a front-burner issue. Inamine enjoys the support of the governing Liberal Democrats and promises to use his Tokyo connections to secure Okinawa's economic future. His election, in effect, was more a measure of popular anxiety than it was of popular choice.

American officers stationed in Okinawa expect Inamine's victory to ease animosities over the U.S. presence. "Most of this is just political," one said when I asked about the renewed stirring of local sentiment. "With the elections over, the bases issue will die down." It might, in the current economic environment. And there is no telling yet what Inamine's impact as governor will be. But this is short-term thinking. Neither recession nor a prefectural governor prone to compromise can do more than obscure a challenge that extends far beyond the Okinawan shoreline.

After half a century of an intimacy that has often suffocated the Japanese, a decade after the Berlin Wall came down, a great divide has begun to appear in U.S. relations with Japan—and indeed across the Pacific region. Viewed with disinterest, this is healthy. And in any case it is inevitable. Okinawa is oddly a kind of epicenter in this seismic shift. Here one sees fully the anachronism of the old relationships. Here in miniature one also sees the potential damage—in antagonism, alienation, even confrontation—that can come of improvising the extension of the past into the future. "As Okinawa goes, so goes Japan," U.S. Ambassador Armin Meyer wrote in a State Department dispatch from Tokyo in 1969 (see LaFeber, p. 350). The context was very different. But the observation seems as true now as then.

"AN ALLIANCE WITHOUT TROOPS"

In 1990, while running the *International Herald Tribune's* Tokyo bureau, I wrote about the thirtieth anniversary of the revised U.S.-Japan Security Treaty. Changes in East-West relations, I observed, were prompting a rethink among scholars, analysts, and political figures—or at least thoughts of a rethink. Beyond the geopolitical considerations, I recorded "a growing restlessness" with security ties first fixed seven years after the war and reaffirmed amid great national controversy eight years later. "Even those who defend the agreement—and they are in the majority—do not question that the U.S.-Japan relationship has changed as much since 1960 as it had when negotiators agreed to replace the arrangement embodied in the San Francisco Treaty of 1952."

According to my 1990 datebook, the piece elicited a dinner invitation from the Foreign Ministry within two days of publication. There were many taboos in Japan's public discourse then, and I had transgressed. We had a private room in one of those expense-account restaurants in the Ginza. The scolding was delivered in friendly terms and came with sumptuous accompaniment—a measure of the severity of the ministry's concern. "Smith-*san*," I recall one of my hosts saying, "no one in Japan, apart from our small, ultraconservative element, ever questions our relations with the United States."

It is a recent and distant memory all at once—less than a decade old, but an era away nonetheless. Changing the

American relationship, and therefore the treaty it rests upon, is now a matter Japanese politicians and officials will as often as not raise themselves in conversing with Western visitors. In December 1998, there were reports from Tokyo that the governing Liberal Democrats were also beginning to debate Japan's "peace" constitution—a development that is both startling and perfectly logical. Altering the constitution, especially its "no-war" Article 9, has long ranked high among Japan's postwar taboos. Yet constitutional revision has been a plank in the LDP's official platform since the party was formed in 1955. Any fundamental change in the security relationship, in any case, would more or less force Tokyo to recast a constitution that requires the nation to remain officially disarmed.

Few Japanese, if any, want to alter the essentially amicable tone of Tokyo's ties with Washington—only the substance. Since the legislative elections of 1998, in which opposition parties made big gains against the Liberal Democrats, even the Japan Communist Party has softened its long-established critique of the U.S.-Japan relationship. The phrase one frequently hears among public figures and policy intellectuals of many persuasions these days sounds like something concocted in Okinawa: "An alliance without troops by 2010." In the July/August 1998 issue of *Foreign Affairs,* former prime minister Morihiro Hosokawa went still further. "The gulf separating American and Japanese perceptions of the U.S. troops stationed in Japan could jeopardize the alliance between these two important countries," Hosokawa asserted. "The U.S. military presence in Japan should fade with this century's end."

It is astonishing what ground the Japanese have covered since my Foreign Ministry reprimand. One may reasonably put this psychic sea change down to the rape incident in 1995. In May 1996, an *Asahi Shimbun* poll found that two out of three Japanese now wanted the Yanks to go home. But more than the deployment of 47,000 troops on Japanese soil is at issue. At issue is sovereignty and the equal partnership the Japanese have demanded at intervals since the early 1950s. Liberals and conservatives, leftists, rightists, moderates—they have all articulated these issues differently over the past fifty years. But the different perspectives obscure common concerns about the unhealthy closeness of the U.S.-Japan relationship. And now this subterranean dimension of things is becoming more evident: Beneath the practical political matters flows a process of self-reappraisal at every level, from the individual to the national.

None of what is now beginning to take shape among the Japanese—a renewed self-confidence, a revalued ethos, even a reinvented nation—would be of any surprise had Americans not purposefully ignored the extent to which the Japanese have always chafed under the postwar order. Of course, the better histories of the relationship are dense with diplomats and State Department officials fretting over a neutral Japan—"Neutrality is immoral," as John Foster Dulles put it—or an assertive Japan, or even a genuinely independent Japan (LaFeber, p. 313). This is not what we remember of the Japanese—or ourselves—during the Cold War era. In memory, we never had much to worry about so far as our Japanese friends were concerned. Who would not wish to host our soldiers? Who would not want pride of place at the table Washington lays for its clients? And so we are surprised now, and clearly cannot cope, as a distance between the two nations reappears. Isn't there something not quite imaginable about a Japan that concerns itself with territorial sovereignty—or a Japan that claims possession of an alternative economic model? This sort of assertiveness is simply "un-Japanese." It is something one expects of third world hotheads—the Nassers and Sukarnos and Mahathirs, men of yesterday, not of our globalized tomorrow.

It may also be hard to imagine that Americans could obscure Japan's true view of things for so long—rather the way U.S. troops have been obscured in Okinawa—except that we are now doing the same thing again. More than six million Japanese protested the security treaty's renewal in 1960—an event of which most Americans have no recollection whatsoever. The Japanese have been complicit in this—and still are—to the extent that Tokyo has grown accustomed to misrepresenting Japan to Americans (and to the outside world in general). Yet this is precisely what Japan and the Japanese are now outgrowing: They are learning to speak their minds. And that is precisely what we fail to understand (or choose to ignore).

THE NYE REPORT

In late November 1998, the Pentagon issued a document called *East Asian Strategy Report* 1998. It is the fourth *EASR* to appear since 1990. Note the time span of this series: The *EASRs* are essentially progress reports on post-Cold War thinking among American defense planners. And indeed, there were clear signs in the first two *EASRs* that the Pentagon would take an imaginative, flexible approach to the Pacific region in acknowledgment of the vast changes sweeping across the East Asian security landscape. Then came the third *EASR,* in 1995. It is commonly known as the Nye Report for its principal thinker, Harvard scholar Joseph S. Nye. In effect, the Nye Report announced to East Asians that they would enjoy no peace dividend at the Cold War's close. Again, note the date: the Nye Report coincided with the Pentagon's development of its "two-war" preparedness strategy and the grim announcement by Colin Powell, then chairman of the Joint Chiefs, that Americans weren't going to see a peace dividend, either.

The Nye Report was greeted with disappointment in many quarters, on both sides of the Pacific. Among its most controversial features was its position on U.S. troops in East Asia. It committed the United States to maintaining troop strength at the long-established level of 100,000 (of which roughly half are in Japan) "for the foreseeable future." This was an especially hard blow to Okinawans. For half a decade they had looked forward to a basic shift in U.S. security strategy that would at last return their land and their cities to them. But you do not have to be Okinawan to understand the report's fundamental flaw on this question: It was a profound error, surely, to attach U.S. credibility to a number.

The Pentagon appears to have learned at least one lesson over the past three years: Its new *EASR* was evidently withheld until after Okinawans chose their next governor on November 15, 1998. While that could hardly be taken as a sign of bold initiatives to come, one still hoped for some sign of innovation in response to circumstances and perspectives in the region that have been changing as fast as one can register them. In particular, wouldn't the new *EASR* have to take into account the evolution of Japanese attitudes that I have briefly reviewed above?

No chance. The presence of U.S. troops in Asian countries is "of fundamental strategic importance," the new *EASR* states. The 100,000 figure is noted five times in the first ten pages—and is reaffirmed in the strongest possible terms. The most prominent examples of U.S. activity in the region since the previous report are the 1996 deployment of the carriers *Nimitz* and *Independence* in the Taiwan Straits and the dispatch of the latter vessel to the Persian Gulf in early 1998. Never mind that both missions demonstrate the increasing irrelevance of troops and the increasing primacy of something far simpler: access to naval and air facilities when needed.

Why do we need 100,000 troops in Okinawa and elsewhere in East Asia? According to the 1998 *EASR,* they "provide U.S. commanders great flexibility in tailoring forces to meet national objectives." They are part of a "strategic mix" that is essential "because it presents an enemy with an overwhelming array of capabilities." They can play a "mitigating role"—one must read this to believe it—in the East Asian financial crisis. None of these assertions, in my view, stands up to scrutiny. There is also the still vaguer matter of "reassurance." Having soldiers in the region "multiplies our diplomatic impact." It "demonstrates professional military ethics." It "encourages pursuit of policies in U.S. and regional interests." Can U.S. troops in Asia credibly claim to do any of these things? Logic this flaccid suggests something disturbing: It suggests that the Pentagon has gone too long without a rigorous, detached civilian review.

One is hard-pressed to accept *EASR* 1998 as anything more than a display of the inertia I have already noted. But this is not to imply that security policy in the region is benignly static, for to stand still in the past is to move in the wrong direction. Consider the May 1996 *Asahi Shimbun* poll noted earlier, or the Japanese Diet's law of 1997 denying several thousand Okinawan landlords the right to repossess acreage leased to the Pentagon: Hasn't the U.S. military become reliant on Japan's attenuated democracy at the very moment the Japanese are trying to reconstruct it? The airlift and fighter wings at Kadena are now evolving into "expeditionary forces," one is told: Those units are on call to project U.S. power throughout the Western Pacific—and, indeed, vastly beyond the Pacific region. While this has been a discernible thread in Pentagon thinking since the early-1960s, it is now being implemented as a new, post-Cold War mission. But has anyone considered the implications of using Japanese territory to fulfill "rapid response" objectives Tokyo may not support—this while Japan is attempting an independent redefinition of its interests?

This is where policy leads when it is formed in the absence of vision: It leads to risks. One is the obvious potential for renewed unrest should there be another serious accident involving a base in Okinawa or (far worse) on the main islands. There is nothing far-fetched about this. In view of the record, it is far-fetched to anticipate a future without damaging mishaps. There is also the danger of rising antagonism borne of the realization that the security treaty operates ever more exclusively to Washington's benefit and has ever less to do with protecting Japan. Japan may have been a strategic platform for the United States military since the treaty was signed, but what happens when the nation discovers it has evolved into that and nothing more? What happens, more specifically, to what the Japanese call the "sympathy budget"—the $5 billion Tokyo now spends yearly on host-nation support?

A third risk is more complicated. It has to do with larger questions—questions of history, nationalism, and of changing attitudes toward the nation that defeated Japan half a century ago. The national reinvention I have already noted is inevitable. Within that process, however, many matters remain unsettled. And what the United States does (or fails to do) in coming years will have much to do with how these unsettled issues are resolved. American conduct, quite simply, will influence the kind of nation Japan makes of itself.

Gradually since the death of Emperor Hirohito a decade ago, and as the baton passes from one generation to the next, the Japanese are finding their way back through the past. This is partly a matter of expedience. Japan's neighbors have been drumming their fingers on the table for years; obstinacy on Tokyo's part is not a match with the region's growing interdependence. Nonetheless, younger Japanese will reach their own understanding of history in coming years. And when they look back, it is with detachment. What will they see, these Japanese whose schooling in history has (to put it mildly) left them wanting? Many Japanese outside the ruling elite are quite prepared to accept their nation's responsibility for the past as it was. But it is not a foregone conclusion that Japan will reconcile itself to history as it urgently needs to do. These same Japanese are far less reticent than their parents in the matter of national pride. This is not unhealthy—not necessarily, at least. But what kind of nationalism will take root in Japan today? It is a mistake not to recognize the role the United States will play—actively or passively, whether it wants to or not—in how these questions are answered.

The point is well-illustrated in a recently published *manga,* the comics that feature prominently in Japanese popular culture. This particular *manga* is called *Senso-ron (War Discourse,* roughly, published in 1998) and is part of a running series by Yoshinori Kobayashi, a young, vigorously opinionated member of Japan's emerging generation. Kobayashi makes a virtue of what he calls *goumanizumu,* a kind of plain-spoken arrogance. He writes and draws for his own cohort, the generation inclined to say, "It wasn't my war"—but not entirely. There are many adults among *Senso-ron's* hundreds of thousands of readers. And what do they read? They read that those who would apologize for the war "are announcing the success of America's War Guilt Information Program" (p. 51). They read that the Japanese have been "brainwashed" by a victor's version of history. "'War' isn't just battles where there is gunfire," one of Kobayashi's commentaries reads. "There are also the wars called 'information war' and 'propaganda war.' Even in the present day, which we call peaceful, this war continues relentlessly" (p. 171).

So runs *Senso-ron,* for 381 pages. As any close reader of the book must conclude, war and history are as much Kobayashi's conceits as his subject. They are his artifice, if you like. *Senso-ron* (along with its multiplying companion volumes by various *manga* artists) is about *ressentiment* and the confinements of Japan's postwar arrangements with the United States. It is about restlessness and the alienation one feels in a society directed by forces beyond one's control. And it is about inequality. It is important to identify these themes, because in expressing them Kobayashi also suggests the simple yet powerful antidote Washington could apply: fresh thinking—an approach to Japan that is at once imaginative in the face of new challenges and an acknowledgment of a nation struggling to assume its rightful place. But there is no fresh thinking—not in security matters, certainly, and not in economic affairs, either.

"THE WARFARE OF PEACETIME"

During the East Asian currency and economic crises that began in mid-1997, the United States has offered Japan a steady stream of policy prescriptions. Chiefly through the Treasury Department, it has advised Tokyo to close the worst of the nation's debt-burdened banks, deregulate the economy at an accelerated pace, reduce taxes, and open up the financial sector, in particular, to free foreign competition. This is the menu of medicines we all know as globalism. I say "offered" and "advised," but "demanded" would in many instances be more accurate, for when globalists speak across the Pacific, they tend to speak in imperative sentences. At one point in the spring of 1998, Washington went so far as to specify its preference for tax cuts and public spending equal to 2 percent of Japan's national output.

The effect of this approach could hardly have been intended—though anyone following events might easily have predicted it. Far from moving Tokyo in its direction in managing Japan's recession, Washington succeeded in once again making economics, not security, the arena where fissures in the relationship are now closest to the surface. It is no wonder that, during 1998, officials from the State Department and the National Security Council began sitting in on strategy sessions at Treasury.

Let us look at these events from both ends of the Pacific. Since the Cold War's end, Washington has asserted with mounting vehemence that globalism is an ineluctable force that allows for only one alternative: Those who do not embrace it will fail. Recent history made it especially easy for Americans to advance this idea to the Japanese. As everyone by now understands and acknowledges, "globalization" is really another term for "Americanization." And Americans have assumed the power to Americanize Japan since the autumn of 1945. To modernize is to Westernize: That has long been the prevailing assumption in the Atlantic community. In our time, Washington has come to insist instead that to modernize is to Americanize: That is globalism's most fundamental tenet.

But this produces a profound irony across the Pacific. For whatever else the Japanese have had to show us over the past 130 years, they began with the lesson that modernizing does not require Westernizing. And they have now started us on Lesson No. 2: It doesn't mean Americanizing, either.

From Japan's perspective, the Americans brought very little news when they arrived with the gospel of globalism. Fundamental reform—economic, social, political—has been on the agenda in Tokyo at least since the "bubble economy" of the 1980s burst, with perfect symmetry, in the first weeks of this decade. Japan Inc., at least in the form it took during the "miracle" years, is a spent asset. To enter the next century the nation will have to open its economy and compete without the protection it has long enjoyed. That will mean renovating institutions across the board. Schools will have to produce more creative thinkers and fewer foot soldiers. Corporations will have to be lighter on their feet. The banking system will have to accommodate what banking professionals call "disintermediation:" Instead of simply recycling household savings as loans to industry, they will have to survive in a world of sophisticated alternatives for both savers and borrowers. The nation's dysfunctional political system—which I consider the largest instance of institutionalized corruption in the developed world—can no longer be sustained. The times demand a more responsible leadership; gradually, the Japanese are coming to demand it, too.

This is the institutional side of the fundamental change in ethos that I touched upon earlier. But what form will all this change take? Will the new, emergent Japan resemble the United States because that is what Americans tell the Japanese to do? Or will it be a renovated, revalued version of itself—reflecting it own deep, extensive roots in its own past? It is slightly bizarre that such a question even has to be asked—except that Americans have been making the same "just like us" error since Commodore Perry's time. There was simply never a chance that Japan would adopt the neoliberal capitalism urged upon it by Adam Smith's most fervent apostles. So the American stance has not been a cause of the friction now evident between Washington and Tokyo so much as a catalyst to an inevitable departure.

Eisuke Sakakibara, former vice minister for international affairs of the Ministry of Finance, once termed the American campaign to reform Japan "nothing less than an act of barbarism against our own cultural values" (LaFeber, p. 400). It may sound like something worthy of Malaysian Prime Minister Mahathir bin Mohamad. Sakakibara, it is true, was something of a hothead before he achieved a high-ranking position in the Japanese bureaucracy, and he made his observation in 1995. What did he mean?

Something quite defensible, in my view. The Japanese—along with the rest of East Asia—are fully cognizant of a simple fact the Treasury ignored in its approach to the Asian crisis: Economic systems tend to reflect the cultures they inhabit. This is not a new idea: Karl Polanyi, the political economist, articulated it in *The Great Transformation,* which he published in 1944. Washington understands it well enough when it looks across the Atlantic: When was the last time it told Bonn or Paris to relegate their long social democratic traditions to history and embrace the Anglo-American model? But when it looks across the Pacific, it fails to see any traditions worthy of respect—again, a problem of vision. No, the Japanese have not resisted Washington's harsh medicine simply because they are too weak-willed to face the social and political consequences. Nor do they balk at swallowing the prescription only because it has proven inappropriate. They think they are engaged in a kind of civilizational clash instigated by the United States.

And they are right. Banks and corporations are no more independent of the societies in which they function than poets or politicians. To deny this is to take one's place in the long line of those who have charged across the Pacific to insist that Asia "open its door." One cannot talk about regulatory reform, to take one simple example, without asking whose standards to apply.

Not quite 130 years ago, when Japan began sending missions abroad to inspect all things foreign, a diplomat named Kunitake Kume took one look at Anglo-American capitalism and pronounced it "the warfare of peacetime."[2] All that furious competition, that unbounded power, the gnashing of so many teeth: So did the Japanese recoil from Adam Smith's legacy in the last century—and so are they likely to seek another way forward once again. Those first impressions launched Japan upon a long fascination with continental Europe—in particular the methods cultivated in Bismarck's new Germany. Like Japan, Germany was a "late developer," in scholarly parlance. And in Japan as in Germany, national development would take precedence over free exchange. Adam Smith never got to name the game when Japan began its modernization project; the Anglo-American way was judged inappropriate technology. Friedrich List, the German-born economist, helped the Japanese name the game in the 1870s. Today we call it developmental capitalism.

Some Japanists assert that the Japanese can make no substantial advances without an external model—and that the model this time, insofar as one can identify a single source of inspiration, is again likely to be Germany. I accept the conclusion but not the premise. What distinguishes the emerging era in Japan, in my view, is precisely the desire among the Japanese to leave their long habit of imitation behind in favor of their own way forward. This is not to say the bureaucrats in Tokyo are not doing their share of look-ing around, as the technocrats of any ordinary nation do. But they still see no benefit in waging the warfare of peacetime.

THE "SEAMLESS WEB"

In the summer of 1961, President Kennedy invited Ha-yato Ikeda to the White House and there lectured the new Japanese prime minister on the need for Japan to play a larger role on the global stage. Ikeda's reply was startling: This would be possible, he told Kennedy, except that the Japanese first had to bring their English up to speed. If disin-genuousness were the point of that summit session, it would be hard to say who came out ahead. Ikeda offered a classic duck-the-issue response from a postwar conservative deter-mined to milk the U.S.-Japan relationship for the maximum economic gain. But Kennedy did no better. "Do more": It has been a constant refrain since this old encounter. But the Americans have never really meant it.

Washington's concerns back in the 1950s and 1960s were Japanese trade with China and its developing relation-ships in Southeast Asia (where the French had been defeat-ed and where America saw not nations so much as teetering dominoes). And it is remarkable how faithfully these same concerns have been transliterated into the language of America's post-Cold War orthodoxy. A few months after the Thai devaluation touched off the Asian economic crisis, Tokyo proposed a $100 billion bailout fund to which it would contribute half. Washington scotched that proposition as quickly as you can say "hegemony"—though the idea still survives in Tokyo and other East Asian capitals. In the autumn of 1998, the Japanese came forward again, this time with a package of grants and trade credits worth $73 billion—vastly more than anything the United States had put on the table. In response, U.S. Special Trade Representative Charlene Barshefsky accused Tokyo of trying to buy influence in the region (*Los Angeles Times*, Nov. 14, 1998).

But if attitudes in Washington have changed little over the decades, they are shifting discernibly at the other end of the Pacific. Japan has no need to buy influence; it is doing more—and winning recognition for it. However long it takes the East Asians to dig themselves out of their current predicaments, they are likely to emerge a more interdependent group of nations whose leaders know they have more to share than they have to fear. This can only enhance Japan's standing among its neighbors, who clearly (and authentically) want a more active Japan. History has long kept Japan from a leadership role in the region. Impressively, its neighbors are beginning to address this problem, too.

For sheer dramatic effect, it would be hard to match the autumn 1998 visit to Tokyo of South Korean President Kim Dae Jung. Kim listened attentively to Prime Minister Keizo Obuchi's ritual apology for Japan's wartime conduct—as all visiting Koreans must. But he was clearly ready to make the most of it. He began his talks by proposing a new era in Korean-Japanese relations and ended with a call for a seven-nation security dialogue in which Japan would figure prominently. The evident point here is to begin developing a form of stability that springs from dynamic intra-regional relationships—and not merely from the projection of power from the far side of the Pacific lake. History must be squared, Kim told his hosts, but in the meantime let's move forward. From a ringside seat in Tokyo, Kim's performance was startling to watch—the more so when put against the American approach to the very same questions.

True, Chinese President Jiang Zemin failed to elicit a matching apology when he visited Tokyo a month later. Tokyo offered a variety of explanations afterward—each one landing it deeper in the familiar swamps of historical revisionism. This was foolish—an immense disappointment all around. But this very disappointment suggested the extent to which Beijing wants seriously to engage the question; it looks as if Beijing may finally prefer to solve the problem of history rather than continue making cynical diplomatic use of it. It is perfectly plausible that Japan and China will eventually find the kind of equilibrium Seoul and Tokyo seem at last destined for—an equilibrium the Sino-Japanese relationship needs if the region is to achieve a stability of its own.

"Asia is a seamless web," the columnist Joseph Alsop wrote in 1955. "If the web is too badly torn anywhere, it will unravel everywhere" (quoted by LaFeber, p. 313). Alsop's remark, singular for its crudity, was no more than the domino theory recast as punditry. But let's turn the thought this way and that; let's put it to work from another perspective. The U.S. now risks damage in its relations with Japan. And whether it occurs first as a matter of security or of economics, any such damage is unlikely to stop at Japan's frontiers. To one degree or another, the tear will run across the region. That is the reality—unseen for lack of vision. From Alsop's day to ours, Washington has cast Japan as a sort of "other"—as potentially neutral in the Cold War, as an industrial rival, now as an alternative economic model. And in this, it must be said, Washington has been right all along. Japan never enlisted in the West's Cold War army—it was a draftee. It does stand now for an alternative path forward. This faces the United States with a choice: to dwell upon these differences, as it now does; or to acknowledge difference so as to begin the worthy business of transcending it.

NOTES

1. LaFeber, Walter, *The Clash: A History of U.S.-Japan Relations* (New York: W.W. Norton, 1997), p. 337. LaFeber's work is a masterful account of its subject—and the first to follow the relationship forward from Commodore Perry's voyage in 1853 to the present.

2. *Tokumei zenken taishi Bei-O kairan jikki* (Journal of the Envoy Extraordinary Ambassador Plenipotentiary's Travels Through America and Europe) was published in Tokyo in 1878. This translated fragment is cited in Eugene Soviak's essay, "On the Nature of Western Progress: The Journal of the Iwakura Embassy," in Donald H. Shively, ed., *Tradition and Modernization in Japanese Culture* (Princeton: Princeton University Press, 1971), p. 15.

[This article first appeared in a slightly different form in *The Washington Quarterly* and is reprinted here with the permission of the Massachusetts Institute of Technology Press.]

Index

Green, Michael, 125-26
Guam, 243-44
Guantanamo Bay, Cuba, 238-39
Gushiken, Soosei, 20
gyokusai (honorable suicide), 27, 29

Hamahiga, Ryoki, 160
Hamilton, Robert, 102-3, 222-25
Haneba, Yasunobu, 26
Hansen, Camp, 116, 161, 284
Harp, Rodrico, 96-97, 116
Harvard University, 120, 290
Hashimoto, Ryutaro, 5, 8, 103, 113,
    218-21
Hateruma island, 271-72
Hatoma island, 277
Hatoyama, Yukio, 235, 237
Hawaii, 243-44, 275
Hayashi, Saburo, 23
Hayashi, Toshio, 99-100
Hearst, Fannie, 77
Heliport, 103, 119, 194-95, 218-20,
    222, 225, 227-31, 247, 279
Henoko, 102, 218
Hicks, George, 40, 42-43
Hideyoshi Toyotomi, 135
Higa, Michiko, 74
Higa, Tetsuya, 103, 220
Higashi, Mineo, 79-80, 90
Higuchi, Kotaro, 125-26
Hinomaru (Japanese national flag), 146-
    47, 155, 167
Himeyuri Student Corps, 144
Hirohito, Emperor of Japan, 6, 48, 77-
    78, 142, 160, 174, 178-79, 292
Hokama, Shuzen, 138
Hokkaido, 138
Hoover Institution, Stanford University,
    56
Hosokawa, Morihiro, 119, 180, 235,
    237, 288
Hosokawa, Morisada, 19-20, 33
Hunter, Duncan, 224

Ichiki, Kitokuro, 140
Iejima, 32
Ienaga, Saburo, 39-40, 45-47
Iha, Fuyu, 143
Iha, Yuka, 202
Ikeda, Hayato, 297
Inamine, Keiichi, 221-22, 231, 247-48,
    250, 258, 286
Inchon landing, 103
India, 237
Indonesia, 124
International City Plan, 249-52, 258,
    279
Iran, 126
Ireland, 178
Iriomote island, 35, 263
Irokawa, Daikichi, 174
Isahama, 54-55

Ishigaki island, 258, 282
    incident at (1945), 35-36
Ishihara, Masaiye, 44, 47-48
Ishii, Torao, 19
Italy, 155, 235
Ito, Masanori, 16, 26, 34
Itokazu, Keiko, 192
Itoman, 6
Iwo Jima, 16

Japan, 117
    educational system of, 282, 292, 295
    militarism in, 104, 241
    Ministry of Agriculture and Fisheries,
    266
    Ministry of Colonization, 152
    Ministry of Construction, 266, 274
    Ministry of Education, 39, 41, 45-48,
    147, 152
    Ministry of Finance, 295
    Ministry of Foreign Affairs, 120, 152,
    222, 232, 287-88
    Ministry of Health and Welfare, 31, 33
    Ministry of Home Affairs, 21-22, 140
    Ministry of Local Autonomy, 179
    Ministry of Transportation, 180, 266
    Okinawa Development Agency, 259
    subsidies to Okinawa, 103, 106, 242-
    43, 249, 266, 284
Japanese-American trade, 103-5, 120-
    21
Japanese army, 14-15, 19-20, 25, 31-
    32, 34, 158
    Imperial Headquarters, 18, 23-28,
    31, 157
    killing of civilian Okinawans, 33, 39-
    49, 78
    Nakano Intelligence Academy, 27-28
    sexual slaves of, 190, 197
Japanese navy, 18, 23, 28, 35
Japanese Supreme Court, 5-6, 40, 45-
    47, 65, 112, 205-14
Japanese International Cooperation
    Agency (JICA), 63
Japan Policy Research Institute (JPRI),
    53-54
Japan-U.S. Security Treaty, 7, 34, 118,
    121, 125, 172, 189, 192-93, 202,
    205, 207, 211-12, 215, 226, 232,
    235-40, 287-92
    Japanese subsidies, 229-30, 238,
    241-43, 292
    Security Guidelines, 216, 264
Japan-U.S. Status of Forces Agreement
    (SOFA), 117-18, 189, 192-93, 200,
    207, 212, 226
Jiang Zemin, 123, 298
Johnson, Chalmers, 53, 109-29, 215-32

Kadena, 15
    Ammunition Storage Area, 253
    Japanese airfield at, 23

305

AUTHORS

Kozy Amemiya holds a Ph.D. degree in sociology from the University of California, San Diego, and is a member of the Board of Advisers of the Japan Policy Research Institute.

Carolyn Bowen Francis was until 1999 an Instructor at Okinawa Christian Junior College and one of the founding members of Okinawa Women Act Against Military Violence. She is today retired and living in Southern California.

Chalmers Johnson is president of the Japan Policy Research Institute and author of *Blowback: The Costs and Consequences of American Empire.*

Gavan McCormack is a professor of Japanese history in the Australian National University and author of *The Emptiness of Japanese Affluence.*

Mike Millard has worked as a journalist and editor in Japan for over ten years. He is author of the forthcoming book *Leaving Japan: Observations on the Dysfunctional U.S. - Japan Relationship.*

Masahide Ota is emeritus professor of humanities at the University of the Ryukyus and author of many books on Okinawan history. He was governor of Okinawa (1990-1998).

Steve Rabson is associate professor of Japanese at Brown University and author and translator of *Okinawa: Two Postwar Novellas by Oshiro Tatsuhiro and Higashi Mineo.*

Masayuki Sasaki is a professor of economics at Kanazawa University and the author of many books on "sustainable development" and the problems of urban areas.

Patrick Smith is author of *Japan: A Reinterpretation*, which won the 1998 Kiriyama Prize for the best book on a Pacific Rim subject.

Koji Taira is emeritus professor of industrial relations at the University of Illinois, Urbana, and coeditor of *The Ryukyuanist,* a quarterly newsletter on Ryukyuan studies.

Shunji Taoka is the military correspondent for the *Asahi Shimbun* in Tokyo. His articles are a regular feature of the weekly newsmagazine *Aera.*

JAPAN POLICY RESEARCH INSTITUTE

JPRI was founded in 1994 by Chalmers Johnson and Steven C. Clemons to promote public education about Japan, its significance in world affairs, and trans-Pacific international relations. It is a non-profit membership organization. One of JPRI's important goals is to bring home to educated people around the Pacific the need for genuine area studies on Japan and other countries in East Asia— serious empirical and inductive research, as distinct from the formal theory dispensed by far too many of our university social science departments. In order to be able to say what needs to be said without censorship of any kind, JPRI depends on the dues of members. It does not take funds from either Japanese or American corporations, and its officials serve pro bono publico without salary. Its concept is not to spend time raising money but rather not to need it. Its reputation rests on three pillars: the reputations and integrity of its Board of Advisers, the fact that it cannot be bought, and the quality of its publications and conferences.

JPRI publishes monthly a series of *Working Papers, Occasional Papers,* and *JPRI Critique,* which is devoted to essays, translations, and reprints of important articles. For a full list of JPRI publications, see the JPRI Internet web site. Members of JPRI automatically receive new issues in the mail. Back issues can be downloaded from the JPRI web site with a special password made available to members. The web site also lists forthcoming events, projects in hand, and recommended readings and links. JPRI collaborates with the New Mexico U.S.-Japan Center and the Asia Technology Information Project in organizing and sponsoring workshops and conferences on topics of major importance.

Annual memberships in JPRI are available in the following categories:

Student or retired person	$25.00 or ¥5,000
Academic, Journalist, or Government Official	$50.00 or ¥10,000
Regular Individual	$80.00 or ¥15,000
Sustaining Individual	$1,000 or ¥200,000

Please indicate type of membership requested and send your name, affiliation, address, phone, fax, and e-mail address with payment to:

JPRI, 2138 Via Tiempo, Cardiff, CA 92007 USA, Tel. (760) 944-3950, Fax: (760) 944-9022. If you are in Japan and would prefer to pay your membership dues in ¥, please write to our Tokyo address: JPRI, Tomigaya City House #303, 2-34-21 Tomigaya, Shibuya-ku, Tokyo 151-0063.

JPRI is a non-profit organization. Contributions to it are tax-deductible.

JPRI'S BOARD OF ADVISERS